SCENIC DRIVING
NORTH CAROLINA

Help Us Keep This Guide Up to Date

Every effort has been made by the editors to make this guide as accurate and useful as possible. However, many things can change after a guide is published—establishments close, phone numbers change, hiking trails are rerouted, facilities come under new management, etc.

   We would love to hear from you concerning your experiences with this guide and how you feel it could be improved and kept up to date. While we may not be able to respond to all comments and suggestions, we'll take them to heart and we'll also make certain to share them with the editors. Please send your comments and suggestions to the following address:

The Globe Pequot Press
Reader Response/Editorial Department
P.O. Box 480
Guilford, CT 06437

Or you may e-mail us at:

editorial@GlobePequot.com

Thanks for your input, and happy travels!

INSIDERS' GUIDE®

SECOND EDITION

SCENIC DRIVING

NORTH CAROLINA

LAURENCE PARENT

INSIDERS' GUIDE®

GUILFORD, CONNECTICUT
AN IMPRINT OF THE GLOBE PEQUOT PRESS

INSIDERS' GUIDE®

Copyright © 2006 Morris Book Publishing, LLC
A previous edition was published in 1998 by Falcon Publishing, Inc.

All interior photos by Laurence Parent.
Maps by Trailhead Graphics © Morris Book Publishing, LLC

Library of Congress Cataloging-in-Publication Data
Parent, Laurence.
  Scenic driving North Carolina / Laurence Parent. —2nd ed.
    p. cm. — (Scenic driving guides)
  Includes bibliographical references and index.
  ISBN-13: 978-0-7627-4061-1
  ISBN-10: 0-7627-4061-2
  1. North Carolina—Tours. 2. Automobile travel—North Carolina—Guidebooks. I. Title.
  II. Series.
  F252.3.P37 2006
  917.5604'44—dc22

                                                                        2006041811

Manufactured in the United States of America
Second Edition/First Printing

CONTENTS

The Scenic Drives

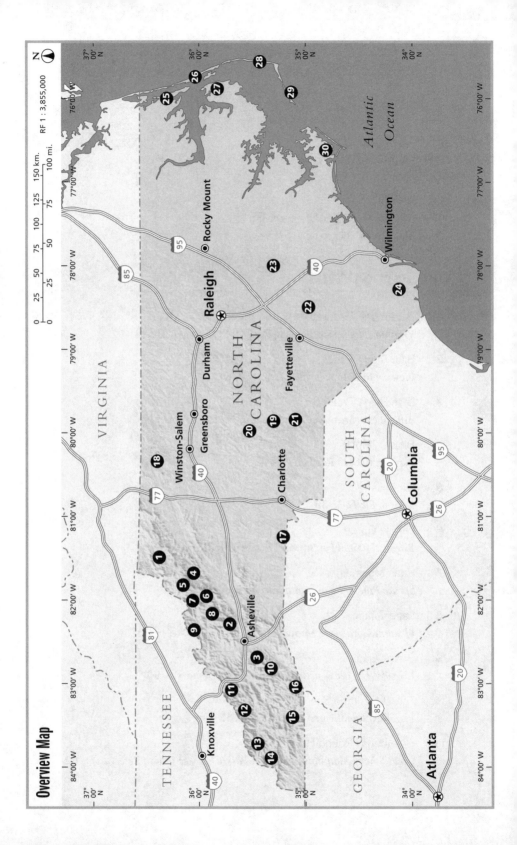

Overview Map

RF 1 : 3,855,000

N

0 25 50 75 100 125 150 km.
0   25   50   75   100 mi.

Map Legend

Transportation

Limited Access Freeway	
U.S. Highway	
Featured U.S. Highway	
State Highway	
Featured State Highway	
Local Road	
Featured Local Road	
Unpaved Road	
Trail	
Interstate Highway	40
U.S. Highway	64
State Highway	28
Local Road	1401
Forest Road	69

Boundaries

State Line	
National/State Park	
National Forest	
Wilderness Area	

Population

City	⊙ Asheville
Town	○ Kitty Hawk

Grids

Latitude / Longitude
Number and Ticks

35°
30' —
N

Hydrology

Reservoir or Lake	Lake
River or Creek	Creek
Marsh/Swamp	
Waterfall	≈

Physiography

Terrain (Shaded Relief)

Mountain,
Peak, or Butte ▲ Peak

Valley

Symbols

Visitor Center	❷
Ranger Station	♟🏠
Point of Interest	▫
Campground	⛺
State Park	🔺
Ski Area	⛷
Museum	🏛
Picnic Area	⛱
Wildlife Refuge	✵
Structure	■
Historic Site	⚐
Lighthouse	🗼

ACKNOWLEDGMENTS

Many people contributed to the completion of this book. Special thanks go to my mother, Annette Richards Parent, who accompanied me on about half of the drives. Thanks also go to my wife, Patricia, for traveling with me on many of the other drives. Although I had traveled quite a bit in North Carolina before starting this book, photographer Kevin Adams of High Point greatly helped me in choosing drives that were truly scenic and interesting in parts of the state that I had not been. Kevin also helped immensely with fact checking in the revised edition of this guide.

Bob Kopetsky, the scenic byway coordinator for the North Carolina Department of Transportation, helped with maps and information on the state scenic byway system. Many friendly people of the USDA Forest Service, the National Park Service, North Carolina state parks, North Carolina historic sites, North Carolina Forest Service, U.S. Fish and Wildlife Service, various chambers of commerce, and many other entities, from museums to roadside businesses, helped with research, maps, and endless questions. David Anderson and Jacque Hopkins helped keep the home fires burning while my wife and I were in North Carolina. Velva Price assisted with airport logistics.

My gratitude also goes to editors Randall Green and Elizabeth Taylor for giving me an excuse to spend a lot of time traveling in North Carolina—which was more fun than writing up the book afterward.

INTRODUCTION

North Carolina is a state with incredible variety. It stretches across hundreds of miles of country, from rugged mountains in the west to sandy beaches in the east. It is blessed with plentiful rain; lush forests and rich farmland cover everything but urban areas and the sandy barrier islands of the coast.

Superlatives abound. People who don't believe the eastern United States has high mountains haven't been to western North Carolina. Mount Mitchell reaches an elevation of 6,684 feet, the highest point in the United States east of the Black Hills of South Dakota. It receives an average of 104 inches of snow a year and has had a record low temperature of minus 34 degrees Fahrenheit, not exactly what you would expect in a southern state. Mount Mitchell isn't the only high mountain getting snow; there are enough others that ski areas have developed in several areas.

The rugged Appalachian Mountains harbor Great Smoky Mountains National Park, the nation's most popular national park and one of the largest in the eastern half of the country. The Appalachian Trail, the longest hiking trail in the United States, winds its way along the spine of the Appalachians in North Carolina. Many large waterfalls splash their way down rocky mountain cliffs, drawing admirers from far away. Tucked away in these mountains are rare virgin groves of trees with hemlocks and tulip poplars that tower more than 100 feet into the sky. Over the years prospectors have unearthed troves of rock from the mountains that contain valuable gemstones, such as rubies and sapphires.

East of the mountains, the land becomes more gentle, forming the Piedmont. The rolling country supports farms, woodland, small towns, and the state's largest cities. Old tobacco farms vie with high-tech manufacturing as part of the state's economy. Gently flowing rivers snake their way toward the ocean, slowed here and there by dams creating large reservoirs.

The Piedmont slowly gives way to the coastal plain as you move farther east. The land flattens and large farms mix with vast sprawling pine forests. Marshes and swamps cover much of the land near the shore. People once thought of these wetlands as worthless and drained many for farmland. Today scientists have discovered these lands' importance as breeding grounds for many ocean creatures, such as fish, shrimp, and shellfish. The areas are also important for land creatures, such as ducks, geese, bears, and red wolves. The marshes lead into the many sounds of the North Carolina coast, some of the largest estuarine areas in the eastern United States.

Lying off the coast are a series of islands that protect the mainland and the sounds behind them from the ocean's fury during storms. These islands, the Outer Banks and other islands, are built of sand and change constantly under the ceaseless assault of wind and wave. Their long, sandy beaches draw an ever increasing number of people to the coast.

In addition to great natural beauty, North Carolina has a tremendous human history, beginning with the many Indian tribes that predated European settlement. The first English settlement in the New World occurred here on Roanoke Island in 1585. Although the colonists disappeared without a trace, they set the stage for successful English settlements in succeeding years. Like the lost colony of Roanoke Island, another event in the state affected human history across the world. On the sandy island flats of Kitty Hawk and Kill Devil Hills, Wilbur and Orville Wright conquered the skies with the world's first powered, controlled airplane flight.

Throughout its long history, North Carolina has seen its share of warfare and tragic bloodshed. Pirates such as Blackbeard sailed the state's coastal waters in the early 1700s, preying upon shipping. As many people know, numerous battles and events of the Civil War played out in North Carolina. However, most people tend to think of the American Revolution as being associated largely with northern cities such as Boston and Philadelphia, even though crucial battles of the war for independence were fought here in North Carolina. Many Americans believe that Pearl Harbor in Hawaii was the only place that the country was directly attacked by enemy forces during World War II. However, during the dark days of early 1942, German U-boats sank American ships with impunity just off the Outer Banks. Recovering bodies from beaches was often a grisly daily chore for coastal residents.

The drives in this guide visit many of the natural and historical wonders of North Carolina. However, like any guidebook, there is often room to hit only the highlights. Use this guide as an introduction. After you have seen the sights along a given route, take off on your own. Something interesting awaits around every turn of the road. You could use up a lifetime and not visit every place worth seeing in North Carolina.

USING THIS GUIDE

Scenic Driving North Carolina describes thirty drives scattered widely across the state. The map at the start of this book indicates their locations. With a current state highway map and the directions given in the descriptions, you should have no trouble locating the start of each drive listed here. Using the guidebook's maps in conjunction with the written directions should make following any of the drives easy.

Please note, however, that not all of the roads within some drives are shown on standard highway maps. A more detailed mapbook of the state, such as the widely available *North Carolina Atlas & Gazetteer,* published by DeLorme Mapping, will help you follow the more remote routes and plan side excursions. Other useful maps are the detailed maps of the national parks and forests through which some of these drives pass. They show additional information that could not be squeezed onto the maps in this guide, such as hiking trails and small side roads. The maps are usually available at park or forest offices and at many outdoors shops in the larger towns.

Generally, the federal highways (both interstates and other federal highways) are the largest and busiest roads. This book uses "US" to designate federal highways, and "I" for interstate highways. North Carolina has a two-tiered system of state highways. The primary highways are paved and well-traveled; we use the abbreviation "NC" followed by the route number to designate these. The secondary North Carolina routes are designated by the abbreviation "SR," for State Road. These routes are usually paved, but some have gravel surfaces. They are often narrower and less traveled than the primary state highways. Look for SR route numbers on the posts of stop signs and other official highway signs at intersections. For national forest roads, I use the abbreviation "FR" for Forest Road. They are usually unpaved and lightly traveled. Their route numbers are marked with thin, short, brown, fiberglass posts.

Unless the drive described is a loop, the length specified is the one-way distance. Distances were measured using several different car odometers. Realize that the figures may not be exact, since different cars vary slightly in their measurements. Even the same car will read slightly differently depending on tire wear or uphill and downhill travel. Be sure to keep an eye open for the specific signs, junctions, and landmarks mentioned in this book's directions, not just the mileage. By watching both signs and mileage, drivers can also do the routes in the reverse direction of how they are described.

The travel season specified for a drive is the optimum or ideal season to visit that route. Except in the mountains, snow rarely closes North Carolina drives for long. Generally, the drives are at their best from spring through fall. Summers can be quite hot and humid on the Piedmont and on the coast. Weather, especially in the mountains, can be quite changeable, so be prepared. Watch weather forecasts and take adequate clothing along with snacks and drinks.

Most of the drives in this guide follow paved roads and all are passable with an ordinary passenger car. A few, as noted, may be difficult for large recreational vehicles or trailers because of their narrowness and sharp turns. Remember that these drives have all the traffic hazards of any road anywhere. Use normal caution and drive defensively, particularly on some of the narrow, winding routes. The terrain these highways pass through is beautiful, but be sure to keep a close eye on the road. Watch out for blind curves and water crossings. Never drive into a flooded stream crossing. Pull well off the road if you stop to sightsee. Watch out for deer and other animals on the road, especially at night (I have had an unfortunate and expensive experience with a deer). Also be aware of stray livestock.

Before setting out, be sure that your car is in good condition. It's always good to top off your gas tank. Though North Carolina isn't the Wild West with vast tracts of wilderness, many of these drives pass through only small towns. It can be difficult to find an open gas station or restaurant late in the day on some of the back roads. It never hurts to carry extra food and water in case you have car trouble or can't find an open restaurant. Snacks will also be useful if you decide to take a hike somewhere along the way. Each write-up notes the availability of food, gas, and lodging along a drive route, but the status can change with time. Before you drive remote and unpaved routes, call the relevant government agency (listed in each description) for current road conditions.

Although crime is unlikely on these rural roads, it never hurts to take precautions. Don't leave valuables in your car when hiking a trail or touring a museum. If you have no choice, lock them out of sight in the trunk—and don't let anyone see you put them in there. If a situation seems unsafe for any reason, just leave.

Many parks, museums, campgrounds, tourist-oriented businesses, and other attractions have seasonal schedules. Days and hours of business tend to be most extensive in summer. Many places have long hours then, with more limited hours in the fall, and restricted or nonexistent hours in winter and early spring. Campgrounds, in particular, tend to be closed in winter and early spring. If you plan to travel in the off-season, call ahead before counting on a given attraction being open.

Please do your part to protect the scenic country through which you pass. Be careful with fire; be sure that you thoroughly put out campfires and cigarettes. Don't litter. Don't disturb historic sites. Stay on designated roads, since the land is fragile. Though many of the drives in this book pass through federal or state land where access is allowed, others pass through private land. In areas of private ownership, respect the landowners and stay within the highway right-of-way.

Use this guide as an introduction to this marvelous state. Follow the intriguing side road that disappears into the pines. Stop in a national forest and hike to a waterfall or fish a rushing stream. Climb to the top of a lighthouse or look for birds in a national wildlife refuge. Browse through a small-town antiques shop or pull into a roadside cafe and sink your teeth into some real southern food. Stay at a bed and breakfast and meet the hosts and other guests. Above all, take your time as you discover all that North Carolina has to offer.

Blue Ridge Parkway

Virginia state line to Blowing Rock

General description: A 75-mile section of the paved recreational Blue Ridge Parkway, which follows the scenic crest of the Blue Ridge Mountains from the Virginia state line to Blowing Rock.

Special attractions: Cumberland Knob, Brinegar Cabin, Doughton Park, Northwest Trading Post, E. B. Jeffress Park, Boone's Trace, Blowing Rock, hiking, scenic views, fall colors.

Location: Northwest North Carolina. The drive starts where the Blue Ridge Parkway enters the state about 17 miles west of Mount Airy.

Drive route name: Blue Ridge Parkway.

Travel season: The best season is April through October, but the route is scenic any time of year. Snow and ice can make travel difficult in winter.

Camping: The National Park Service maintains a campground at Doughton Park and at Julian Price Memorial Park a short distance south of Blowing Rock on the parkway. Nearby Stone Mountain State Park also has a campground.

Services: Gas, food, and lodging are located on the parkway itself at Doughton Park. Towns near the parkway, such as Sparta, Blowing Rock, and Boone, all have visitor services.

Nearby attractions: Stone Mountain State Park, New River State Park, Mount Jefferson State Park, ski areas near Boone, Tweetsie Railroad, sections of the parkway to the north and south.

For more information: Blue Ridge Parkway (National Park Service), Mount Jefferson State Park, Stone Mountain State Park, Blowing Rock and Boone Chambers of Commerce. See Appendix for addresses and phone numbers.

The Drive

This drive follows the northern section of the Blue Ridge Parkway within North Carolina from the Virginia state line to Blowing Rock. The well-known scenic route was designed as a recreational road along the crest of the Blue Ridge and other mountains of the Appalachian chain. Hence there is little commercial truck traffic and few business establishments along the parkway itself. The road passes through a seemingly endless array of deep forests, pastoral fields, and breathtaking views. Historic sites, hiking trails, and numerous overlooks break up the trip. Though the parkway is hardly undiscovered, it is still one of the premier touring routes of the eastern United States.

The Blue Ridge Parkway got its start in the 1930s, when the nation was in the depths of the Great Depression. To boost morale, President Franklin Delano Roosevelt visited Civilian Conservation Corps facilities at Shenandoah National Park

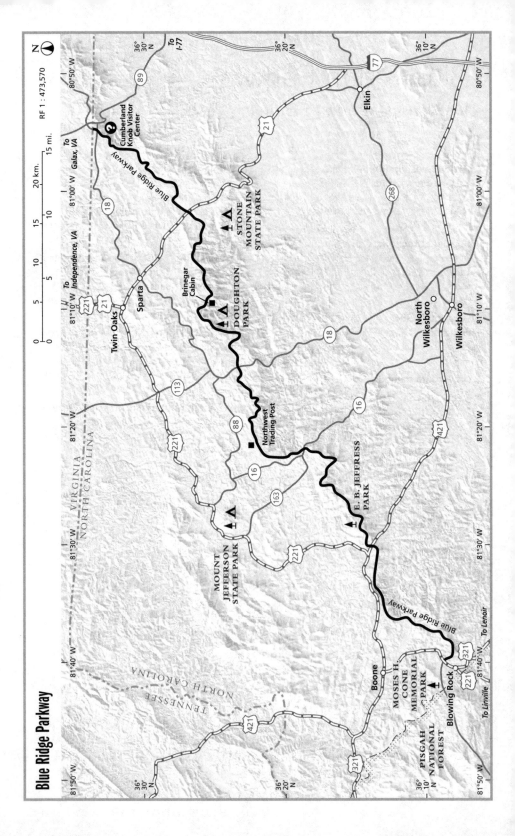

Blue Ridge Parkway

in Virginia. The Civilian Conservation Corps (CCC) was established to provide jobs to unemployed young men in difficult economic times. During his visit, Roosevelt particularly enjoyed the scenery and views along Skyline Drive. When Virginia senator Harry Byrd proposed building a scenic drive along the crest of the Appalachians between Shenandoah and Great Smoky Mountains National Parks, the idea fell on receptive ears. It would not only create a long scenic drive, but would offer new employment opportunities.

The states of North Carolina and Virginia purchased rights-of-way and donated them to the project. In 1936, Congress approved legislation, creating the parkway and placing it under the National Park Service's authority. Construction was soon underway, but completing the route took many years. The last segment, near Grandfather Mountain, was not finished until the 1980s. As you follow the parkway, notice the excellent stonework on its bridges and embankments.

The drive starts in rolling, wooded country at the North Carolina border just a few miles south of Galax, Virginia. It immediately passes a junction with NC 18. The Cumberland Knob Recreation Area is on the left, only a mile into the drive. The first of many recreation sites built along the parkway, it's also the first of many worthwhile stops. The visitor center here was built by the CCC in 1937 in a rustic style, using durable native materials. The visitor center offers information, books for sale, and a great view. From here, a short paved trail leads to the top of 2,885-foot Cumberland Knob; other longer trails wind through the area, some offering southeast views of the valleys below. Picnic tables entice hungry visitors to eat lunch here on nice days.

A short distance farther down the parkway lies Fox Hunter's Paradise, an overlook on the left. The overlook and the next 0.5 mile or so of road offer great views southeast down to the Piedmont, the area of rolling country between the mountains and the coastal plain. The site's quaint name comes from a nearby knoll, which was a favorite gathering place of local fox hunters in earlier days. The hunters sat around a campfire here after a day of listening to the barks and howls of their dogs pursuing a fox.

The parkway crosses US 21 about 13 miles from the state line at Roaring Gap, a small pass in the ridge. A worthwhile side trip on US 21 leads to Stone Mountain State Park, a large granite mass rising 600 feet from its base. Stone Mountain is part of an igneous intrusion that formed when molten rock hardened here, deep underground, about 350 million years ago. Erosion of softer overlying rock layers later exposed the granite. Not surprisingly, Stone Mountain is popular with rock climbers and hikers. The large state park includes granite faces, waterfalls, a campground, trout fishing, and other attractions.

Just past the US 21 junction is Little Glade Pond, which offers a picnic area and fishing opportunities. About 2.5 miles farther down the road is an overlook with a good view of Stone Mountain. Soon other views begin to appear on the right (west) side of the parkway. The country on the east side of the ridge is generally much lower than that on the west because it slowly slopes down to the Atlantic

The road gains altitude for the next few miles. The ridge it follows is narrow in the vicinity of Air Bellows Overlook, with views on both sides of the drive. Just beyond the overlook is Air Bellows Gap, named for the fierce winds that blow here in winter. Brinegar Cabin lies about 1.5 miles beyond Air Bellows Gap on the left side of the road. This historic cabin displays weaving exhibits and has a million-dollar view.

The site was settled by Martin and Caroline Brinegar in about 1880. With their family, they cleared fields, raised crops, and tended livestock to support themselves. In about 1885, they began building the present cabin and outbuildings. A reliable spring supplied them with clear, cold water. To get cash to purchase the few things they could not raise or build themselves, Caroline and the children collected herbs and sold them to local druggists, while Martin earned money as a cobbler.

A staunch Baptist, Martin looked down on drinking, dancing, and even the playing of musical instruments during church services. Since stills and bootlegging were rampant here during Prohibition, Martin was probably one of the few people in the area to get along with revenue officers. Martin Brinegar died in 1925, leaving the property to his wife, Caroline. She continued to live in the cabin until the land was purchased by the government for the parkway in the late 1930s. She lived her last few years with her daughter Rene in nearby Pine Swamp Valley and died in 1943.

When you reach the cabin, the parkway has entered Doughton Park, a recreation area of about 6,000 acres. The park was named for Robert Lee Doughton, a longtime North Carolina congressman and supporter of the Blue Ridge Parkway. The park flanks the next 6 miles of parkway. You will reach the campground first, followed by Low Notch, a pass over the mountains. "Notch" is a term used more commonly in New England for a mountain pass; in this part of the South, the term "gap" is generally used. About a mile farther, you will come across a large complex with gas, food, lodging, and picnic sites. Trails lead from parking areas at Alligator Back and Wildcat Rocks through forest and clearings to great views.

You'll get even more views as you continue southwest along the parkway, with frequent overlooks. In a few miles the parkway drops into the small Meadow Fork Valley and crosses NC 18. (Yes, this is the same NC 18 you crossed near the start of the drive; it's not a particularly straight highway.) Meadow Fork Creek flows into the New River, and its waters eventually spill into the Gulf of Mexico. The divide between the Atlantic and Gulf of Mexico watersheds follows the Blue Ridge here.

The Northwest Trading Post lies on the right about 10 miles from the junction with NC 18. The store sells many old crafts and products made by people in the northwestern eleven counties of North Carolina. Although these items are not

The Blue Ridge Parkway near Blowing Rock

cheap, they are often very attractive and well made. Two miles past the trading post is Jumpin' Off Rocks, where a short 0.5-mile trail leads to a rock outcropping and a view almost worth jumpin' off for.

Just beyond Jumpin' Off Rocks, drivers come to the junction with NC 16 at Horse Gap. Unlike most sites on the parkway, the gap's name is not especially historic. Locals had never heard of the name until the state government put up a sign here in the 1930s after moving NC 16 to its present route. Views start improving beyond the gap as the parkway ridge gets higher. The Lump, a large rounded hill, offers sweeping views about 3 miles from the gap.

Mount Jefferson Overlook, a short distance down the road, offers a great view north to the mountain that was renamed for Thomas Jefferson in 1952. Jefferson's father, Peter, was a member of the party that surveyed the nearby Virginia–North Carolina boundary in 1749. The mountain's original name, Negro Mountain, dates to the 1700s. The name may have come after an escaped slave was captured there during the American Revolution. Alternately, the name may have originated from the mountain's dark appearance at sunset. Before and during the Civil War, runaway slaves sometimes hid on the mountain on their way north, giving it a reputation as a stop on the underground railroad.

The mountain's 4,683-foot summit looms over the small town of Jefferson, where a small state park offers views and hiking trails. The peak lies on the divide between the two main forks of the New River, which is thought to be the oldest river in North America (its name is slightly off the mark!). Geologists believe that this waterway predates the uplift of the mountains. It has followed roughly its present course for millions of years.

E.B. Jeffress Park lies about 5 miles from the Mount Jefferson Overlook, farther southwest along the parkway. The 600-acre park was named for the state highway commission chairman who persuaded the federal government to build the parkway in its present location. The park has picnic tables and a short nature trail leading to cascades on Fall Creek, ample reasons for a rest stop. Another trail within the park leads to the old Cool Spring Baptist Church and Jesse Brown Cabin.

The parkway crosses US 421 at Deep Gap, a few miles past Jeffress Park. In the last days of the Civil War, Union troops occupied this gap and raided nearby towns. In another 4 miles, an access road leads to US 421 (which roughly parallels the parkway here) and US 221. US 421 leads to nearby Boone, the largest town in the area. Home to a university, ski areas, and other attractions, Boone is more fully described under this guide's Drive #5, Elk Falls.

A pullout on the left about 4 miles down the road marks Boone's Trace, the route believed to have been used by frontiersman Daniel Boone on his westward treks. Boone settled on the North Carolina Piedmont in 1751, but he wasn't much suited to the farming life. He soon left his family for frequent hunting and exploration trips as far west as Tennessee and Kentucky. He became an excellent woodsman during his years of travel. He is probably most noted for guiding settlers through Cumberland Gap into Kentucky, one of the first steps toward opening the American West.

This drive ends about 7 miles past Boone's Trace at the junction of US 221/321 at the edge of the town of Blowing Rock, an attractive tourist town. For more details about the town, see Drive #4. Visitors could spend several days exploring Boone and Blowing Rock and the surrounding area.

2

Blue Ridge Parkway
Blowing Rock to Asheville

General description: A 90-mile paved segment of the Blue Ridge Parkway, the famous scenic drive that connects Shenandoah and Great Smoky Mountains National Parks.

Special attractions: Blue Ridge Parkway, Blowing Rock, Moses H. Cone Memorial Park, Julian Price Memorial Park, Linn Cove Viaduct, Grandfather Mountain, Linville Falls, Museum of North Carolina Minerals, Crabtree Meadows and Falls, Mount Mitchell State Park, Craggy Gardens, Folk Art Center, hiking, views, fall colors, fishing, rockhounding.

Location: Western North Carolina. The drive starts on the Blue Ridge Parkway at its intersection with US 321/221 in Blowing Rock, just a few miles south of Boone.

Drive route name: Blue Ridge Parkway.

Travel season: The best season is from April through October. Although the route is scenic all year, snow and ice can make travel treacherous in winter.

Camping: Campgrounds are located along the parkway at Julian Price Memorial Park, Linville Falls, and Crabtree Meadows. Other public campgrounds are located in Mount Mitchell State Park (tent only) and the Pisgah National Forest.

Services: On the parkway food is available at Crabtree Meadows. Full services are available nearby in the towns of Boone, Blowing Rock, Linville, Spruce Pine, and Asheville. Other smaller towns sometimes have at least some visitor services.

Nearby attractions: Sections of the Blue Ridge Parkway to the north and south, Pisgah National Forest, Biltmore Estate, Roan Mountain, Linville Caverns.

For more information: Blue Ridge Parkway (National Park Service), Pisgah National Forest, Mount Mitchell State Park, Grandfather Mountain, and Chambers of Commerce in Blowing Rock, Boone, Mitchell County (Spruce Pine), Avery County (Newland), and Asheville. See Appendix for addresses and phone numbers.

The Drive

The Blue Ridge Parkway is one of the most scenic routes in the eastern United States. It follows a 469-mile route along the crest of the Blue Ridge and other mountain ranges between Shenandoah National Park in Virginia and Great Smoky Mountains National Park in North Carolina. The road was designed as a recreational route and is remarkably free of commercial establishments, subdivisions, and truck traffic. Its roots lie in the Depression of the 1930s; see Drive #1 for details of its history. Although visitors can travel this scenic section of the parkway in a day, its many attractions can fill two or three days.

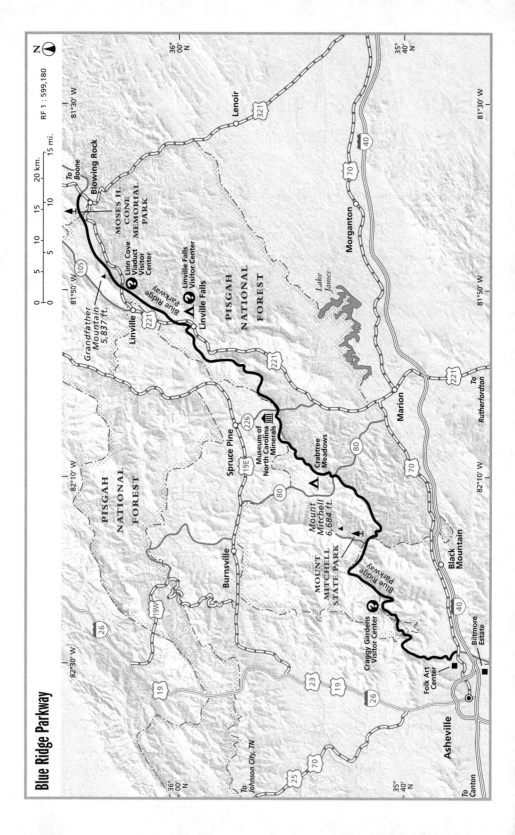

Blue Ridge Parkway

The drive starts in Blowing Rock, an attractive resort town described fully in Drive #4. From town the drive climbs into 3,500-acre Moses H. Cone Memorial Park. It winds its way through the park for almost 2.5 miles. Activity centers on Flat Top Manor, an imposing 20-room home built by Moses Cone in the middle of this large property.

Moses Cone was born in 1857 in Jonesboro, Tennessee, to German immigrants. Thirteen years later the Cone family moved to Baltimore, Maryland, and built a thriving wholesale grocery business. Moses and his brother Ceasar went to work as salesmen for the business, taking trips into textile communities in the Carolinas and elsewhere. As the years went by, the brothers became more involved in the textile business and in 1891 became selling agents for the southern mills. In 1895, the brothers built their own mill in North Carolina. Initially they produced heavy-duty blue denim, leading to Moses' informal reputation as the "Denim King." Later the company branched into other fabrics. In time, it operated more than thirty plants, producing many items.

By 1897, Moses was prosperous enough to create an estate of his own design. Since the southern Appalachians were becoming a popular place to escape the summer heat and mosquito-borne diseases of the lowlands, Moses began to buy land near Blowing Rock. He allowed tenant farmers there to stay on. He added three lakes to the property and stocked them with fish. He planted apple orchards and pines. In the center of his land he created the elaborate Flat Top Manor, reached by a network of carriage roads. During his life here, Moses contributed money to local schools and helped found what would become Appalachian State University in Boone. He died relatively young and childless, in 1908, and was outlived by his wife, Bertha. When she died in 1947, she left the intact estate to the Cone Memorial Hospital in Greensboro. The hospital donated it to the U.S. government three years later.

Today the mansion has a shop that sells informational books on the parkway and surrounding area, plus an impressive collection of high-quality Appalachian handicrafts. Visitors can purchase everything from handmade quilts and weavings to jewelry to hardwood kitchen utensils. When you tire of shopping, take a walk on the miles of carriage paths and enjoy the cool mountain air, lush woods, and broad views. There is an access point to US 221 only 0.5 mile beyond Flat Top Manor.

Beyond Cone Park, the Blue Ridge Parkway enters Julian Price Memorial Park. The park is slowly reverting to forested wilderness after being heavily logged from 1912 to 1930 by lumber magnate William Whiting. Before it was logged, the area was noted for its virgin forest of huge tulip poplars, hemlocks, American chestnuts, and other trees. Although the poplar and hemlock are recovering, the formerly dominant chestnut is not. Once important for its nuts and decay-resistant wood, the chestnut is now virtually extinct. A blight imported from Asia swept through the tree's entire range, killing every standing example. Chestnut trees still sprout occasionally from old roots or stumps, but the blight usually strikes before the trees get much larger than saplings. Many of the picturesque split-rail fences that you see along the parkway were made of chestnut wood, which split easily and resisted rotting. With the tree's demise, the fences are getting more and more difficult for the National Park Service to repair and replace.

Julian Price acquired the Price Park property in the late 1930s and early 1940s to create a vacation retreat for employees of Jefferson Standard Life Insurance Company. After he died an untimely death in 1946, the company donated the land to the National Park Service. Within the park, Sims Pond offers hiking and fishing right alongside the parkway. A half mile or so past the pond is another picnic area, followed by trout fishing at Price Lake and the campground. Drivers can access US 221 about 2 miles past Price Lake.

Several overlooks in the next few miles along the parkway have hiking trails that connect to the Tanawha Trail, a 13.5-mile path that winds along the slopes of Grandfather Mountain and parallels about 7 miles of the parkway to Beacon Heights. The trail is spectacular, with tremendous views of the valley below and the Linn Cove Viaduct, an engineering marvel that comes farther down this drive.

The road slowly climbs from Price Park onto the slopes of Grandfather Mountain. About 3 miles beyond Price Lake, look for views of Calloway Peak. At 5,964 feet, it is not only the highest point on the long, rocky ridge of Grandfather Mountain, but is also the highest point on the entire Blue Ridge. As the parkway climbs, it offers increasingly impressive views to the southeast at several overlooks.

You'll soon drive onto the S-shaped bridge of the Linn Cove Viaduct. This impressive feat of engineering was one of the last parts of the parkway to be completed, in 1983. Here engineering becomes art. Rather than blast road cuts and build straight bridges across the steep, rocky mountain face, the parkway builders decided to design a viaduct that curved with the mountain slope, allowing a large section of delicate mountainside to remain unscarred.

The 0.25-mile long viaduct was built with precast concrete segments on seven vertical piers spaced 180 feet apart. Other than drilling and pouring concrete for each pier base, the builders carried out all construction from above. One by one, each custom segment was attached to the end of the preceding segment, starting at the south end of the bridge. When the segments extended outward 90 feet, a temporary support pier was installed. More segments were then added, reaching to 180 feet. Then the permanent support pier was constructed with workers lowering sections to the base. Be sure to stop at the Linn Cove Viaduct Visitor Center and parking area on the left, at the viaduct's south end, to view the result. A short paved trail and the longer Tanawha Trail lead from the visitor center to great views of the viaduct and the valley below.

A junction with US 221 lies about a mile past the viaduct visitor center. To get

Along the Blue Ridge Parkway

to Grandfather Mountain, a worthwhile side trip, turn here and follow US 221 a short distance west to the entrance. Forty-two endangered and rare species live on this mountain preserve. Designated an International Biosphere Reserve by the United Nations, Grandfather Mountain is the only privately owned site so honored. After paying an entry fee, visitors follow an access road as it snakes up to a nature museum, picnic area, and restaurant. Many visitors like to walk across the pedestrian suspension bridge connecting two rocky crags, although acrophobic folks will avoid it. Covered by miles of hiking trails, Grandfather Mountain offers some of the most impressive views in the Blue Ridge Mountains.

Back on the Blue Ridge Parkway, drivers soon come to the Beacon Heights parking area. Here a trail leads a short distance to a rocky viewpoint overlooking Beacon Heights, the Tanawha Trail, and other routes. Another mile or so of parkway leads visitors to a good view of Grandfather Mountain at its namesake overlook. About 2 miles past this point, a sign marks the boundary of Pisgah National Forest. Much of the terrain along the parkway between Blowing Rock and Asheville lies within the national forest. A trail at the Flat Rock parking area, on the right, leads to another rocky outcrop with views.

The parkway crosses NC 181 a few more miles down the road. About 4 miles past this junction, be sure to stop at Linville Falls Recreation Area. This rugged

Linville Falls

440-acre area was given to the National Park Service by John D. Rockefeller. Its visitor center, picnic area, and campground are all along a short spur road. The big attraction here is the trail system, which leads to overlooks of the Linville River where it roars over a cliff into a deep plunge pool. The easy trail on the south side of the river leads to several dramatic overlooks of the falls and downstream views. A more difficult trail on the north side of the river descends to the base of the falls. In late spring, prolific rhododendrons bloom here, adding splashes of color. Because of the rough terrain, much of the area was never logged. Virgin hemlocks and white pines tower into the sky in both the recreation area and nearby Linville Gorge Wilderness Area, which is described in more detail in Drive #6.

A mile past the Linville Falls spur, the Blue Ridge Parkway crosses US 221 again. For the next few miles, various overlooks line the route. A sign at Heffner

Gap Overlook describes the importance of apple trees to early settlers. Untended apple trees in fields and forests often mark the site of abandoned homesteads. A viewpoint about 2.5 miles past the Heffner Gap Overlook looks down on the Loops, large curves on the Clinchfield Railroad line where it climbs over the Blue Ridge and crosses the road. Years of struggle, first to raise the capital and then to build the tracks, culminated in these steel rails. Completed in 1909, the line required eighteen tunnels and 31.5 miles of track to ascend the Blue Ridge. In 1915, the tracks were tied into rail systems in the Piedmont and Midwest. Even today, the Clinchfield Railroad is the only line to cut a path across the southern Appalachians.

In another 2 miles, the parkway crosses NC 226 at Gillespie Gap. The town of Spruce Pine lies just off the parkway on NC 226. Spruce Pine is the center of North Carolina's mining industry. Prospectors have dug into the rocky, wooded hills here in search of riches since before the American Revolution. Some of the country's first gold rushes occurred in this area, and for many years North Carolina was the nation's leading gold producer. (See Drive #7 for more area mining history.) If mining intrigues you, be sure to stop at the Museum of North Carolina Minerals at the NC 226 junction. The museum describes North Carolina mining activity and exhibits native minerals, showcasing everything from rubies to tungsten to gold nuggets. It was enlarged and renovated in 2002.

The first of many tunnels on the remainder of this drive appears about 2.5 miles from the NC 226 junction. A short distance past the tunnel, NC 226A leads to Little Switzerland. This settlement got its name when a person who had recently visited Switzerland suggested that the area resembled the Swiss Jura Mountains. The Wildacres Tunnel follows in about 3 more miles.

Next comes Crabtree Meadows Recreation Area, which has a campground, picnic area, restaurant, and crafts shop. Several families once lived here, raising crops, tending livestock, and grinding corn at a mill built by Billy Bradshaw. As standards of living improved early in this century, people slowly drifted away from the hard mountain life. Once you fill your stomach, stretch your legs on a 0.9-mile hike down to 70-foot-high Crabtree Falls, one of the most scenic waterfalls in the area. The trail starts from the parking area just inside the Crabtree Meadows campground.

Farther down the road, the Black Mountains Overlook is particularly interesting. There is no mistaking the looming crest of the Black Mountains, the highest range east of the Mississippi River. Its green mantle of cool Fraser firs and red spruces appears very dark from a distance, giving the range its name. The average elevation of the mountains exceeds 6,000 feet, very high by eastern standards. From the overlook, visitors can see the eastern section of the J-shaped range. It includes Mount Mitchell, the highest point and center of a state park that you will visit later in this drive.

The parkway crosses NC 80 in Buck Creek Gap about 2 miles past the Black Mountains Overlook. It then passes through two more tunnels, generally climbing as it travels southwest toward the Black Mountains. After going through another tunnel, it passes more overlooks with impressive views. Near mile marker 354, the Blue Ridge Parkway leaves the Blue Ridge and crosses to the Black Mountains. For more than 200 miles, the parkway has roughly followed the divide between the Gulf of Mexico and Atlantic watersheds along the crest of the Blue Ridge. Here, it finally leaves it. A nearby summit, the Pinnacle, is the second highest point in the Blue Ridge Mountains.

NC 128 turns right just after Black Mountain Gap, climbing into Mount Mitchell State Park. This 4.8-mile side trip is well worth the time. The highway climbs steadily, passing a restaurant and a small tent campground on its way to the summit parking lot. There, a short trail climbs to the observation tower on the 6,684-foot summit. As of fall 2005, plans were under way to tear down and rebuild the tower. Bring a jacket, since summit temperatures are almost always cool, even in summer. The record high here is only 81 degrees F; the record low is minus 34 degrees F, a bit chilly for a southern state. Winds in excess of 100 miles per hour are common here, where the average annual snowfall is 104 inches. Altogether it's a hostile climate, explaining the spruce-fir forest that blankets the mountain's upper slopes; the forest type is more common in cooler places such as Canada.

Unfortunately, Mount Mitchell's conifer forest is not healthy. A tiny imported aphid called the balsam woolly adelgid is the main culprit. The aphid kills off Fraser firs by injecting a substance into the trees that eventually blocks the flow of nutrients and water through the trees' vascular system. The red spruce here also have been growing much more slowly in recent decades, and have a higher mortality rate, due to acid rain created by sulfur dioxide emissions from power plants and nitrous oxides emitted by vehicles. In addition, ozone levels have been increasing. What with the adelgid, the chestnut blight, Dutch elm disease, and pollution, visitors have to wonder how much forest will eventually be left in the East.

Elisha Mitchell, the mountain's namesake, is buried on the summit below the tower. Mitchell began his long career as a teacher at the University of North Carolina in 1824. He first visited the Black Mountains in 1835. Using a barometer to measure atmospheric pressure, he calculated the height of several peaks and concluded that the range was higher than Mount Washington in New Hampshire. Enlisting the aid of local guide Big Tom Wilson, he came back in 1844 and measured the mountains' elevations more precisely.

That same year, a North Carolina congressman and senator, Thomas Clingman, also visited the range and calculated the height of several of the peaks. He asserted that he had found a peak higher than that of Mitchell, opening a dispute between the two men. To settle the matter, Mitchell made another trip to the mountains in 1857. Sadly, he fell to his death over a waterfall when traveling alone to Big Tom Wilson's house. For days searchers combed the mountain looking for him. Finally Wilson found the body, which later was buried on the summit of the range.

After his death, people sided with Mitchell and the mountain was officially named in his honor. Remarkably, Mitchell's measurement was only 12 feet off the actual height, when measured with modern scientific instruments. In time, Clingman also found his place in history. Clingman's Dome is the highest point in the Smokies and one of the highest peaks in the East. Another high peak in the Black Mountains is named for Big Tom.

As loggers approached the crest of the Black Mountains at the turn of the twentieth century, people in the area agitated for its protection. North Carolina's first state park was established near Mount Mitchell in 1915, through the efforts of Governor Locke Craig, Theodore Roosevelt, and others. If you enjoy the high elevations of Mount Mitchell, consider hiking some of the other trails in the state park and adjacent Pisgah National Forest.

From the turnoff to Mount Mitchell State Park, continue to drive toward Asheville on the parkway. For several miles, the road passes through high spruce-fir woodland to Balsam Gap, the dividing point between the Black Mountains and the Great Craggy Mountains. From here the parkway follows a sharp ridge to Craggy Gardens in the Great Craggies. Stop to look at Glassmine Falls, a very high seasonal waterfall, at an overlook soon after Balsam Gap.

Just past another tunnel is the Craggy Gardens Visitor Center, where great views open up on both sides of the ridge. The Craggy Gardens are a large heath bald, an area of thick shrubs rather than trees. One of most common plants here is the rhododendron, with colorful blooms that open in mid-June. One theory of the balds' evolution postulates that Native Americans burned the area long ago to create openings for game. Grass grew back first, followed by brush. Several hiking trails start in the gardens and lead through this fragile terrain. All have tremendous views. Stay on the trails, which lead to many possible destinations, including the summit of Craggy Pinnacle and 70-foot Douglas Falls.

Back on the parkway, drivers go through yet another tunnel to reach a picnic area with hiking trails that go back to the Craggy Gardens Visitor Center and other destinations. From here, the road steadily descends toward Asheville. Several more overlooks offer views as you drop off the Craggy Mountains.

The Folk Art Center of the Southern Highlands Craft Guild lies on the right in about 17 miles. This spacious center, opened in 1980, has a large museum with changing displays of guild members' work and traveling exhibits, plus an elaborate shop with a broad array of excellent local crafts. If you didn't find enough crafts to satisfy you at Moses H. Cone Memorial Park, you'll find them here. Hardwood fan pulls, silver dogwood jewelry, quilts, creative cutting boards—the Folk Art Center has it all. There is also a bookstore with titles relevant to the area.

Just past the Folk Art Center is the parkway's junction with US 70 at the edge of Asheville, marking the end of this drive. The next segment of the parkway, from Asheville to the Great Smokies, is described in Drive #3. For now, relax and enjoy the plentiful restaurants and lodging facilities in Asheville, the largest city in western North Carolina. If the drive hasn't worn you out, consider a tour of the Biltmore Estate. The estate started when George Vanderbilt began buying land in the area, eventually amassing 125,000 acres (a large portion of which later became part of the Pisgah National Forest). Vanderbilt's massive 255-room home was modeled after French chateaux and took hundreds of workers five years to construct. The house is huge—it's the largest private residence in the world—and lavishly furnished. Tours visit "only" fifty of the rooms. You also can explore the estate's elaborate gardens designed by Frederick Law Olmsted, the winery, or nearby Biltmore Village before you collapse in your Asheville motel room.

3

Blue Ridge Parkway
Asheville to Great Smoky Mountains National Park

General description: A 75-mile paved section of one of the most famous routes in America, following the dramatic crest of the Pisgah and Great Balsam Mountains to Great Smoky Mountains National Park.

Special attractions: Blue Ridge Parkway, Pisgah National Forest, Devils Courthouse, Graveyard Fields, Shining Rock Wilderness, Middle Prong Wilderness, Cherokee Indian Reservation, Great Smoky Mountains National Park, hiking, scenic views, fall colors.

Location: Southwestern North Carolina. The drive starts on the southwest side of Asheville, at the junction of the Blue Ridge Parkway and NC 191. To get there from I–26, take exit 2 and follow NC 191 south about 2.5 miles.

Drive route name: Blue Ridge Parkway.

Travel season: Spring through fall is the best travel time. Snow and ice can make travel treacherous and even close the parkway in winter.

Camping: The National Park Service maintains campgrounds at Mount Pisgah on the parkway, and at Balsam Mountain and Smokemont in Great Smoky Mountains National Park. The Pisgah National Forest manages several campgrounds within a few miles of the parkway.

Services: All services are available in Asheville, Mount Pisgah, and Cherokee.

Nearby attractions: Other sections of Great Smoky Mountains National Park and the Pisgah National Forest, other segments of the Blue Ridge Parkway, Nantahala National Forest, Cradle of Forestry in America, Looking Glass Falls, Looking Glass Rock, and Biltmore Estate.

For more information: Blue Ridge Parkway (National Park Service); Pisgah National Forest (Pisgah Ranger District); Great Smoky Mountains National Park; Cherokee Visitor Center; and the Asheville, Brevard, and Maggie Valley Area Chambers of Commerce.

The Drive

The Blue Ridge Parkway is one of the premier drives in the United States. It generally follows the crest of the Blue Ridge and other Appalachian mountains for 469 miles, from Shenandoah National Park in Virginia to Great Smoky Mountains National Park in North Carolina and Tennessee. Though it is rooted in the Great Depression (see Drive #1), the parkway was not completed until the 1980s. Driving the entire route takes several days if you want to see its many sights. Even this 75-mile segment of parkway, the southernmost section, can take more than a day if you spend a lot of time hiking and taking side trips.

Drive #3 travels from the southwest side of Asheville to Great Smoky Mountains National Park, both worthy destinations in themselves. Drive #2 describes the section of parkway just north of this one, from Blowing Rock to Asheville. Two

Blue Ridge Parkway

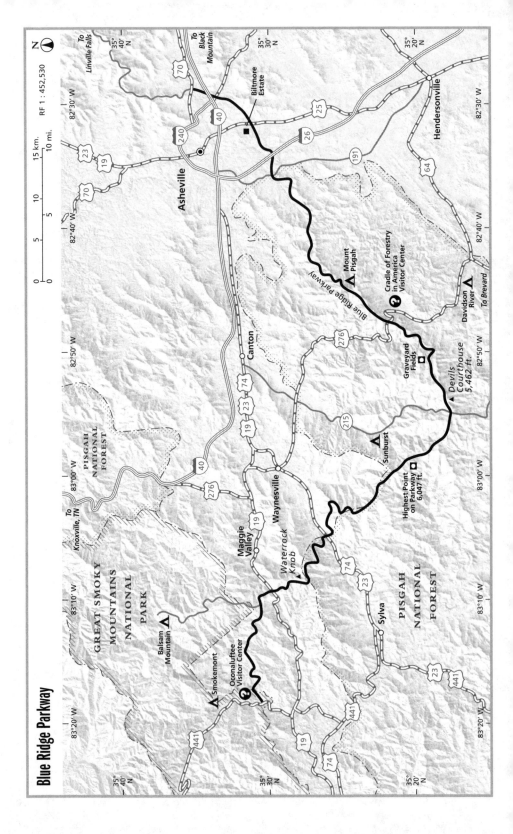

other drives in this guide—Drive #11, Heintooga–Round Bottom Road, and Drive #12, Newfound Gap Road—describe drives within Great Smoky Mountains National Park. Between Asheville and the Smokies, the Blue Ridge Parkway reaches its highest point (6,047 feet) and some of its most spectacular views. It crosses a large portion of public lands in the Pisgah and Nantahala National Forests, leading to exceptional opportunities for hiking, fishing, camping, and other activities.

Start the drive on the edge of Asheville where the parkway crosses NC 191 and the French Broad River, a large waterway flowing west toward Tennessee. The river's wide banks encouraged its use as a travel route through these mountains during the early days of area settlement. In warm weather you may see boaters floating downstream here. The parkway's first overlook, on your left, offers good views of the river and boaters.

From here, at about 2,000 feet above sea level, the parkway climbs and climbs. It enters the Pisgah National Forest almost immediately. The 87,000-acre heart of this forest unit was once part of the Biltmore Estate, established by George Vanderbilt (see Drive #2). The U.S. government purchased the land after Vanderbilt's death in 1914. As you continue up the road, you will get occasional views back toward Asheville and the old Biltmore Estate.

By the time you arrive at Chestnut Cove Overlook in another 4.9 miles, you will have climbed to an altitude of 3,035 feet. Until 1904, the American chestnut was one of the dominant trees in this cove. In that year, a blight introduced in New York City began wiping out all the chestnuts in America. A favorite shade tree, the chestnut provided wood for split-rail fences like those seen along the parkway. Both humans and wildlife ate its flavorful nuts. Today, chestnuts that sprout from old root systems still cannot survive the blight. Forest specialists are trying to hybridize a resistant variety.

Drivers along this stretch will have passed through the Grassy Knob Tunnel before reaching Chestnut Cove. Now, in less than a mile, you will reach Pine Mountain Tunnel. At 1,462 feet long, this tunnel is the longest of the twenty-six found on the parkway. All but one of the tunnels lie in the southernmost 136 miles of the parkway; eighteen of them lie along this segment alone. Only one tunnel is in Virginia, near the parkway's northern end.

The parkway next climbs a long ridge leading to Mount Pisgah, with numerous overlooks and tunnels. Drivers pass the 4,000-foot mark just before the Mills River Valley Overlook, about 11 miles into the drive. The river that runs far below this overlook was named for William Mills, an early settler in the area. In the early 1800s, Mills saw an elk near the river; it was the last reported elk in North Carolina. Even in the early nineteenth century, mankind had a significant impact on this natural area.

The road continues to climb. In another 3 miles, it reaches the 4,995-foot Mount Pisgah parking area. Mount Pisgah was named for the biblical mount from

Boaters in the French Broad River

which Moses first viewed the Promised Land after leading his people out of slavery in Egypt. From the parking area, a moderately strenuous hiking trail climbs more than 700 feet to the mountain's summit. One mile beyond the parking area is Pisgah Lodge on the mountain crest. With attendant great views, visitors can find food, lodging, campsites, a picnic area, and a gift shop here. The lodge tends to book up early, so reserve a room ahead of time if you want to stay.

The parkway now follows the crest of the mountains on a nearly level route. Look for the Frying Pan Fire lookout tower on a ridge above the road, a little past the lodge. After some distance, the Cradle of Forestry Overlook appears on the left. Signs at this overlook tell about the birth of modern forestry in the valley far below when it was part of the Biltmore Estate. About 0.8 mile past the forest overlook, drivers reach the junction with US 276. If you do not plan to drive the entire Forest Heritage Scenic Byway (Drive #10), consider making a short side trip down US 276 south toward Brevard to the Cradle of Forestry in America Visitor Center. The center's historic buildings, displays, and living history demonstrations are all very interesting.

Pigeon Gap lies less than a mile past the US 276 junction. Passenger pigeons once flew through here in immense flocks that sometimes numbered in the millions. Hunting and possibly diseases from domestic fowl led to their extinction early in this century. The area along the road to the right after the gap is part of the Shining Rock Wilderness, a 19,000-acre preserve favored by hikers and back-packers. Many miles of trails wind through its high peaks, lush forests, and past rushing streams.

An overlook about 5 miles from the US 276 junction offers a good view of Looking Glass Rock. This rocky knob lined with curving cliffs got its name from the sparkling reflections it gives off when wet or icy. Hikers and rock climbers love this peak, which is accessible from trails along Drive #10.

In another 1.9 miles, a pullout marks the site of Graveyard Fields. Much of the area here is open or brushy. In 1925, after a long dry spell, hunters started a fire here on Thanksgiving eve. Burning out of control, it decimated 25,000 acres. The blaze destroyed standing trees, cut timber, logging camps, and slash piles. The fire was so hot that it burned up stumps, roots, and much of the soil itself. Because it so damaged the soil, the area has been slow to recover. Graveyard Fields is a well-known hiker destination because it offers easy access to the Shining Rock Wilder-ness and high peaks such as 6,214-foot Black Balsam Knob. Another area attraction is Yellowstone Prong (a prong is a creek), visible below the road. The Graveyard Fields Loop Trail leads to three attractive waterfalls and many smaller cascades. In summer, don't expect to have this popular area to yourself.

After another 1.4 miles of parkway, you will pass another trailhead on the right. Routes lead from here to the Shining Rock Wilderness. Another popular parkway stop, known as the Devils Courthouse, follows in 2.2 miles. Legend tells us that the devil holds court in a cave within the bowels of this mountain. The Cherokee people also speak of a "nice" devil in this place. According to their story, a giant named Judaculla sat in judgment here, condemning people who lacked courage or strayed from virtue. The Devils Courthouse viewpoint lies at 5,462 feet. A short trail climbs nearly 300 feet to the knob's summit. The top is bare and rocky; without trees to get in the way, the 360-degree views are incredible.

In less than a mile, the parkway reaches Beech Gap and NC 215, which is part of the Forest Heritage Scenic Byway (Drive #10). Beyond Beech Gap the parkway turns northwest and passes between two prominent peaks, Mount Hardy and Tanasee Bald. Great views are plentiful in the next few miles as you travel along the crest of the Great Balsam Mountains. Along the right (north) side of the road, the Middle Prong Wilderness contains rugged terrain. The Cowee Mountains Over-look, about 7.4 miles past the NC 215 junction, gives visitors an impressive panorama of the mountains and valleys to the south and west.

The road soon climbs to an elevation of more than 6,000 feet and reaches the highest point on the entire Blue Ridge Parkway at 6,047-foot Richland Balsam Overlook. Nearby Richland Balsam Mountain is the highest peak in the Great Bal-sams, rising 6,410 feet. If you hike the short nature trail that leaves from the over-look, wear a sweater; it's usually quite cool up here, even in summer. The

View of misty mountains from near Balsam Gap

surrounding forest of Fraser fir and red spruce indicates a cool, wet climate. During cooler times, such as during the last ice age, this Canadian-type forest grew farther down the mountain slopes. As the climate warmed, the trees retreated upward to scattered high peaks and ridges. Sadly, as is obvious here, many of the Southern Appalachian firs are dying from an insect pest known as the balsam woolly adelgid. The red spruces are also not very healthy, victims of acid rain.

From Richland Balsam Overlook, the parkway begins to head downhill. The town of Waynesville and a large, ugly quarry soon become visible below you, on the right. The town is noted for its apple orchards. After a long, 12.5-mile descent, you will reach a low point of 3,370 feet at Balsam Gap. The gap has long been a travel route across the Great Balsam Mountains and was used by the Cherokees before Europeans arrived. Later settlers adopted the route when they arrived on the scene. In 1883, the Southern Railroad built a line through the gap, the highest point on a standard-gauge railroad in the eastern United States. Busy US 23/US 74 also crosses the gap and the parkway here. After traveling down the quiet parkway, the roar of trains and heavy traffic here can be a bit of a shock.

From Balsam Gap, the parkway once again begins a long climb, reaching a second high point in 7.6 miles. Here, at 5,718-foot Waterrock Knob Overlook, visitors can look at exhibits in the visitor center, walk a trail, and find a bathroom. Waterrock Knob rises in the distance to 6,292 feet, making it the second highest peak in the Great Balsam Mountains. It also marks the point where the Plott Balsam Mountains join the Great Balsams. The knob was named for a popular spring that once poured over the rock. Not surprisingly, the all-encompassing view from the top is wonderful.

From Waterrock Knob, the parkway descends once again, this time to Soco Gap and a junction with busy US 19. Like other similar gaps, this one has long been a popular travel route. The Cherokee people remember the gap as a place where they ambushed and defeated a large group of invading Shawnees in the mid-1700s. From Soco Gap, the parkway climbs yet again, reaching the boundary of the Cherokees' Qualla Reservation in about 1.8 miles. A series of wars with white settlers and other Indian tribes pushed the Cherokees out of North Carolina by 1838. They were forcibly removed to a reservation in Oklahoma via the well-named Trail of Tears. During the removal, a band of refugees hid in these mountains while their white agent, Will Thomas, purchased land for them. In time they were allowed to return to this land, which makes up part of the present-day reservation.

About 2.7 miles from Soco Gap, the parkway arrives at 5,100-foot Wolf Laurel Gap. Here Balsam Road leads into Great Smoky Mountains National Park, where there is a campground, picnic area, hiking trails, overlooks, and a back route to the town of Cherokee (see Drive #11). Beyond this junction, the parkway descends through the reservation, dropping off the Balsam Range past overlooks and through tunnels. In about 11 miles, the parkway ends after crossing the Oconaluftee River at Newfound Gap Road. You are now in Great Smoky Mountains National Park. Turn left to go a short distance into the busy tourist town of Cherokee. Turn right to get to the Oconaluftee Visitor Center and a route into the heart of the park (see Drive #12).

4

Blowing Rock
Blowing Rock to Roseboro

General description: A 26-mile paved and gravel road from the busy resort town of Blowing Rock deep into the tranquil Pisgah National Forest and past the tiny communities of Globe, Edgemont, Mortimer, and Roseboro.

Special attractions: Blowing Rock, Pisgah National Forest, Coffey's General Store in Edgemont, hiking, fishing, fall colors, waterfalls.

Location: Northwestern North Carolina. The drive starts in Blowing Rock (a few miles south of Boone) at the junction of US 221 and Business US 321 at the north end of the downtown business district.

Drive route name/number: Business US 321/Main Street, SR 1367/Johns River Road, SR 1362/Anthony Creek Road, NC 90, FR 981/Roseboro Road, SR 1511.

Travel season: April through October. Winter snow can make travel difficult or impossible.

Camping: The Pisgah National Forest maintains Mortimer Campground.

Services: All services available in Blowing Rock. Snacks are sometimes available in Mortimer and Edgemont.

Nearby attractions: Blue Ridge Parkway, Grandfather Mountain, Linn Cove Viaduct, ski areas around Boone, Linville Falls, Linville Caverns, Moses H. Cone Memorial Park.

For more information: Pisgah National Forest (Grandfather Ranger District), Blue Ridge Parkway (National Park Service), Blowing Rock Chamber of Commerce. See Appendix for addresses and phone numbers.

The Drive

This drive starts in the mountain resort town of Blowing Rock and winds along back roads in the Pisgah National Forest. On its way to the Blue Ridge Parkway, it passes tiny communities, rushing streams, and waterfalls. Consider purchasing a copy of the Pisgah National Forest district map and the forest's Wilson Creek Area Trail Map, along with the book *North Carolina Waterfalls: A Hiking and Photography Guide,* before you do this drive.

The town of Blowing Rock developed in the 1880s as a mountain resort. Vacationers and seasonal residents came here to escape the heat, humidity, and insects of the lowlands during summer. Temperatures rarely climb above 80 degrees F in this town, which is 4,000 feet above sea level. While the town has only about 1,500 permanent residents, its population swells to 6,500 in summer and fall.

Blowing Rock is named for a large cliff on the south side of town, which looks out over the Johns River Valley. Because of the rocky cliff's exposed position, winds usually blow up from below and cause leaves or snowflakes to float upward

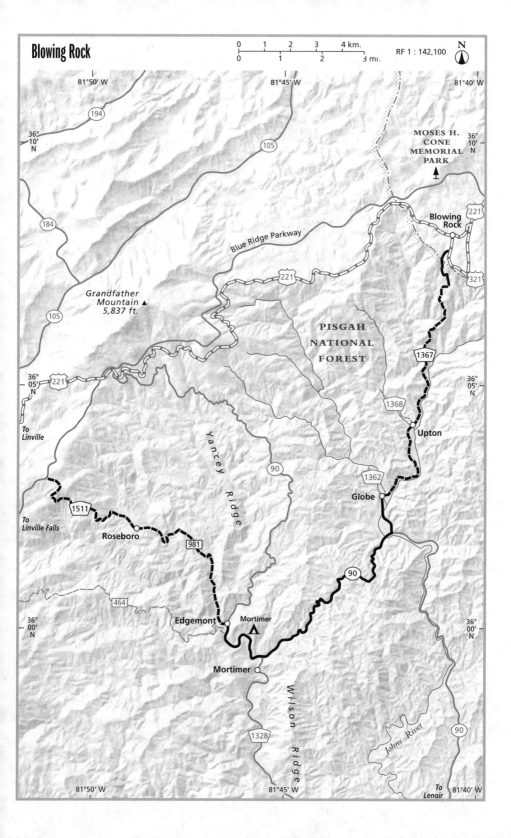

Blowing Rock

RF 1 : 142,100

N

0   1   2   3   4 km.
0   1   2   3 mi.

81°50' W   81°45' W   81°40' W

194

105

MOSES H.
CONE
MEMORIAL
PARK

36°
10'
N

184

221

Blowing
Rock

221

321

Blue Ridge Parkway

221

Grandfather
Mountain ▲
5,837 ft.

PISGAH
NATIONAL
FOREST

1367

105

1368

36°
05'
N

221

Upton

36°
05'
N

To
Linville

Yancey Ridge

90

1362

Globe

To
Linville Falls

1511

981

Roseboro

90

464

90

Edgemont

Mortimer
▲

36°
00'
N

Mortimer

36°
00'
N

Wilson Ridge

1328

Johns River

90

To
Lenoir

81°50' W   81°45' W   81°40' W

instead of falling downward. Various legends have tried to explain the upward-blowing wind. One story tells of an old-time blacksmith who got fed up with his nagging wife and tossed her off the edge into the void. Because her life had been less than upright, she wound up in hell. The devil got so tired of her nagging that he threw her back up, causing the wind to always blow upward.

A more romantic explanation revolves around a Chickasaw chief's beautiful daughter. Fearing that white men were becoming too interested in her, the chief brought her up to the mountains, where she fell in love with a young Cherokee man. When battle fires lit the sky, the young man felt obligated to return to his tribe. When the chief's daughter begged him not to leave, he was torn between his love and his obligations. He threw himself off the rock into the valley below. The girl was heartbroken and prayed for his return, and her prayers were answered when winds blew him back up to her. Since that time, the winds have blown upward from the valley. Today Blowing Rock is a small tourist attraction, with tremendous views from its clifftop and observation tower.

Start the scenic drive by following Business US 321/Main Street south from its intersection with US 221 in Blowing Rock. The road passes the busy, tourist-oriented shops of the town's central business district. Restaurants, clothing stores, gift shops, and other establishments all vie for your attention. The Blowing Rock Chamber of Commerce, located on the right only two blocks into the drive, provides loads of information. Among its other offerings is a brochure that outlines a historic walking tour of the downtown area.

One of the more interesting sites on the walking tour is St. Mary of the Hills Episcopal Church, on the left about three blocks down Main Street at the corner of Chestnut and Main. The church is known for its connection to the artist Elliot Daingerfield, who came to Blowing Rock from New York in the 1880s to recover from an illness. Over the next thirty years, Daingerfield fell in love with the area. In 1918, when a wealthy Alabama resident made a donation that allowed the community to build a new Episcopal church, he asked Daingerfield to contribute a painting. The artist proceeded to paint his *Madonna of the Hills*, which hangs in the church. In time, Daingerfield became a well-known artist; some of his works now hang in the National Gallery of Art in Washington, D.C.

Just down Main Street from the Episcopal church is the turnoff for the town of Globe on the opposite side of the street. Watch carefully and turn right onto Johns River Road/SR 1367. The pavement ends almost immediately. Though the gravel surface is good, the road is narrow and winding with blind corners. People with large RVs or trailers should not take this road.

The road descends steeply into the Johns River Valley, reaching the bottom in about 4.5 miles. Go left at a junction 5.6 miles from the start and continue downstream along the river. If you look back, you can see some of the houses of Blowing Rock perched high on the ridges above. The area around the junction is known as Upton. Not much is left of this community other than a few homes and a Baptist church. Large tree and shrub nurseries appear to be among the area's main businesses.

After another 2.5 miles the road intersects paved SR 1362/Anthony Creek Road in the tiny settlement of Globe. The small Globe Baptist Church, organized in 1797, waits at the junction. The town's most exciting days occurred during the Civil War. Although most people in the area supported the South, a substantial number sided with the Union. One of the sad effects of the war was its brother-against-brother violence. Some feuds that survive in the area to this day have their roots in the War Between the States.

An example of the war's odd alliances was Keith Blalock. A Globe resident, Blalock wanted to join the Union forces but had no opportunity to do so after the war broke out. To avoid being drafted into the Confederate States Army, he joined it as a volunteer instead. Since Blalock's wife, Malinda, didn't want to be left alone, she disguised herself and joined the war effort too. She claimed she was Keith's brother Sam, and amazingly, the disguise worked. Unhappily, the couple found no chance to join the Union forces. To get out of the Confederate army, Keith rubbed himself with poison oak and gave himself a rash. He was discharged after convincing army doctors that it was incurable. Malinda was also granted a discharge, when her gender was revealed. After leaving the army, the Blalocks hid out on Grandfather Mountain and aided the Union by recruiting others. Their little group constantly raided the Globe area, to the chagrin of Southern sympathizers. The Confederates retaliated by killing Blalock's stepfather, and the violence only escalated. Blalock survived the war, although he lost an eye in the conflict.

From the junction at the Globe Baptist Church, go left on paved SR 1362. After only a mile, the road intersects paved NC 90. Turn right on NC 90 and cross the Johns River. The pavement ends beyond the bridge, but the road has a good gravel surface. It winds and climbs steeply into a smaller valley with scattered farms and houses. Passing in and out of the national forest, the road heads upstream past more plant nurseries. It soon climbs over a small divide into another drainage, then descends into the tiny settlement of Mortimer. A small, rustic general store marks its junction with SR 1328, about 15 miles from the start of this drive in Blowing Rock.

Mortimer is quiet now but was once a thriving town. Right after the turn of the twentieth century, the Ritter Lumber Company began operations here and created the town for its workers. Soon Mortimer was booming, with more than one hundred houses, several churches, a hotel, a school, and other facilities. A railroad line was built to haul timber and supplies to the area. Then, in July 1916, thirty-six hours of torrential rain washed away the railroad, the logging operations, and much of the town. Heavy logging worsened the effects of the flood by hastening

Baptist church in Edgemont

runoff and creating landslides. The railroad and town were rebuilt, but the timber was already running out. Mortimer soon declined.

In 1922, a cotton mill helped the town rise again for six years until the mill closed. In the 1930s, the village was revitalized once more by a Civilian Conservation Corps camp and the reopening of the old cotton mill to produce hosiery. In spite of these high points, Mortimer was doomed to fail. In 1938 the railroad ceased service to the area, and in 1940 another flood occurred here, spawned by a hurricane. Most of the town was washed away once again. The general store at the road junction was one of the few surviving buildings. According to its proprietor, Mortimer has a population of seven these days. Drive a short distance left on SR 1328 to see the last remains of its old mill.

If you're tired of driving, consider a side trip to beautiful Harper Creek Falls. Turn left on SR 1328 and follow it 1.2 miles to a small pullout on the right, marking the start of the Harper Creek Trail. Using the national forest map or directions in the aforementioned waterfall book, follow the trail for about 1.6 miles past several junctions to the falls. On warm summer days expect to meet swimmers here.

Continue the scenic drive from Mortimer by going straight on NC 90. Just past the general store, look for the attractive Mortimer Campground and Picnic Area, on the right along a side creek in Pisgah National Forest. From here the gravel road follows Wilson Creek upstream about 2 miles to the village of Edgemont. Along the way you will pass the turnoff to FR 464. If you like hiking or waterfalls, consider a side trip up this road. Several trails lead from FR 464 into the proposed Lost Cove and Harper Creek Wilderness Areas, and to multiple cascades.

Take time to explore the village of Edgemont. Unlike Mortimer, this town survived both the 1916 and 1940 floods. An old white building on the left side of NC 90 was once the town's railroad depot; it is now a private residence. Edgemont was the end of the rail line for people traveling to resorts such as Blowing Rock. From here visitors took carriages or horses to their destinations. The crisp white Edgemont Baptist Church still stands across the creek on a small hill above the floodplain. Continue a short distance up NC 90 into the center of the settlement. The most interesting building is Coffey's General Store. The old store appears to have changed little since it was built early this century, though it has been moved twice because of the floods. An old pressed-tin ceiling and wooden floors complete the historic effect. Archie Coffey ran the store and the town post office for more than forty years.

To continue along the main drive route, backtrack to the junction across from the Baptist church turnoff and turn right onto Roseboro Road/FR 981. A sign here directs you to US 221. The road is narrow but has a good gravel surface like the others. It winds up a scenic stretch of national forest along Rockhouse Creek. Tall trees arch over the road as the crystal-clear creek tumbles over numerous cascades. Look for a particularly nice cascade right before the road crosses the creek on a small bridge. Beyond it, the road climbs steeply out of the creek bottom through lots of rhododendrons. After going over a divide and dropping down to the stream known as Gragg Prong, it follows that creek upstream a short distance to the small settlement of Roseboro.

Roseboro has a small church and a number of homes. Stay left on FR 981 at a junction at the edge of the village. Past the town, the unpaved road climbs steeply back into national forest and becomes SR 1511. Views begin to open up as the road climbs onto a ridge. It soon reaches the Blue Ridge Parkway and the end of the drive. For an easy loop, turn right on the parkway and follow it back to Blowing Rock, past Grandfather Mountain and over the Linn Cove Viaduct. Drive #2 describes this section of the parkway.

5

Elk Falls

Vilas to Elk Falls

General description: A 25-mile mostly paved road through rugged mountains, past a historic general store to a large, accessible waterfall.

Special attractions: Mast General Store, Elk Falls, Pisgah National Forest, fall colors, scenic views, hiking, fishing.

Location: The drive starts at the junction of US 321/421 and NC 194 about 5 miles west of Boone in the small settlement of Vilas.

Drive route names/numbers: NC 194, US 19E, SR 1303/Main Street, SR 1305/Elk River Road.

Travel season: April through October. Winter snows can make the drive quite treacherous.

Camping: The nearest public campgrounds are at Julian Price Memorial Park and Linville Falls along the Blue Ridge Parkway, and at Roan Mountain State Park in Tennessee.

Services: All services are available in Boone. Elk Park and Banner Elk have limited food, gas, and lodging. Limited food and lodging are available at Valle Crucis.

Nearby attractions: Blue Ridge Parkway, Grandfather Mountain, Tweetsie Railroad, Linn Cove Viaduct, Linville Falls, Linville Caverns, Moses H. Cone Memorial Park, Sugar Mountain, Ski Beech ski areas.

For more information: Pisgah National Forest (Grandfather Ranger District), Boone and Avery/Banner Elk Chambers of Commerce. See Appendix for addresses and phone numbers.

The Drive

This drive follows a winding route through the mountains west of Boone, past the historic Mast General Store and an Episcopal mission to thundering Elk Falls in the Pisgah National Forest. Parts of the road are very narrow and winding, with blind curves (particularly between Valle Crucis and Banner Elk). Large RVs and trailers are not recommended. Much of the route is a state scenic byway.

The drive starts just outside Boone, the largest town in this part of North Carolina. Appalachian State University is here, along with extensive tourist-oriented businesses. About 5 miles west of town, from busy US 321/421 in Vilas, take NC 194 and climb out of the valley. The road follows a fairly narrow, winding route. You will soon leave most of the traffic behind.

After about 9 miles from Boone, the highway enters the wide valley of the Watauga River. The river gets its name from an Indian term meaning "beautiful water." Within a mile you reach the village of Valle Crucis, a small farming community that was founded around 1780 by Samuel Hix and is listed on the National

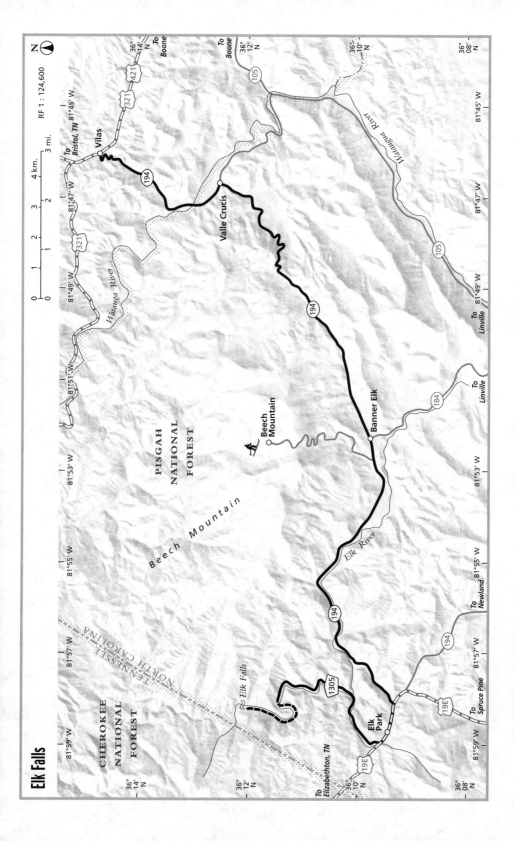

Elk Falls

RF 1 : 124,600

Register of Historic Places. The obvious stop here is the Mast General Store. This general store has become such an attraction that on weekends with pleasant weather, you may have trouble parking nearby. The store was founded in 1882 by Henry Taylor, and W. W. Mast later bought a half interest. In 1913, Mast bought out Taylor to own the store for himself. He and his family ran it for sixty years, building it into a thriving business.

Mast tried to stock everything for everybody. He is often quoted as saying, "If you can't buy it here, you don't need it." Current owners John and Faye Cooper have tried to maintain this tradition. They carry an incredible hodgepodge of items while still retaining the store's historic ambience. (Its plain white siding and tilted wooden floors appear to have not changed in a hundred years.) You can buy everything from cast-iron skillets to candy bars, from hiking boots to wooden handicrafts, from blue jeans to coffins. You can mail a letter here while you buy hardware. After you tour the maze of the first floor, head up for more in the second. If that's not enough, go a short distance past the main store to the Mast General Store Annex for an encore.

A bit past the store's annex lies the Mast Farm Inn. This inn was the main house on a farm started in 1812 by David Mast. Over the years, Mast's farm grew into a prosperous establishment with a large frame house and many outbuildings. Today the historic farm buildings have been converted into a bed and breakfast inn. Continue the drive just past the Mast General Store by turning right and staying on NC 194. The road follows Dutch Creek upstream and soon passes the Taylor House Bed and Breakfast. This elegant farmhouse within a bucolic setting is a tranquil place to spend the night.

In another mile or so you pass the Valle Crucis Episcopal Mission. The mission was founded in 1842 when Bishop Levi S. Ives purchased a large tract of land here and created the first Anglican monastic order since the Reformation. Bishop Ives gave the valley its name when he climbed a ridge and saw the interesting alignment of its creeks, which converge with the river here to form the shape of a crucifix. In Latin, the name Valle Crucis means "Valley of the Cross." The bishop's monastic order was short-lived, disbanding in 1852 because of disagreements within the church about its direction, but Ives's historic log cabin still stands.

After many years, Bishop Joseph Blount Cheshire visited the area and revived the church's activities. The new church community he founded, in 1895, included a mission school that was active until World War II. The attractive stone church here was built in 1925. Its interior is ornate, with a wood floor that uses the end cuts of lumber, rather than the more common side grain. The Episcopal Diocese of Western North Carolina now operates the mission as a camp and conference center.

Beyond the mission, NC 194 winds its way up out of the valley. The road is narrow with very sharp curves, some of them blind, so drive with care. Stay with

Elk Falls, Pisgah National Forest

NC 194 at junctions. The road eventually reaches an upper valley with scattered homes and farms. It follows the valley upstream past some great old wooden barns, and finally reaches Bowers Gap at the Avery County line. It then descends into the village of Banner Elk.

Banner Elk was named for the Banner family, early area settlers, and perhaps for the elk that once roamed these mountains. The center of town lies at the junction of NC 194 and NC 184. A short distance southeast on NC 184 is Sugar Mountain, one of the largest ski areas in North Carolina. Continue the drive by staying on NC 194. The attractive campus of Lees–McRae College is along the highway just past the junction. On the right side, a continuation of NC 184 leads to Ski Beech, another good-size ski area. Stay on NC 194.

From Banner Elk, the highway follows the Elk River downstream to Elk Park. On your left is the ritzy Elk River subdivision, complete with its own airport runway. At the junction with US 19E at the edge of Elk Park, turn right and drive 0.7

mile into the center of the small town. The elk that once roamed the region gave the town its name. Elk Park was founded in 1885.

Turn right in the center of Elk Park and then immediately turn left onto SR 1303/Main Street. Go just more than 0.3 mile and turn right on SR 1305/Elk River Road. Follow it downstream along the river for 4.0 miles to a parking lot and picnic area within the Pisgah National Forest. The pavement ends at the national forest boundary. A short walk downstream leads to Elk Falls, a large 65-foot waterfall that roars into a deep plunge pool. The pool is a popular place for swimming in the summer. The trail leads to the base of the falls for easy access. Don't approach the brink of the falls too closely; it can be slippery and dangerous.

Relax here for a while before continuing your travels. If you are returning to Boone and want a scenic alternate route, take NC 194 south to Newland from Elk Park. Turn left in Newland on NC 181 and go to Linville. From there, take NC 105 back to Boone.

6

Linville Gorge

Pisgah National Forest near Linville Falls

General description: A 19-mile gravel and paved route that encircles rugged Linville Gorge.

Special attractions: Linville Gorge Wilderness, Linville Falls, Pisgah National Forest, Wiseman's View, Hawksbill Mountain, Table Rock, hiking, scenic views, fall colors.

Location: Northwest North Carolina. The drive starts in the village of Linville Falls at the junction of NC 183 and SR 1238. Linville Falls lies just off the Blue Ridge Parkway about 30 miles southwest of Boone.

Drive route numbers: SR 1238, NC 183, NC 181, SR 1265, FR 210, FR 210B, FR 99.

Travel season: April through October. Snow in winter can make parts of the route difficult or impossible to travel.

Camping: The National Park Service manages a campground on the Blue Ridge Parkway at Linville Falls.

Services: There is limited food, gas, and lodging in Linville Falls. Spruce Pine, Linville, Boone, and Blowing Rock offer more extensive services.

Nearby attractions: Blue Ridge Parkway, Linville Caverns, Grandfather Mountain, Linn Cove Viaduct, Roan Mountain, Mount Mitchell State Park.

For more information: Pisgah National Forest (Grandfather Ranger District), Blue Ridge Parkway (National Park Service), and chambers of commerce in Mitchell County/Spruce Pine, Avery County/Banner Elk, Boone, and Blowing Rock. See Appendix for addresses and phone numbers.

The Drive

This drive partially encircles Linville Gorge, a yawning chasm where the Linville River tumbles 2,000 feet in 14 miles. The route offers spectacular views into the deep canyon. Access trails lead to Linville Falls and the summits of prominent peaks such as Table Rock and Hawksbill Mountain. Although the drive is only 19 miles long, plan on a full day of travel. Most of the road is gravel-surfaced, winding, and slow, and many nearby hikes are extremely scenic and worthwhile. Although the road is suitable for passenger cars, it is not meant for large RVs or trailers, especially in the section just before Table Rock picnic area.

I describe the drive in two segments, both starting in the village of Linville Falls. Start at the junction of NC 183 and SR 1238, about 0.7 mile south of US 221. The junction is marked by Pisgah National Forest signs pointing to the Linville Gorge Wilderness. Turn here onto SR 1238, a good gravel road. Almost immediately you will pass a parking area on the left for Linville Falls—the waterfall, not the town. If you haven't seen the falls from the Blue Ridge Parkway (Drive #2), be

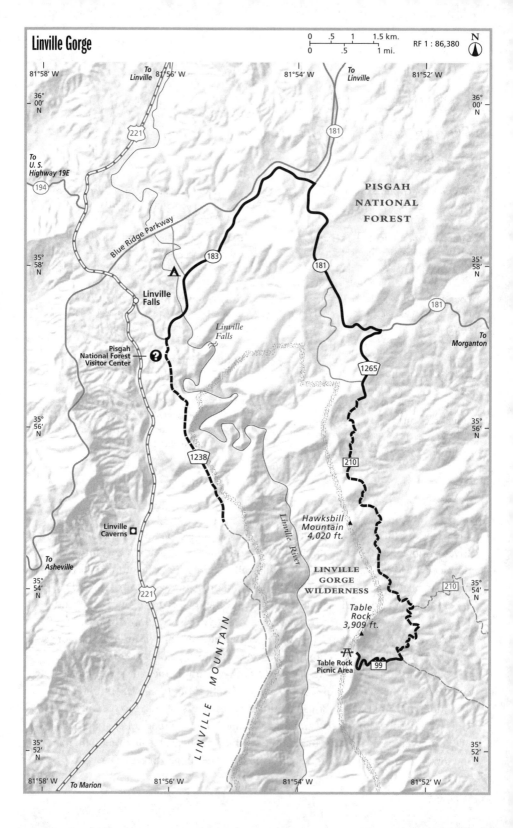

Linville Gorge

RF 1 : 86,380

N

0   .5   1   1.5 km.
0   .5   1 mi.

81°58' W
81°56' W
81°54' W
81°52' W

To Linville

To Linville

36°00' N

221

181

To U.S. Highway 19E

194

PISGAH NATIONAL FOREST

Blue Ridge Parkway

183

181

35°58' N

Linville Falls

Linville Falls

181

To Morganton

Pisgah National Forest Visitor Center

❓

1265

35°56' N

1238

210

Linville Caverns

Hawksbill Mountain 4,020 ft.

Linville River

LINVILLE GORGE WILDERNESS

210

35°54' N

To Asheville

221

Table Rock 3,909 ft.

Table Rock Picnic Area

99

LINVILLE   MOUNTAIN

35°52' N

81°58' W
To Marion
81°56' W
81°54' W
81°52' W

Linville Gorge, Wiseman's View

sure to stop now. It's a short walk from here down to one of the best waterfalls in the state.

Continue down SR 1238 for about 0.4 mile to the Pisgah National Forest information center on the right in an old, interesting cabin. You can get maps and information here. Particularly useful are maps of this district, the national forest, and the Linville Gorge Wilderness. Beyond the information center, the road continues south along the high ridge separating Linville Gorge from a fork of the Catawba River. Here and there you can peek through the trees for views in both directions. Trailheads appear with regularity on the left side of the road.

At about 3.9 miles from the start, be sure to take the very short side road on the left to Wiseman's View. A short, paved, barrier-free trail leads from the parking area, at the end of the spur road, to the overlook. The view may not make you any wiser, but it will take your breath away. Cliffs and steep, wooded slopes drop off abruptly to the Linville River, 1,300 feet below. Across the gorge tower the rocky crags of Table Rock and Hawksbill Mountain, which you'll visit in the second segment of this drive. Mountains are visible all around, and views stretch far over the Piedmont on a clear day.

Because of the rugged terrain, much of the 11,000-acre Linville Gorge Wilderness Area was never logged. Today it is forested with tall virgin timber. The area was first designated as a wilderness in 1951 by the USDA Forest Service and became an official wilderness area in 1964. Because it is the most popular of North Carolina's wilderness areas, the Forest Service limits the number of backpacking permits on summer and fall weekends. Contact the Pisgah National Forest information center for details about the permit system.

In recent years, SR 1238 has been improved, making it possible to do this drive as a loop if armed with a good map. However, I chose to retrace the route on SR 1238 to Linville Falls.

For the second half of the drive, turn onto NC 183. The road crosses the Linville River upstream from Linville Gorge and intersects NC 181 after about 3.8 miles. Turn right on NC 181 and reset your odometer. The highway soon passes through the tiny community of Jonas Ridge, where you can get gas if necessary. At 3 miles from the junction of NC 183 and NC 181, turn right onto a small paved road. The junction is marked by a Gingercake Acres sign on the left and a Table Rock picnic area sign on the right. At a "Y" in 0.3 mile, go left on paved SR 1265. The road passes through a subdivision where homes, on the left, have a tremendous view from the mountainside. The pavement ends in less than a mile where the road becomes FR 210 and enters the national forest.

Narrow FR 210 descends through lush forest, passing the Sitting Bear trailhead on the right in about 1.5 miles. Trails lead from here along the rim of the gorge and down into the gorge itself. Get a copy of the Linville Gorge Wilderness map if you plan to walk any of these area trails. Drivers get occasional great views to the southeast through the trees.

In another mile you will pass the Hawksbill Mountain trailhead on the right. If you're tired of driving, the trail here makes a particularly fine hike. Follow it uphill about 0.5 mile to a junction. Turn left and climb about 0.7 mile to the mountain's rocky 4,020-foot summit. The bare rock allows views in all directions over a huge swath of country, ranging from Grandfather Mountain to the Piedmont. A mile past the Hawksbill turnoff, the Spence Ridge trailhead provides yet another opportunity to hike into the gorge from FR 210.

From here the road descends steadily for another mile to a junction marked with a Table Rock picnic area sign. Turn right and go uphill for a change, on FR 210B. The North Carolina Outward Bound School is on the right after 0.6 mile. The school teaches self-confidence and awareness of nature, primarily through outdoor activities such as backpacking, rock climbing, and wilderness solitude. Continue straight past the school's driveway. The road turns into paved FR 99 about 0.9 mile past the school. Although paved, the final steep climb to the picnic area is very narrow, with sharp curves.

The road ends at the picnic area on the rim of Linville Gorge. Cliff-lined Table Rock looms over the north side of the area, enticing rock climbers from all over. Relax, eat lunch, and consider taking the 1-mile trail to the top of the mountain.

View of Linville Gorge from summit of Table Rock Mountain

The trail starts from the north end of the parking lot, up a series of rocky steps. Ignore the unmarked climbers' trail that forks right after the trail levels. At about 0.3 mile, the proper trail turns right at a junction, heading up the mountain. In a short distance the trail forks again; the Mountains-to-the-Sea Trail turns left here. Go right again and continue climbing. Before too long, you'll reach the rocky, 3,909-foot summit and its incredible views.

The views here are even better than those at Wiseman's View, since the summit is higher. The gorge spreads out below you and mountains extend to the horizon in all directions except southeast, where the mountains flatten into the Piedmont. A network of informal trails crisscrosses the summit, leading to different viewpoints and vertigo-inducing cliffs favored by rock climbers. From the top you can pick out much of the route you followed as you nearly circled the gorge. Because of its distinctive, rocky shape, Table Rock is a famous mountain landmark. Most people only see it from a distance, so enjoy being one of the select minority that has made it to the spectacular summit.

7

Roan Mountain

Spruce Pine to Roan Mountain

General description: A 25-mile paved route from the historic mining town of Spruce Pine to the extensive rhododendron gardens on the summit of Roan Mountain.

Special attractions: Roan Mountain, Pisgah National Forest, Cherokee National Forest (Tennessee), Museum of North Carolina Minerals, rhododendron gardens, rockhounding, hiking, scenic views, fall colors.

Location: Northwestern North Carolina. The drive starts in Spruce Pine at the junction of US 19E and NC 226.

Drive route numbers: NC 226, NC 261, SR 1348/FR 130.

Travel season: April through October. Winter snow closes the upper part of the route, except to cross-country skiers.

Camping: There are no public campgrounds along the route, but a campground in Roan Mountain State Park in Tennessee is nearby.

Services: All services are available in Spruce Pine. Limited services are available in Bakersville.

Nearby attractions: Blue Ridge Parkway, Penland School of Crafts, Linville Falls, Linville Gorge, Linville Caverns, Grandfather Mountain, ski areas.

For more information: Pisgah National Forest (Toecane Ranger Station), Blue Ridge Parkway (National Park Service), Mitchell County Chamber of Commerce (Spruce Pine). See Appendix for addresses and phone numbers.

The Drive

This drive travels north from the old mining area surrounding Spruce Pine to the rhododendron gardens atop one of the highest mountains in the southern Appalachians. It offers a broad array of recreational activities, from searching for precious gems to hiking and viewing wildflowers. The drive's starting point, Spruce Pine, is the center of the North Carolina mining region. Miners have dug here since prehistoric times and continue to do so today.

Spruce Pine was founded relatively recently by North Carolina standards, in 1908. In that year the Clinchfield Railroad opened a station here to handle shipping for the logging industry. The Clinchfield line was built with great effort over the Blue Ridge Mountains, connecting the Piedmont of North Carolina with the Midwest via Tennessee. It is still the only railroad to cut directly through the southern Appalachians' formidable barrier.

When most people think of hard-rock mining, they think of western states such as California and Colorado. Before the California gold rush of 1849, however,

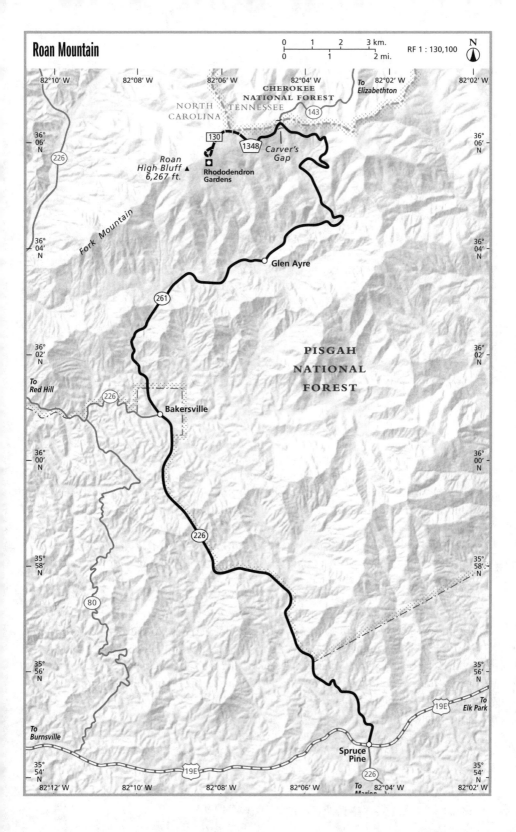

A stormy view of Roan Mountain

North Carolina led the nation in gold production. Precious and semiprecious gems such as rubies, emeralds, sapphires, and amethysts also have been mined for years in the mountains of North Carolina. Geologists and prospectors have found hundreds of minerals here, many with commercial value. Although gold and precious gems are no longer produced commercially in large quantities, other minerals are still quite important to the area's economy. North Carolina is the country's largest producer of feldspar, a mineral used in many industrial processes, including manufacture of glass, paint, and ceramics. The Spruce Pine area is known for its extremely pure quartz deposits; much of the world's quartz comes from here. Some of the area's quartz was used to make the 200-inch mirror of the Mount Palomar telescope in California, one of the world's largest. Pure quartz is also very important in electronics. The silicon crystals used for computer chips are created by using specially treated quartz. North Carolina is also home to the nation's largest tungsten mine. A metal with a very high melting point, tungsten is used in lightbulb filaments, drill bits, saw blades, missile and space components, and many other applications.

Before you head north on the main scenic drive route, consider making a short side trip south from Spruce Pine on NC 226 toward Marion and the Blue

Ridge Parkway. Where the highway meets the parkway, the Museum of North Carolina Minerals has exhibits detailing the mining history of North Carolina. It also displays a wide range of gems and minerals, from gold nuggets and rubies to tungsten and quartz. One of the most interesting exhibits holds a display of plain-looking rocks that fluoresce with brilliant colors when bathed with ultraviolet light. The museum underwent a major renovation and enlargement in 2002.

Some people get so excited about minerals that they want to hunt for their own. If you drive to the museum from Spruce Pine on NC 226, you pass several gemstone mines that allow you to wash ore in search of treasures. Other gemstone mines are located near Little Switzerland, a few miles away. The ore buckets that you purchase to wash with water are often enriched, so the odds are good that you will find something, maybe even something valuable. After all, the famous Tiffany Jewelers of New York operated an emerald mine near Little Switzerland at the turn of the twentieth century. The gemstone mines also have shops that sell all kinds of mineral specimens.

After hunting for treasure, return to Spruce Pine and begin the drive. Busy NC 226 winds through the center of town and heads northwest toward Bakersville. In about 7.6 miles, you'll pass a historic marker that tells of the old Sinkhole Mine, about 4 miles southwest. The mine is believed to be one of the oldest in the area, with early excavations by local Indians. Legend says that Spaniards worked the mine in the 1500s and 1600s, digging for silver. United States senator Thomas Clingman hunted for silver here after the Civil War, but was unsuccessful. Commercial quantities of mica were removed from the mine in later years.

Shortly beyond the historic marker, drivers get a good view of Roan Mountain, looming on the horizon. The road soon carries you into Bakersville. The Mitchell County Courthouse lies at a junction in the center of this small town. This interesting building, built in 1907 in a neoclassical revival style, is worth a look. From the courthouse junction, follow NC 261 out of town.

Once you are past Bakersville, the traffic gets much lighter and the countryside is less developed and more scenic. The road now starts to climb slowly toward Roan Mountain. It reaches a gap between the Pumpkin Patch and Meadlock Mountains about 3 miles from Bakersville, then drops into the Little Rock Creek valley. After passing scattered homes, Christmas tree farms, and the small village of Glen Ayre, the road begins to climb in earnest. Seemingly endless mountain views to the southwest get better and better as you ascend the flanks of Roan Mountain.

The highway finally reaches its high point of 5,512 feet at Carver's Gap, on the crest of Roan Mountain. The gap holds the state line between North Carolina and Tennessee, and the boundary between the Pisgah and Cherokee National Forests. The boundary lines follow the crest of Roan Mountain, as does the Appalachian Trail. A parking area at the gap is often used by hikers along the Appalachian Trail. On bare eastern slopes above the gap, the trail is clearly visible.

A grassy bald, Roan Mountain in background

From Carver's Gap, follow SR 1348/FR 130 the rest of the way to the summit of Roan Mountain. If you are driving this route in early spring or late fall, you may want to call the Pisgah National Forest ahead of time to make sure the road is open. It climbs steadily through a thick forest of Fraser fir and spruce. Because of the high elevation and cool climate, the forest resembles that which would be found much farther north in Canada at lower elevations. The conifers here are in better shape than the spruce-fir forests in the Great Smokies and Black Mountains. Fraser firs, such as the ones found here, are commonly raised in commercial nurseries for Christmas trees.

Scientists are not sure why some Southern Appalachian mountaintops, such as the crest of Roan Mountain, are not forested. Some have speculated that Indians occasionally burned the summits, creating these "balds." One legend tells of a time when many local tribes were allied against the Catawbas and determined to possess their land. The Catawbas challenged the other tribes to a battle for supremacy on the summit of Roan Mountain. The Catawbas overcame their adversaries with great bloodshed in three battles. Afterward, the Great Spirit caused the forest on the battlegrounds to die. Today the rhododendrons that grow here have blooms of red and pink because of the blood of the many Indians killed in battle.

The pavement ends at the Cloudland parking area after about 1.7 miles. From here a short trail leads to a great overlook into Tennessee. The Cloudland Trail parallels the gravel road beyond the parking area. Both trail and parking area were named for the Cloudland Hotel, which once operated on one of Roan Mountain's summits. The 166-room hotel was built in 1885 and enjoyed modest fame for the cool temperatures in summer and tremendous views. Because of its remote location, visitors had to make lengthy journeys by railroad and carriage to reach it.

Beyond the Cloudland parking area, a good gravel road leads a short distance farther to another parking area on the left. From the small information center here, a short multiloop trail, partially barrier-free, winds through the rhododendron gardens. Several hundred acres of the shrubs bloom profusely in June, coloring the mountaintop with red, pink, and lavender. Thousands of people come to see the display every year. A small fee is now charged to enter the area part of the year.

The road goes only a short distance farther, ending in a large loop. From the end of the loop, the Cloudland Trail continues along the crest of the mountain to 6,267-foot Roan High Bluff. The first 0.5 mile of the trail climbs to a wooden observation deck on the bluff's summit, offering tremendous views. Roan High Knob, the highest peak on the mountain, is only 19 feet higher and can be reached via the Appalachian Trail from Carver's Gap. Enjoy the views, flowers, and cool fresh air before returning to the valley visible far below.

8

Lake Tahoma
Pleasant Gardens to Micaville

General description: A 27-mile paved route up over the Blue Ridge Mountains and down the South Toe River.

Special attractions: Blue Ridge Parkway, Pisgah National Forest, Lake Tahoma, Black Mountains, fishing, hiking, scenic views, fall colors.

Location: Western North Carolina. The drive begins in the village of Pleasant Gardens at the junction of NC 80 and US 70. Pleasant Gardens is about 30 miles east of Asheville near Marion.

Drive route number: NC 80.

Travel season: April through October. Winter snow can make travel difficult.

Camping: The Pisgah National Forest operates Black Mountain and Carolina Hemlock Campgrounds.

Services: Pleasant Gardens has limited food and gas. There are some gas and food sources available along the route and in Micaville. Nearby Asheville, Spruce Pine, and Marion have more extensive visitor services.

Nearby attractions: Mount Mitchell State Park, Linville Falls, Linville Caverns, Linville Gorge, Roan Mountain, Biltmore Estate.

For more information: Pisgah National Forest (Grandfather and Appalachian (Toecane) Ranger Districts), Blue Ridge Parkway (National Park Service), Mitchell County Chamber of Commerce (Spruce Pine). See Appendix for addresses and phone numbers.

The Drive

This is a short, easy drive from the town of Pleasant Gardens, past a small resort lake, up to the Blue Ridge Parkway. From there the road drops down the other side of the mountains and follows the South Toe River to Micaville.

The drive starts in Pleasant Gardens, a small town at the foot of the mountains. The town was named for property purchased in the area by an early settler, John McDowell. McDowell's son Joseph went on to become a Revolutionary War hero; the county was named for him. John McDowell built a large house near here in the 1780s, close to the junction of US 70 and US 221. Another large, historic house nearby was built at about the same time by Colonel John Carson. Carson's first wife was Rachel McDowell, Joseph's sister, with whom he had several children. Pleasant Gardens must have been a small community then. Carson's second wife was Joseph McDowell's widow, with whom he had several more children. Carson's well-maintained home is now used as a museum.

Drive north out of Pleasant Gardens on NC 80 past farms and scattered homes in a broad valley. The valley slowly narrows until you reach the Lake

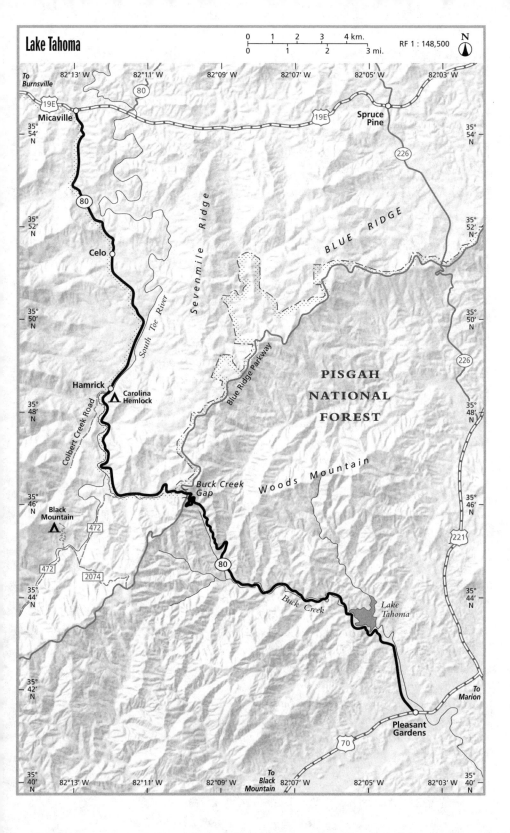

Lake Tahoma in fall

Tahoma Dam after about 2.5 miles. This small lake was created on Buck Creek in 1924 by private investors as part of a real estate development. The lake's name came about as part of a promotional contest. It is a made-up Indian name that is supposed to mean "God's mountain lake." The developers constructed a notable stone building out in the lake, attached to shore by a causeway. The building was a prospering dance hall and casino until the Great Depression hit. Today the old casino still stands out in the lake, and cabins line the quiet lakeshore.

Highway NC 80 hugs the shore of Lake Tahoma for more than a mile, then follows the heavily wooded, narrow canyon of Buck Creek upstream, past occasional homes. It reaches the Blue Ridge Parkway about 8 miles from the lake. The upper part of the road, in undeveloped Pisgah National Forest, winds its way through numerous 180-degree turns; drive carefully. At the crest of the ridge, in Buck Creek Gap, the Blue Ridge Parkway crosses NC 80 via an overpass. The parkway offers many possible side trips, as described elsewhere in this guide.

From Buck Creek Gap, NC 80 descends into the watershed of the South Toe River on a less winding road. You will pass Christmas tree farms that have been carved out of the forest here, plus a gas station and restaurant in about 1.5 miles. Just beyond is a bed and breakfast inn.

Forest Road 472 turns left about 2.3 miles below Buck Creek Gap. That road heads deep into a scenic area of the Pisgah National Forest, at the foot of the towering Black Mountains. After reaching Black Mountain Campground, it eventually climbs back up to the Blue Ridge Parkway. Battle-hardened hikers can take the arduous trail from Black Mountain Campground to the summit of Mount Mitchell, the highest peak in the eastern United States. The hike is spectacular, with an elevation gain on the order of 4,000 feet. It's not exactly a stroll in the park.

Just past the turnoff of FR 472 is the ritzy Mount Mitchell Golf Club. It's not an ugly spot for a game of golf. The Black Mountains loom over the lush fairways, inspiring extra effort by the golfers. Past the greens, the road continues to wind down the South Toe River valley, passing occasional homes. The Black Mountains loom above you, their upper slopes darkly colored by a forest of fir and spruce.

The Carolina Hemlock Campground and Recreation Area is on the left about 3 miles below the golf club. In summer, locals flock here to swim and ride innertubes in the river's rapids and swimming holes. More trails for the Black Mountains and Mount Mitchell begin in the recreation area. To get to them, continue down NC 80 a very short distance from the campground and cross a bridge to a junction with a gas station and restaurant. Turn left here and follow Colbert Creek Road to the trailheads.

Below the Carolina Hemlocks Campground and Recreation Area, the valley slowly widens. A few miles after passing through the small settlements of Hamrick and Celo, drivers arrive in Micaville. Mines visible on the slopes here hint at the origin of Micaville's name. Much of the early local mining was done to obtain mica, a transparent, glassy mineral that forms in sheets. Other important minerals mined in the area include feldspar and pure quartz, a key ingredient of modern computer chips. The drive ends here. More discussion of the area's mining history can be found in Drive #7, Roan Mountain.

9

Spivey Gap

US 19W/US 19E junction to Earnestville, Tennessee

General description: A 29-mile paved road that climbs up and over a remote, rugged mountain area into Tennessee.

Special attractions: Pisgah National Forest, Appalachian Trail, old barns, waterfalls, hiking, fishing, fall colors.

Location: Northwestern North Carolina. The drive starts at the junction where US 19 splits into US 19W and US 19E about 30 miles northeast of Asheville.

Drive route number: US 19W.

Travel season: April through October. Winter snow can make travel difficult and treacherous.

Camping: The Pisgah National Forest maintains only a picnic area at Spivey Gap. The nearest public campgrounds are in the Mount Mitchell area; see Drive #2.

Services: Only limited gas and snacks are available along the route. Full services are available nearby in Asheville, Mars Hill, Burnsville, and Johnson City, Tennessee.

Nearby attractions: Blue Ridge Parkway, Mount Mitchell, Roan Mountain, Wolf Laurel Ski Resort, whitewater rafting.

For more information: Pisgah National Forest (Appalachian (Toecane) Ranger District), Asheville Convention and Visitors Bureau. See Appendix for addresses and phone numbers.

The Drive

This drive winds through the rugged Bald Mountains, over a divide, and into Tennessee. It follows a quiet route off the beaten path that can easily be extended into a loop. Start at the junction where US 19 splits into US 19W and US 19E, just a few miles west of Burnsville. Burnsville was named for Otway Burns, a patriot during the War of 1812. After building a very fast sailing ship, Burns made himself extremely unpopular with the British navy by capturing and destroying many of its vessels. Even though the British officers put a price on his head, he was never captured—although his ship finally was taken.

From the US 19 junctions, take US 19W downstream along the Cane River. This watercourse apparently was named for the extensive canebrakes growing along its banks. Many of the river's tributaries roll off the slopes of the Black Mountains and Mount Mitchell, the highest peak in the eastern United States. Scattered homes and farms dot the Cane River valley. Many old wooden tobacco barns, most still in use, add a rustic charm to the drive.

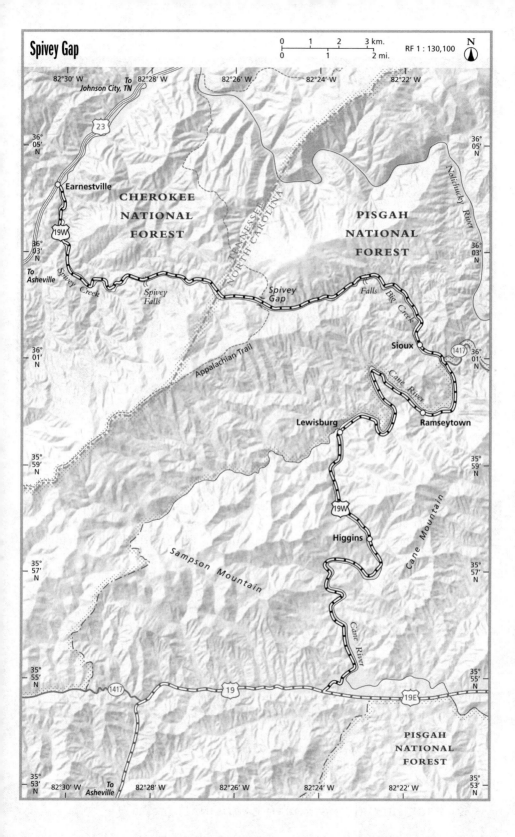

Spivey Gap

0 1 2 3 km.
0 1 2 mi.

RF 1 : 130,100

N

82°30' W
82°28' W
To
Johnson City, TN
82°26' W
82°24' W
82°22' W

36°
05'
N

23

Earnestville

CHEROKEE
NATIONAL
FOREST

PISGAH
NATIONAL
FOREST

Nolichucky River

36°
05'
N

19W

36°
03'
N

To
Asheville

Spivey Creek

*Spivey
Falls*

TENNESSEE
NORTH CAROLINA

*Spivey
Gap*

Falls

Big Creek

36°
03'
N

Sioux

1417

36°
01'
N

Appalachian Trail

Lewisburg

Cane River

Ramseytown

36°
01'
N

35°
59'
N

19W

Higgins

Cane Mountain

35°
59'
N

35°
57'
N

Sampson Mountain

Cane River

35°
57'
N

35°
55'
N

1417

19

19E

35°
55'
N

PISGAH
NATIONAL
FOREST

35°
53'
N

82°30' W
*To
Asheville*

82°28' W

82°26' W

82°24' W

82°22' W

35°
53'
N

Barns in Yancey County

On the right in less than 6 miles is a large, impressive stone building that seems out of place in the tiny rural settlement of Higgins. This structure and several smaller outbuildings were once the home of the Markle Handicraft School. The school, now abandoned, was once sponsored by the Presbyterian Church to foster traditional mountain crafts.

Beyond Higgins, the valley narrows as it follows a path along the rushing Cane River. In less than 3 miles you reach the settlement of Lewisburg, which is today little more than a scattering of houses. Stay right here, on US 19W, and cross the river. The valley stays narrow. Many homes on the far side of the river have pedestrian suspension bridges to connect their homes to the highway. This area has a poor economy, as evidenced by the condition of many of the homes. Its residents have found it increasingly difficult to make a good living off the land. Here and there kudzu vines thrive, smothering the trees and shrubs that they climb. Kudzu was imported to control erosion, but it is now considered a scourge because of its rapid, suffocating growth.

In less than 5 miles, the road passes through another hamlet, Ramseytown. A short distance beyond this community, the highway leaves the Cane River and

Big Creek waterfall in Pisgah National Forest

begins to climb the narrow valley carved by Big Creek. You can continue to follow the Cane River a few miles downstream on a gravel road to where it joins the North Toe River to become the Nolichucky River. The Nolichucky has become popular for whitewater boat trips. The Clinchfield Railroad, the only line to cut straight through the Southern Appalachians, follows the path the river has carved through the mountains.

The road passes through the village of Sioux about 0.7 mile after leaving the Cane River. The road and creek climb steadily and soon enter undeveloped woods that are part of the Pisgah National Forest. The rapid elevation change creates many cascades on the creek. Watch carefully for an unmarked gravel pullout on the left side of the road about 1.8 miles past Sioux. A small but quite attractive waterfall lies just below the road here. On a hot, sticky summer day, the plunge pool at its base looks inviting.

From the waterfall, the road climbs another 3-plus miles into the Bald Mountains to Spivey Gap. The Pisgah National Forest manages a small recreation area with picnic tables where the Appalachian Trail crosses the road. This famous path follows the Appalachian Mountains from Maine to Georgia and stretches more than 2,000 miles. Every year, a select group of people attempt to hike its entire length in one season. Millions of others hike much smaller segments along its scenic route. From here the trail heads northwest toward Roan Mountain and southwest toward the Great Smoky Mountains.

From Spivey Gap, US 19W descends the other side of the Bald Mountains. It leaves the Pisgah National Forest and enters Tennessee in less than a mile. The road follows Spivey Creek downstream. Watch for an unmarked overlook on the left, a little more than 2 miles from the state boundary; there's a nice waterfall below the road here in the tumbling creek. The drive ends in a few more miles at the junction with I–26, where Spivey Creek joins Indian Creek near Earnestville.

For a quick return to the Asheville area, turn left and follow I–26 back into North Carolina. The highway is a four-lane freeway, which connects Johnson City, Tennessee, with Asheville. The busy freeway is fast and convenient, but it doesn't have the charm of a scenic drive.

10

Forest Heritage Scenic Drive

Pisgah National Forest near Brevard

General description: A 65-mile paved road through the heart of the Pisgah Ranger District of the Pisgah National Forest, past waterfalls, historic sites, mountain overlooks, and miles of lush, undeveloped forest.

Special attractions: Pisgah National Forest, Cradle of Forestry in America Visitor Center, Pink Beds, Looking Glass Falls, Looking Glass Rock, Sliding Rock, Shining Rock Wilderness, Middle Prong Wilderness, rock climbing, hiking, fishing, swimming, fall colors, scenic views.

Location: Southwestern North Carolina. The drive starts at the junction of US 276 and US 64 on the northeast edge of Brevard.

Drive route number: US 276, NC 215.

Travel season: The best time for travel is spring through fall. Winter snow can make travel difficult at times.

Camping: The Pisgah National Forest manages Davidson River and Sunburst Campgrounds along the route.

Services: All services are available in Brevard.

Nearby attractions: Nantahala National Forest, Blue Ridge Parkway, Great Smoky Mountains National Park, Biltmore Estate, Whitewater Falls, Cullasaja Gorge.

For more information: Pisgah National Forest (Pisgah Ranger District), Brevard Chamber of Commerce. See Appendix for addresses and phone numbers.

The Drive

This drive takes you on a big loop through the Pisgah Ranger District in 495,000-acre Pisgah National Forest, past enough sights to keep you occupied for days. The Pisgah is the second-largest national forest in North Carolina. The Pisgah Ranger District is one of four districts within the forest; it's noteworthy since it is the place where modern American forestry practices were developed. Covering about 157,000 acres, the district ranges in elevation from 2,000 feet above sea level to a 6,140-foot peak at Richland Balsam Mountain.

The drive starts on the northeast end of Brevard at the big, commercial intersection of US 64 and US 276. Take US 276 north into the Pisgah National Forest. As you enter the forest, you will almost immediately leave behind the commercial bustle. Although US 276 is a relatively busy highway, it's still calm compared to what you've just come through.

You'll soon pass Sycamore Flats picnic area on the left, followed shortly by Davidson River Campground. The Davidson River was named for Benjamin

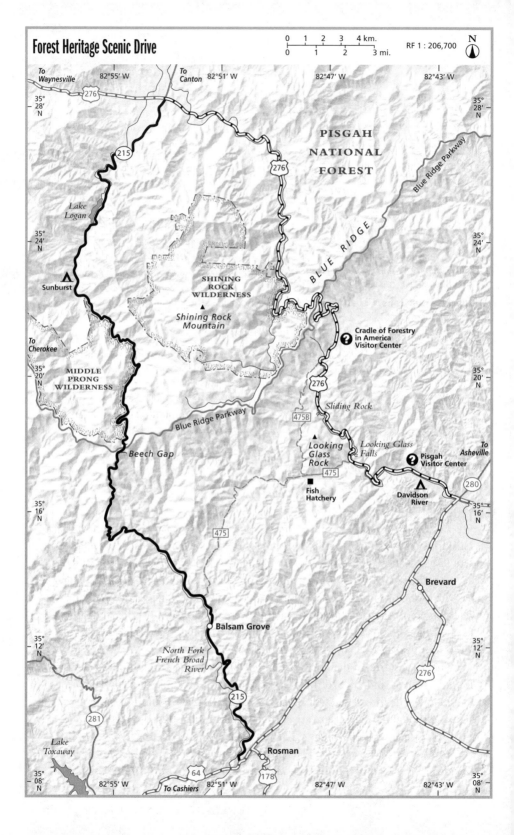

Forest Heritage Scenic Drive

RF 1 : 206,700

N

0   1   2   3   4 km.
0   1   2   3 mi.

To Waynesville

To Canton

82°55' W 82°51' W 82°47' W 82°43' W

35° 28' N

276

215

Lake Logan

PISGAH

NATIONAL

FOREST

Blue Ridge Parkway

276

35° 24' N

B L U E   R I D G E

Sunburst

SHINING ROCK WILDERNESS

Shining Rock Mountain

To Cherokee

35° 20' N

MIDDLE PRONG WILDERNESS

Cradle of Forestry in America Visitor Center

276

Sliding Rock

475B

Blue Ridge Parkway

Looking Glass Falls

Beech Gap

Looking Glass Rock

Pisgah Visitor Center

To Asheville

475

35° 16' N

Fish Hatchery

Davidson River

280

35° 16' N

35° 12' N

475

Brevard

Balsam Grove

North Fork French Broad River

276

35° 12' N

281

215

35° 08' N

Lake Toxaway

Rosman

64   178

35° 08' N

To Cashiers

82°55' W 82°51' W 82°47' W 82°43' W

Davidson, a Revolutionary War veteran who settled here. The Pisgah Visitor Center is just beyond the campground on the right. You may want to stop in for national forest maps and information. From the visitor center, the road follows the river upstream past Coontree Picnic Area.

FR 475 forks off to the left about 0.5 mile past Coontree, following the Davidson River upstream. The road is worth a side trip. In about 0.4 mile it leads to a trailhead for Looking Glass Rock. A fairly strenuous hiking trail leads about 3 miles to the top of the rocky peak, a great spot for dramatic views of the surrounding mountains. The peak's slopes are cliffs, some of which are not quite vertical. After a rain or a frosty night, water runs down the cliff faces, making the shiny rock reflect the sun like a mirror. Climbers are attracted to the rock faces here.

Farther up FR 475, a little past the Looking Glass Rock trailhead, you can visit a trout hatchery run by the North Carolina Wildlife Resources Commission and the new Pisgah Center for Wildlife Education. Trout are raised here for stocking in area streams. For a cheap thrill, buy some fish food here and watch as the trout go into a feeding frenzy when you toss it into the water. For another hiking option, follow the trail that leads into the John Rock Scenic Area next to the hatchery.

Back road fans can continue up gravel FR 475B past the hatchery. The road climbs out of the river bottom in about a mile, leading to a very short trail to Slick Rock Falls. This modest waterfall drops over an overhanging ledge and is well named; don't go anywhere near its top. The trail continues above the falls toward Looking Glass Rock. FR 475B continues circling Looking Glass Rock, passing another Looking Glass trailhead and eventually rejoining US 276. If you follow FR 475B all the way to US 276, be sure to turn right and go back down US 276 to the junction of FR 475, or you will miss Sliding Rock and impressive Looking Glass Falls.

From the US 276 and FR 475 junction, continue up US 276, 0.3 mile to the large pullout on the right at Looking Glass Falls. On weekends and in summer, this is a busy spot. The falls plunge over a dark rock ledge in a single 60-foot cascade. The clean drop, high water volume, and rocky setting make for a very attractive waterfall. A short trail leads from the road down to the base of the falls.

Farther up US 276, trees arch over the road as it climbs higher into the mountains alongside Looking Glass Creek. Small picnic spots dot the route. A parking area about a mile past Looking Glass Falls has a 0.7-mile trail that leads to Moore Cove Falls. This 50-foot cascade drops off an overhang, so you can walk behind it for a cool shower on a hot summer day. The next major attraction (and in summer it *is* major) along the route is Sliding Rock, about 1.2 miles above the Moore Cove Falls parking area. Sliding Rock is a long, smooth, slanting cascade that drops into a deep plunge pool. A bathhouse, large parking lot, and even a lifeguard in summer facilitate what kids have been doing here since the turn of the last century—sliding down the rock into the pool, only to come up gasping from the cold mountain water.

Looking Glass Falls, Pisgah National Forest

Be sure to stop in at the Cradle of Forestry in America Visitor Center on the right about 2.4 miles up the road from Sliding Rock. The large visitor center here, with several historic buildings and attractions plus two trails, will keep you busy for some time as you learn about the birth of modern forestry.

Until late in the nineteenth century (and in some areas well into the twentieth century), logging was done by lumber companies that came into an area, cut all usable trees, then moved on to the next untouched forest. Little effort was made to make forestry a sustainable business by doing such things as replanting seedlings and controlling erosion on logged land. That all began to change in the late 1880s when George Vanderbilt began buying land for his immense Biltmore Estate. Eventually acquiring some 125,000 acres in North Carolina, Vanderbilt named his land the Pisgah Forest after the biblical mountain from which Moses got his first view of the Promised Land. To manage his forest, he hired Gifford Pinchot in 1892.

Pinchot was trained in European forestry practices. He knew the benefits that came from managing forests for sustained profitability, rather than cut-and-run logging. He was dismayed to see how Vanderbilt's land had been abused in earlier years and set about establishing better forestry practices. Pinchot recommended that Vanderbilt add to his holdings. Successful here, he later became the founding chief of the USDA Forest Service under President Theodore Roosevelt.

In 1895, a German named Carl Schenck succeeded Pinchot in managing Vanderbilt's forest lands. Three years later Schenck opened the first forestry school in America at the Biltmore Estate. Winter classes were held at the estate proper near Asheville, and summer classes were held here in the forest in buildings once used by residents of the mountain community called Pink Beds. The buildings were restored and reconstructed as rangers' homes, school buildings, student dwellings, and for other uses. Until Schenck and Vanderbilt parted ways in 1909, Schenck worked to teach his students modern forestry practice. He also educated owners of timberland about topics such as replanting and selective cutting, ensuring sustainable production in the future.

Federal legislation passed in 1911 and supported by North Carolina lawmakers authorized the purchase of land for national forests in the eastern United States. Vanderbilt died soon after the law was passed. The U.S. government purchased the Pisgah Forest from his widow in 1916, creating the nucleus for the national forest we see here today. The processes begun here led to the creation of all other eastern national forests.

Start your visit at Cradle of Forestry at the large visitor center by viewing a short film and exhibits about the site. Then follow either or both of two easy, paved 1-mile loop trails. The Biltmore Campus Trail winds through the old buildings of Schenck's school, including the schoolhouse, ranger homes, blacksmith shop, commissary, office, and the student quarters. Students were told to find themselves a place to stay, and they sometimes settled in abandoned mountaineer cabins and farm homes. They named their humble abodes Hell Hole, Little Hell Hole, the Palace, Little Bohemia, and Rest for the Wicked. Craftspeople often give demonstrations here of skills ranging from blacksmithing and woodcarving to weaving. The second loop trail, the Forest Festival Trail, relates some of Schenck's work in the Vanderbilt forests and features exhibits on tree nurseries, portable sawmills, conifer plantations, logging railroads, and other related subjects.

After touring the Cradle of Forestry center, continue your drive on US 276. Just past the center is Pink Beds picnic area on the right. The name probably comes from the colorful blooms of rhododendron and mountain laurel. Past the picnic site, the road climbs steadily up to a junction with the Blue Ridge Parkway, another beautiful and very worthwhile drive. The adjacent section of the parkway is covered in Drive #3. You can make Drive #10 shorter and return to Brevard by taking the parkway toward the Great Smoky Mountains and rejoining the drive at

Historic ranger residence at the Cradle of Forestry in America Center

NC 215. You can get to Asheville by taking the parkway in the other direction. There are great views both east and west from the parkway junction atop the mountain crest.

On the other side of the parkway, US 276 descends steeply toward the East Fork of the Pigeon River. The traffic now gets a bit lighter. You will soon pass a marked parking area on the left, one of several trailheads for the Shining Rock Wilderness. Many high peaks dot this 19,000-acre wilderness area, along with rushing, wild creeks. Miles of trail wind through the area, including the lengthy Art Loeb Trail. With its high summits and spectacular views, the area attracts many hikers every year. One of the first designated wilderness areas in the east, Shining Rock was named for a peak capped with white quartz that rises from the center of the preserve.

Next the highway temporarily leaves the national forest and enters a moderately developed farming valley. Quite a few commercial campgrounds line the route here, as does a golf course and country club. You will hit the junction with NC 215 about 15 miles from the Blue Ridge Parkway. Turn left onto NC 215. The quiet road heads south up the broad rural valley of the West Fork of the Pigeon River.

At a junction about 2.9 miles up the valley, stay left on NC 215. The valley soon narrows and the road climbs a bit to get around small Lake Logan. After you re-enter the Pisgah National Forest, about 9.3 miles from the US 276 junction, you leave development behind. Sunburst Campground lies on the right just inside the forest. The campground was built on the former site of one of Champion Paper Company's early logging camps.

Beyond the campground, the road continues to follow the West Fork upstream as the grade steadily steepens. The Middle Prong Wilderness, created in 1984, lies on the right; the Shining Rock Wilderness sits on the left. The road crosses an attractive stone bridge over a small gorge of tumbling cascades and waterfalls about 4.3 miles above the campground. Unfortunately, there are no good parking spots here since the road clings to a steep mountainside. Above the cascades the road climbs into a wooded upper valley and reaches the crest of the mountains at 5,340-foot Beech Gap. The Blue Ridge Parkway crosses NC 215 here.

Heading south now, the road descends a steep and rocky mountainside, allowing drivers open and dramatic views. Rhododendrons bloom profusely here in late May and early June. About 3.2 miles down the road, you pass a junction with SR 1756, a gravel road that leads down to Balsam Lake and other Nantahala National Forest destinations. After another 3.4 miles of steady descent, the road grade lessens at the North Fork of the French Broad River. The river was so named by early explorers because it flowed west toward lands claimed by France and because it had a broad river valley for much of its course.

If you haven't tired of waterfalls yet, turn left on FR 140 and follow it upstream along the river. Three modest falls can be reached after a short drive and some hiking. For more details on these pretty waterfalls, get the waterfall book by Kevin Adams, which is listed in Suggested Reading at the back of this guide. Alternatively, you can get directions from the national forest visitor center or from local residents.

Farther along the drive route, you begin to hit private inholdings with scattered development in the broadening river valley. Beyond the quiet village of Balsam Grove, the road begins a winding descent along the French Broad River through a small gorge. After a few more miles, Drive #10 ends at the junction with US 64 on the edge of the small town of Rosman. Turn left if you wish to return to Brevard; turn right to go to Lake Toxaway, Cashiers, and Highlands.

11

Heintooga–
Round Bottom Road

Great Smoky Mountains National Park/Cherokee Indian Reservation

General description: A 35-mile paved and gravel road through a scenic but lightly visited part of Great Smoky Mountains National Park.

Special attractions: Great Smoky Mountains National Park, Blue Ridge Parkway, Cherokee Indian Reservation, Mingo Falls, hiking, fishing, fall colors, mountain biking, scenic views.

Location: Southwestern North Carolina. The drive starts at the edge of Great Smoky Mountains National Park at the junction of the Blue Ridge Parkway and Balsam Mountain Road (about 11 miles from the park's Oconaluftee Visitor Center).

Drive route names: Balsam Mountain Road, Round Bottom Road, Big Cove Road.

Travel season: April through October. Most of the route is closed in winter.

Camping: The national park maintains Balsam Mountain Campground along the route in summer and Smokemont Campground just off the route. Both the park and the Cherokee Reservation manage other nearby campgrounds.

Services: All services are available in the towns of Cherokee and Maggie Valley.

Nearby attractions: Other sections of Great Smoky Mountains National Park, including Clingmans Dome, Cades Cove, Cataloochee, and the Newfound Gap Road; Blue Ridge Parkway; Nantahala National Forest.

For more information: Great Smoky Mountains National Park, Blue Ridge Parkway (National Park Service), Cherokee Visitor Center, and Maggie Valley Area Chamber of Commerce. See Appendix for addresses and phone numbers.

The Drive

If you are tired of the crowds in some parts of Great Smoky Mountains National Park, try the Heintooga–Round Bottom Road. I took my time along the gravel section of the road and saw only a half-dozen cars in three hours on a fall-color weekend. The road offers great views from the top of Balsam Mountain, plus lush forest and rushing mountain streams. Part of the route is a narrow, one-way gravel road, which is not suitable for trailers or large RVs. However, it is generally well graded. Sedans can easily drive this circuit if reasonable care is used.

The drive starts at the junction of Balsam Mountain Road and the Blue Ridge Parkway at Wolf Laurel Gap. You can get there by following the parkway 2.6 miles toward Great Smoky Mountains National Park from its junction with US 19, or by

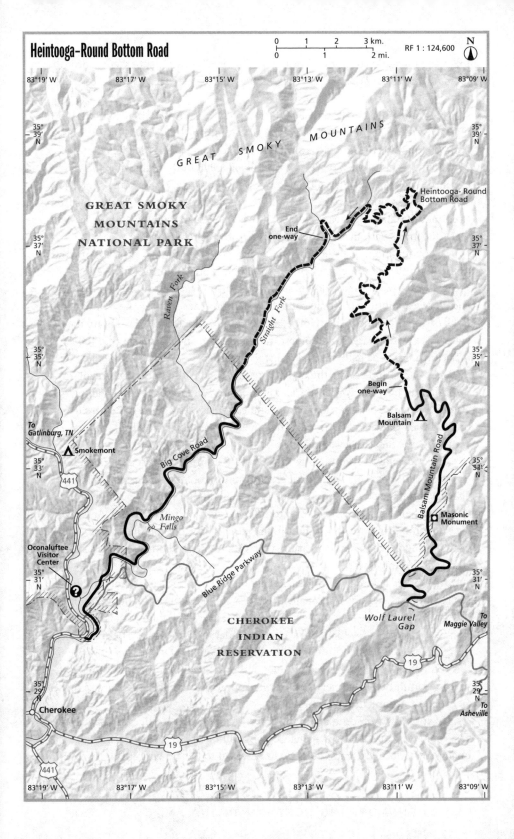

Heintooga–Round Bottom Road

0 1 2 3 km.
0   1   2 mi.

RF 1 : 124,600

N

83°19′ W 83°17′ W 83°15′ W 83°13′ W 83°11′ W 83°09′ W

GREAT   SMOKY   MOUNTAINS

35°39′ N

GREAT SMOKY

Heintooga-Round
Bottom Road

MOUNTAINS

35°37′ N

NATIONAL PARK

End
one-way

Raven Fork

Straight Fork

35°35′ N

35°35′ N

Begin
one-way

To
Gatlinburg, TN

Balsam
Mountain

35°33′ N

Smokemont

35°33′ N

Big Cove Road

441

Balsam Mountain Road

Mingo
Falls

Masonic
Monument

Oconaluftee
Visitor
Center

35°31′ N

Blue Ridge Parkway

35°31′ N

?

CHEROKEE

Wolf Laurel
Gap

To
Maggie Valley

INDIAN

19

RESERVATION

35°29′ N

To
Asheville

Cherokee

19

441

83°19′ W 83°17′ W 83°15′ W 83°13′ W 83°11′ W 83°09′ W

following the parkway 11 miles east from the Oconaluftee Visitor Center near the town of Cherokee. At 5,100 feet, the junction lies in one of the parkway's higher sections.

From the junction, the road climbs onto the crest of Balsam Mountain to Mile High Overlook—a misnomer, since the viewpoint is actually 30 feet short of a mile high. On one side of the road, you can look into the heart of the Great Smoky Mountains where sixteen peaks rise over 6,000 feet. On the other side, the view encompasses Maggie Valley, although not the resort town of the same name. The road continues along the crest beyond this viewpoint with more great vistas from overlooks. Because the area is so high, it may be gray and wintry up here in spring when the lower park near Oconaluftee is already lush and green.

A pullout about 3.5 miles into the drive allows you to walk a very short trail to the Masonic Monument. The marker was built in 1938 through the efforts of Freemasons around the world. Its stones come from various states, 41 countries, and all seven continents. Some come from famous sites, such as the Alamo, the Rock of Gibraltar, the White House, and Plymouth Rock. The Masons are members of the world's largest and oldest fraternal order, and they have held their summer North Carolina gathering here since 1935.

As you continue along the drive, note that trailheads appear with regularity. The Smokies have many miles of hiking trails, with numerous routes leading to waterfalls, views, rushing streams, and endless miles of lush forest. Be sure to get out and walk down a path or two. The quiet and solitude of the trail will make you appreciate the Smokies even more.

The road slowly climbs along the crest of Balsam Mountain and soon enters a forest of spruce and fir. These dark green conifers are found near sea level in Canada; here, the climate is only cool and wet enough for them to thrive at high elevation. Balsam Mountain Campground lies on the left in 8.2 miles. At 5,310 feet, the campground is the highest in the park. Pleasantly cool in summer, the campground is only open part of the year. Call the park about its current status if you want to camp there.

In another 0.5 mile you reach the end of the paved Balsam Mountain Road at the Heintooga Overlook and picnic area. At 5,535 feet, this is the highest point on the drive. Beyond the Heintooga Overlook Trail, the route follows narrow, gravel Round Bottom Road, which looks a bit intimidating at the start. The road disappears downhill into the forest, but it really isn't that bad. Drivers can only travel this route one-way, which makes it safer and more relaxing. Still, once you start, you are committed. With very light traffic and no oncoming cars, the road makes an excellent mountain bike route.

As you slowly descend along the gravel road, note its steady, gradual grade. The route was once a narrow-gauge logging railroad bed. Since locomotives are unable to climb steep grades, the tracks here had to be laid without sudden ups or

Heintooga–Round Bottom Road in fall, Great Smoky Mountains National Park

Straight Fork in fall, Great Smoky Mountains National Park

downs. The roadbed climbs through an area that was logged from 1900 to 1928. Although there is little virgin timber left along the route, beech and yellow birch trees have recovered well.

Occasional numbered signs along this drive mark interpretive stops. To follow the numbered tour, pick up a copy of the useful park guidebook called *Smokies Road Guide*. Stop 8 marks a hog exclosure, an area fenced to keep feral hogs out for research purposes. Many years ago exotic hogs were introduced to this area. Without natural predators, they have thrived and done considerable damage while rooting and foraging in the forest. In some active hog areas, the forest floor looks like it has been rototilled. These destructive animals are smart and adaptable and thus difficult to control.

In another 1.2 miles look for an overlook that has a good view and a sign about the old logging railroad. After another 0.5 mile, the road crosses a divide into another drainage basin. Here, at Stop 11 in the park guidebook, there is a view of a heath bald, an area almost completely dominated by rhododendron and mountain laurel. Because these two plants can grow into dense thickets that make travel almost impossible, these areas are sometimes called rhododendron hells.

After Stop 13, the road changes its overall direction from north to southwest and descends toward the stream known as Straight Fork. A series of nice cascades on the left marks one of its tributaries. Where the road reaches the canyon bottom, two-way traffic begins again. The grade lessens considerably as the road follows the Straight Fork, a classic tumbling mountain stream with clear, cold water and moss-covered rocks. The road crosses the stream and passes through Round Bottom, a flat, somewhat round area along the creek. A horse camp here requires reservations for use.

About 3 miles below Round Bottom, the road leaves Great Smoky Mountains National Park and enters the Cherokee Reservation. Just past the boundary, look for a fish hatchery where the Cherokee people raise trout for stocking their reservation's creeks. The drive route becomes paved again in the reservation section. In a mile, the road intersects Big Cove Road. Go left here and follow rushing Raven Fork downstream.

Occasional homes and public reservation campgrounds line the rest of the drive route. Consider stopping at Mingo Falls Campground, on the left about 5 miles into the reservation. Cross the bridge into the campground and stop at a small parking lot. A steep trail (mostly stairs) climbs 0.25 mile to Mingo Falls. The upward hike is worth it. Waterfall expert Kevin Adams considers the 150-foot waterfall to be the most spectacular in the Great Smoky Mountains and one of the finest falls in North Carolina.

About 2 miles below Mingo Falls Campground, the road reenters the national park again. It stays within the park boundary for about 2 miles, then leaves the park again at the town of Cherokee. The drive ends here, back at tourist central, where Big Cove Road meets Newfound Gap Road at the edge of town. To reach the national park's Oconaluftee Visitor Center and the start of the Blue Ridge Parkway, turn right and follow Newfound Gap Road a short distance into the park.

12

Newfound Gap and Clingmans Dome

Great Smoky Mountains National Park

General description: A 24-mile paved road that climbs from the base of the Great Smoky Mountains to the highest peak, past historic sites, rushing mountain streams, numerous overlooks, and lush forest.

Special attractions: Great Smoky Mountains National Park, Mountain Farm Museum at Oconaluftee Visitor Center, Newfound Gap, Mingus Mill, Appalachian Trail, Clingmans Dome, hiking, scenic views, fall colors.

Location: Southwestern North Carolina. The drive starts on the north side of Cherokee at the entrance to Great Smoky Mountains National Park.

Drive route names/number: Newfound Gap Road/US 441, Clingmans Dome Road.

Travel season: Spring through fall. Snow in winter can temporarily close Newfound Gap Road. Clingmans Dome Road, one of the highest in North Carolina, is generally closed in winter.

Camping: The national park has a large campground at Smokemont along the route and several others in other parts of the park.

Services: All services are available in Cherokee and nearby Bryson City and Maggie Valley, as well as in Gatlinburg, Tennessee.

Nearby attractions: Other parts of Great Smoky Mountains National Park, Blue Ridge Parkway, Nantahala National Forest, Pisgah National Forest, Nantahala River, Cherokee Indian Reservation.

For more information: Great Smoky Mountains National Park, Cherokee Visitor Center, and Maggie Valley and Swain County Chambers of Commerce. See Appendix for addresses and phone numbers.

The Drive

When combined, the Newfound Gap and Clingmans Dome roads may well be the most popular scenic drive in North Carolina and Tennessee. With beautiful scenery and numerous historic sites, the roads' popularity is well deserved. Most people take this drive at some point during their visit to Great Smoky Mountains National Park, the most-visited national park in the country. However, such popularity often means heavy traffic. If possible, avoid this drive during summer and on fall weekends. Otherwise, try to get a very early start. Both of these roads have numbered interpretive stops that match the park book *Mountain Roads and Quiet Places,* available at the Oconaluftee Visitor Center.

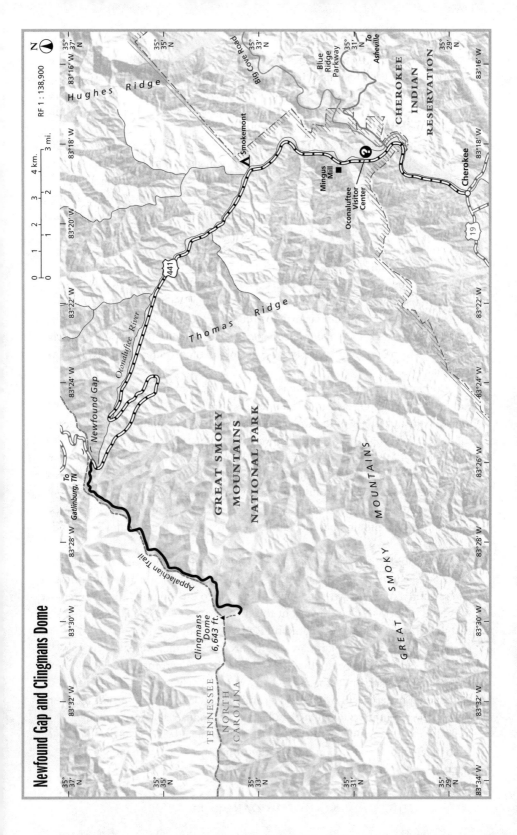

Newfound Gap and Clingmans Dome

RF 1 : 138,900

N

Hughes Ridge

Smokemont

GREAT SMOKY
MOUNTAINS
NATIONAL PARK

Thomas Ridge

Oconaluftee River

Newfound Gap

441

To Gatlinburg, TN

Appalachian Trail

Clingmans Dome
6,643 ft.

TENNESSEE
NORTH CAROLINA

GREAT   SMOKY   MOUNTAINS

Mingus Mill

Oconaluftee
Visitor
Center

Big Cove Road

Blue Ridge
Parkway

To
Asheville

CHEROKEE
INDIAN
RESERVATION

Cherokee

19

0   1   2   3 mi.
0   1   2   3   4 km.

35°37'N
35°35'N
35°33'N
35°31'N
35°29'N

83°16'W 35°35'N
35°33'N
35°31'N
35°29'N 83°16'W

83°18'W
83°20'W
83°22'W
83°24'W
83°26'W
83°28'W
83°30'W
83°32'W
83°34'W

83°18'W
83°22'W
83°24'W
83°26'W
83°28'W
83°30'W
83°32'W

All along this drive are trailheads for paths that lead deep into the lush forests of the Smokies. Be sure to try a few hikes here. Trails give you a better feel of the mountains, the smells, the sounds, the sights, and the textures; otherwise, you are isolated by a cocoon of steel and glass in your car. The park has something on the order of 900 miles of trails to choose from.

Start the drive at the edge of the busy tourist town of Cherokee. You immediately leave the commercial bustle behind when you enter Great Smoky Mountains National Park. The road initially follows the Oconaluftee River upstream. The river's name is derived from a Cherokee term meaning "place by the river." In about 0.5 mile, you will pass the junction with the Blue Ridge Parkway. In another 0.7 mile, you will reach the Oconaluftee Visitor Center and Mountain Farm Museum. Plan to stop at the visitor center, particularly if you have never been to the park before. You can get maps and information, view exhibits, and purchase park-related books. The Mountain Farm Museum is one of the area's highlights. By moving historic buildings here from other parts of the park, the museum has recreated life on a mountain farm about 100 years ago. Explore the pioneer cabin, barns with livestock and farm implements, the garden, and other features of early rural life. The museum often hosts living history demonstrations of crafts such as quiltmaking.

Continue up the road to Mingus Mill, which appears on the left in about 0.6 mile. This turbine-powered mill still operates, using the power of flowing water drawn from a tributary of the Oconaluftee River. A turbine mill is more efficient, though less picturesque, than mills powered by a waterwheel. This mill was built in 1886 for John Mingus, a local physician. Gristmills were a vital component of rural life in this mountain country, since grain had to be ground before it could be used as food. The Mingus Mill ground corn using stones made of local granite. For wheat it used harder, fine-grained stones imported from France. At various times you can view the mill in operation and even purchase cornmeal that was ground there.

The road next passes the entrance to Smokemont Campground in another 2.6 miles. Smokemont was once a booming logging village with a railroad terminus and sawmill. From here, railroad spurs climbed into the mountains to help remove harvested timber. Much of the rest of this drive crosses a huge 93,000-acre tract that was once owned by the Champion Paper Company.

Although these mountains are now lushly forested, they were not always so vegetated. Early in the twentieth century, more than 75 percent of the Great Smokies had been logged. Initial logging activity was relatively minor: settlers cut trees for building materials, firewood, and clearing small fields. By the turn of the twentieth century commercial logging had begun. The industrial loggers initially looked for more valuable hardwoods, such as walnut and cherry. As demand strengthened for construction lumber, they took oaks, pines, tulip poplars, and

Mingus Mill, Great Smoky Mountains National Park

other trees. When paper production demanded pulp, they cut almost everything. Fortunately this forest has recovered.

Little remains of the former logging town at Smokemont. A new transient village, the campground, has replaced it. This large campground usually fills up during summer and on spring and fall weekends, so consider reserving a site before your trip if you wish to camp here. Beyond Smokemont, which lies at a major fork in the river, the valley begins to narrow. As you pass the Collins Creek Picnic Area the road grade begins to steepen. Soon it rises away from the river in switchbacks, climbing onto Thomas Ridge. Stop at any of the several overlooks here for views that become increasingly extensive as you climb in elevation.

A short distance up Thomas Ridge, the road reaches 5,048-foot Newfound Gap, the lowest point on the crest of the Great Smoky Mountains. Marking the boundary between North Carolina and Tennessee, this high mountain backbone includes sixteen peaks that exceed 6,000 feet in elevation. For many years, surveyors believed Indian Gap, 2 miles west, was the lowest point in the mountain crest. Surveys later proved that this gap was slightly lower, hence the "newfound" name.

Stop and park your car here. The popular lot is an access point for the Appalachian Trail, probably the best-known trail in America. This long trail crosses Newfound Gap as part of its trek from Maine to Georgia, while running through 70 miles of Great Smoky Mountains National Park. A popular day hike follows the AT east from Newfound Gap, passing three of the Smokies' best viewpoints: the Jumpoff (7.4 miles round-trip), Charlie's Bunion (8.8 miles round-trip), and the Sawteeth (11.2 miles round-trip). Compared to the traffic at Newfound Gap, this popular trail is a tranquil escape, though it is heavily used. If you hike here, note all the downed trees that have had to be cleared from the route. In the mid-1990s, hurricanes caused considerable damage all over North Carolina.

Once you are done exploring Newfound Gap, take the turnoff to Clingmans Dome. Leaving from the gap's left side, the road climbs along or just below the crest and the Tennessee–North Carolina state line. The Appalachian Trail parallels the route. As on the Newfound Gap Road, several trailheads and overlooks line the route. The views into North Carolina are great, but only a warm-up for what lies ahead.

At Indian Gap, marked with a number "1," old toll roads once crossed the mountains. Pioneers hacked a route across the mountains here along old Indian trails. Today the forest has mostly reclaimed these traces. A spruce-fir forest thrives on these high, cool, wet upper peaks. Unfortunately, many of the native Fraser firs are dead, victim of an imported insect pest. Unlike in Europe, firs here have little resistance and usually die when attacked. Imported insects and diseases have greatly hurt American forests; two other notable victims are the American elm (devastated by Dutch elm disease) and the American chestnut (virtually extinct now from chestnut blight). A third factor, acid rain, has weakened other trees here, especially red spruce. Dogwoods, beeches, and hemlocks are also under assault by various diseases and insects. The forests of the Southern Appalachians are struggling to survive.

The road ends at the enormous Clingmans Dome parking lot. Even if you don't walk to the summit, you will enjoy great views into North Carolina. If you can pry yourself out of bed early enough, this high peak is a great place to watch the sunrise. The mountain was named for Thomas Clingman, a Civil War general and a U.S. senator for North Carolina. In the mid-1800s, he and Elisha Mitchell, a university professor, disputed which Black Mountains peak was highest. Ultimately, the peak that Mitchell claimed proved to be higher and was named Mount Mitchell after his untimely death (see Drive #2). Clingman, however, got a good consolation prize. His name rests forever here on Clingmans Dome in the Great Smokies.

A broad paved trail climbs a steep 0.5 mile to the summit through dying stands of fir and spruce. The mountaintop straddles the state line, ranking as the highest point in Tennessee and the third-highest point in North America east of the Black Hills. A curving ramp leads to an observation tower with 360-degree views of the Smokies and the rest of the Southern Appalachians. An endless series of steel-blue ridges marches into the distance in every direction.

Clingmans Dome view, Great Smoky Mountains National Park

The weather changes often on this summit. Rain and fog often blanket Clingmans Dome, and snow and ice shroud it in winter. Howling winds and temperatures below zero are not uncommon. Even in summer, you may sometimes want a sweater on the summit. The haze from which the Smokies got their name often obscures the horizon; it is a mix of natural moisture and manmade pollution. A cold front can blow out the haze temporarily, opening up views to a seeming infinity. On other days, the clouds limit views to only a few miles. Before you descend back to the starting point of this scenic drive, consider another hike. Several trails lead from Clingmans Dome, including the Appalachian Trail. When you are done exploring this high area, you can return to Cherokee via the same route or continue along the Newfound Gap Road into Tennessee and other parts of the Great Smoky Mountains.

13

Fontana Lake

*Robbinsville to the NC 28 and US 19/US 74
junction, Indian Lakes Scenic Byway*

General description: A 50-mile paved route
that winds through the lush Nantahala
National Forest along the edge of Great
Smoky Mountains National Park past
Fontana, Cheoah, and Santeetlah Lakes.

Special attractions: Fontana Lake, Lake
Santeetlah, Lake Cheoah, Nantahala National
Forest, Great Smoky Mountains National
Park, hiking, horse trails, fishing, boating,
scenic views, fall colors.

Location: Southwestern North Carolina. The
drive starts at the junction of US 129 and NC
143 in Robbinsville, a small town near the
southwest side of Great Smoky Mountains
National Park.

Drive route numbers: US 129, NC 28.

Travel season: All year. Travel is most pleasant from spring through fall. Snow can make
the route treacherous in winter.

Camping: The Nantahala National Forest
operates three campgrounds along the route:
Cheoah Point, Cable Cove, and Tsali. The Tennessee Valley Authority manages a campground at Fontana Dam.

Services: All services are available in Robbinsville and Fontana Village. There is a motel
in Almond, gas and a motel in Tuskeegee,
and a few other scattered services along the
route.

Nearby attractions: Joyce Kilmer Memorial
Forest, other sections of Great Smoky Moun-
tains National Park, other sections of the
Nantahala National Forest, Nantahala River
Gorge, gemstone mines.

For more information: Nantahala National
Forest (Cheoah Ranger District), Great
Smoky Mountains National Park, Graham
County Chamber of Commerce. See Appen-
dix for addresses and phone numbers.

The Drive

This drive is an easy route past three lakes tucked into the lush forested mountains
of the Nantahala National Forest and Great Smoky Mountains National Park. If
you like water activities such as boating, swimming, and fishing, you could probably spend several days on this drive. This route lies mostly within Graham County,
one of the most isolated, least populated, and most scenic counties in North Carolina. It follows much of the official Indian Lakes Scenic Byway. A few sections are
steep and winding and can be somewhat difficult for large trailers and RVs.

Start the drive at the junction of US 129 and NC 143 in the small town of
Robbinsville. The town's economy depends upon diverse industries, including
tourism, furniture making, and logging. Junaluska, a Cherokee chief and warrior
who saved future President Andrew Jackson's life at the Battle of Horseshoe Bend

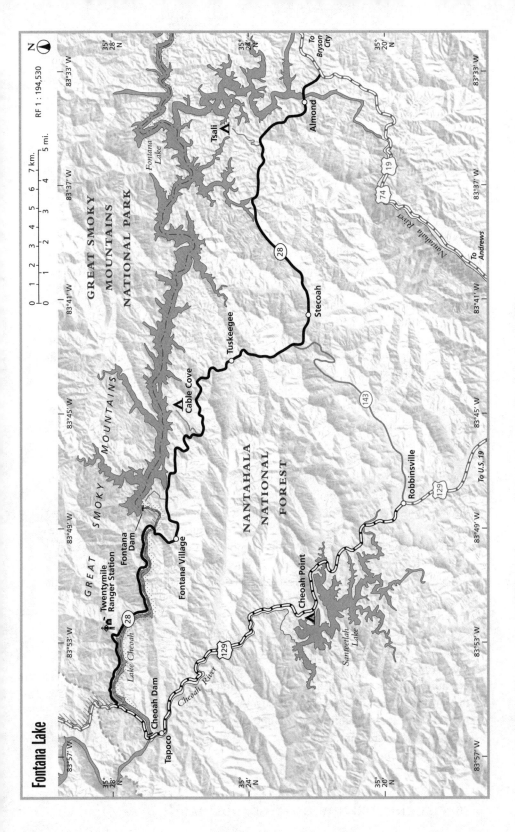

Fontana Lake

RF 1 : 194,530

N

0 1 2 3 4 5 mi.

0 1 2 3 4 5 6 7 km.

83°57' W 83°53' W 83°49' W 83°45' W 83°41' W 83°37' W 83°33' W

35°28' N 35°24' N 35°20' N

GREAT SMOKY MOUNTAINS NATIONAL PARK

GREAT SMOKY MOUNTAINS

NANTAHALA NATIONAL FOREST

Fontana Lake

Lake Cheoah

Cheoah River

Sampeetlah Lake

Nantahala River

Twentymile Ranger Station

Tapoco

Cheoah Dam

Fontana Dam

Fontana Village

Cable Cove

Tuskeegee

Tsali

Stecoah

Almond

Cheoah Point

Robbinsville

To Bryson City

To Andrews

To U.S. 19

28

129

129

143

74

19

28

in 1812, is buried here. Head northwest out of town on moderately busy US 129 toward Lake Santeetlah and the Tennessee border. About 1.5 miles from the center of town, you will pass a turnoff on the left for the western continuation of NC 143 and the Cheoah Ranger District Office of the Nantahala National Forest. You may want to stop here to pick up a forest map and other information.

As you continue along the road, you get periodic views of Lake Santeetlah on the left. The lake has numerous sinuous arms that reach up the channels of its tributaries. The lake was created when the Cheoah River was dammed early in this century. Its name comes from an Indian word meaning "blue waters." The road crosses an arm of the lake 3.1 miles from the national forest office; there's a good overlook in another 1.6 miles. Cheoah Point Recreation Area lies on the left in another mile. This campground has picnic facilities and a boat ramp. A side road continues past the recreation area to a view of the dam. In another 1.1 miles, Forest Road 416 turns left. It leads eventually to Joyce Kilmer Memorial Forest (see Drive #14), a majestic virgin woodland that lies hidden in the verdant Unicoi Mountains across the lake.

About a mile past the turnoff to Kilmer Forest, you will pass a large flume and a swing bridge over the Cheoah River. The flume is part of an aqueduct and tunnel system that taps Lake Cheoah for hydroelectric power generation. From here the highway heads downstream through the scenic gorge of the Cheoah River. The route lies mostly within the Nantahala National Forest and is little developed. An exception is where you cross the river at attractive Tapoco Lodge, about 6 miles past the flume.

The name Tapoco isn't as exotic as it seems; it's an acronym for Tallassee Power Company. The lodge was built as a retreat for industrialist Andrew Mellon shortly after the end of the nineteenth century. At that time, Mellon was head of the Aluminum Company of America (today's Alcoa), which had begun studying ways of damming the Little Tennessee River to produce hydroelectric power. The company needed electricity to smelt its aluminum. Although aluminum is very common in the earth's crust, it takes vast amounts of electricity to separate and purify it. When World War I increased demand for the lightweight metal, workers were brought into this remote area; they began pouring concrete for Cheoah Dam in early 1917.

Two years later, the dam and hydroelectric plant were completed. At the time, the 225-foot-high dam was the highest of its type in the world and its power turbines were the world's biggest. A dozen years later, the Tallassee Power Company built the dam that created Calderwood Lake downstream in Tennessee. Though the town of Tapoco once housed 2,000 workers, today only a handful of people live here. The most prominent remnant of its early days is the well-kept Tapoco Lodge with its restaurant, pool, tennis court, and other facilities, all open to the public except during the winter.

Lake Santeetlah, Nantahala National Forest

Just below the lodge, the Cheoah River flows into the Little Tennessee River. The highway crosses a large bridge just below the towering Cheoah Dam. The tall structure is impressive and makes you realize that you would not want to be standing on this bridge during an earthquake. The hero in the movie *The Fugitive* jumped off this dam. On the other side of the bridge, the road climbs toward the dam along a narrow, snaking path. It passes the top of the dam and follows narrow Lake Cheoah about 2 miles to the junction with NC 28. A gas station and small motel mark the junction.

Turn right onto NC 28 and drive upstream along the lake. The quiet highway winds between the water and Great Smoky Mountains National Park. After 2.8 miles, you will pass the park's Twentymile Ranger Station on the left. If you're tired of crowds in other parts of the park, come here. Several quiet hiking trails start at the ranger station, leading up creeks or over ridges. If you are feeling very energetic and miss the crowds, you can even hike over the mountains to popular Cades Cove.

Past the ranger station, the drive continues along the lake. This area is very scenic; it's almost entirely national forest and national park land, so there's little development. Look for a small hydroelectric plant by the lake in about 2 miles. Water is carried to this station via the aqueduct that you saw earlier below Lake

Santeetlah. In another 3.1 miles, watch for a turnoff on the left by a huge quarry. This side road leads to the base of Fontana Dam, the highest concrete dam (480 feet) east of the Mississippi. The dam and powerhouse tower above the end of the road, holding back 11,685-acre Fontana Lake. If you were nervous below Cheoah Dam, this spot will really get you going.

Fontana Dam was begun by the Tennessee Valley Authority (TVA) in January 1942 as part of an elaborate system of dams, locks, and power plants built largely in the Tennessee River watershed. The TVA was created during the depths of the Great Depression to fill multiple needs. The system of dams and lakes facilitated navigation along the Tennessee River and controlled flooding. During economic hard times, the dam construction projects provided jobs. Hydroelectric plants brought power into areas that never had it. In later years, the TVA' s power generation activities greatly increased with the addition of coal-fired and nuclear power plants.

Because of wartime pressures, Fontana Dam was built in record time. About 5,000 men and women moved into this area to work around the clock, seven days a week, in three shifts. The lake began to fill in November 1944, and two months later the dam generated its first watts of power.

Return to NC 28 and continue the drive. Almost immediately, you will cross the river. Just beyond the bridge, on the left, a turnoff leads to a campground at the base of the dam. Past this turnoff, the road climbs away from the river to Fontana Village on the right in about a mile. Built in the 1940s to house dam workers, this former construction boomtown is now a resort village. You can get food, gas, and lodging here. Notice all the 1940s-vintage buildings.

A mile past the village, drivers can stop and follow a short interpretive walking trail. Before you drive much farther, be sure to follow the side road on the left, which leads to the Fontana Dam Visitor Center. Near the top of the dam, this visitor facility offers a great view. You can ride an inclined tram down to the dam's powerhouse for a tour of the massive, rumbling electrical generators. If you want to walk what is possibly the easiest section of the Appalachian Trail between Maine and Georgia, step out onto the top of the dam. The AT descends from Great Smoky Mountains National Park, crosses the dam here, and heads back into the woods of Nantahala National Forest on the other side.

From the visitor center turnoff, NC 28 slowly climbs up and away from the lake, offering drivers occasional views of the water through the trees. The Nantahala National Forest's Cable Cove Recreation Area is on the left in about 3.7 miles. This site has facilities for camping, boating, hiking, and picnicking. In another 3 miles, you hit the small, sleepy village of Tuskeegee, where there are small motels and a gas station. From Tuskeegee, the highway climbs over mountains to the junction with NC 143. If you need to return to Robbinsville, this road makes a good shortcut.

Beyond the junction, you pass through the small village of Stecoah; you can get gas here if you need it. The road then passes an arm of Fontana Lake. The Forest Service manages Tsali Campground on the left about 8 miles after the NC 143 junction. The campground is notable for its lake access and long horse trail along Fontana Lake. Mountain bikers flock to this area. Tsali was a Cherokee Indian who resisted removal from his lands near here by U.S. Army troops in 1838.

About 1.7 miles past the campground turnoff, you hit the hamlet of Almond. Past this small town and its motel, you cross yet another arm of Fontana Lake. Fontana is a big lake, with 240 miles of shoreline. This arm is where the Nantahala River adds to the reservoir. In another mile the drive ends at the junction with US 19/US 74. To return to Robbinsville, turn right and follow the Nantahala River upstream along the Mountain Waters Scenic Byway (Drive #15).

14

Joyce Kilmer Memorial Forest

Joyce Kilmer Memorial Forest to Tennessee state line

General description: A 25-mile paved road through beautiful, undeveloped Nantahala National Forest, including old-growth trees at Joyce Kilmer Memorial Forest and tremendous views from the crest of the Unicoi Mountains.

Special attractions: Joyce Kilmer Memorial Forest, Maple Springs Observation Point, Nantahala National Forest, Joyce Kilmer Slickrock Wilderness, old-growth forest, hiking, scenic views, fall colors, fishing.

Location: Southwestern North Carolina. The drive starts at Joyce Kilmer Memorial Forest. To get there, start at the junction of US 129 and NC 143 in Robbinsville and go north 1.5 miles on US 129 toward Lake Santeetlah and Tennessee. Turn left on NC 143/Cherohala Skyway, marked with signs for the Cheoah Ranger District of the Nantahala National Forest and the Joyce Kilmer Memorial Forest. Watch for and follow signs for the Kilmer forest at junctions.

You soon pass the ranger station. Continue 2.3 miles past it to a junction. Go right, staying on NC 143. You soon pass the Snowbird picnic area on the right. After 0.8 mile go right again, staying on NC 143. In 4.7 miles, it reaches the top of Santeetlah Gap and a road junction. SR 143 turns left and climbs up from the gap. You will return here on the scenic drive. For now, continue down the other side of the gap onto SR 1127/Santeetlah Road. Turn left in 2.3 miles and enter Joyce Kilmer Memorial Forest. In 0.5 mile, you reach the parking lot at the end of the road.

Drive route name/numbers: Joyce Kilmer Memorial Forest entrance road, SR 1127/Santeetlah Road, NC 143.

Travel season: Spring through fall. Snow can close part or all of the route in winter, especially NC 143.

Camping: The Nantahala National Forest manages Horse Cove Campground just off the route.

Services: Full services are available in Robbinsville, though choices are limited.

Nearby attractions: Great Smoky Mountains National Park, Lake Santeetlah, Fontana Lake, Nantahala River.

For more information: Nantahala National Forest (Cheoah and Tusquitee Ranger Districts), Graham County Chamber of Commerce.

The Drive

This drive winds through a large block of undeveloped Nantahala National Forest. It starts in Joyce Kilmer Memorial Forest, one of the most impressive remnants of old-growth forest in the eastern United States. From there, the drive climbs up to Maple Springs Overlook, a high point on the slopes of the Unicoi Mountains. It

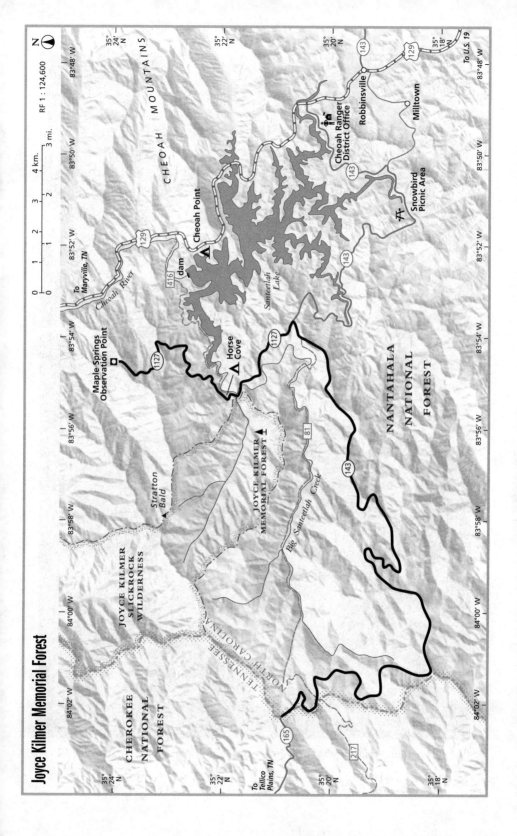

Joyce Kilmer Memorial Forest

Old-growth tulip poplars in the Joyce Kilmer Memorial Forest, Nantahala National Forest

then backtracks and climbs completely over the mountains into Tennessee on a new highway, NC 143. Plan to stop at the Cheoah Ranger District Office near Robbinsville on your way to Joyce Kilmer. A forest map is helpful for finding your way through the forest.

The Joyce Kilmer Memorial Forest lies in a cove, or mountain valley, that somehow escaped logging earlier this century. It contains more than one hundred species of trees, some individual examples of which, particularly hemlocks and tulip poplars, are more than 6 feet in diameter and 100 feet tall. Many trees here may have been standing when Christopher Columbus set foot in the New World. The preserve was created in 1936 as a memorial to Joyce Kilmer, a poet best known for his work "Trees." Its opening lines are famous: "I think that I shall never see/A poem lovely as a tree." Kilmer died in France fighting in World War I.

A beautiful 2-mile, double-loop trail winds through some of the forest monarchs on slopes above the rushing waters of Little Santeetlah Creek. Expect the trail to be busy on summer and fall weekends. Other trails lead from the memorial forest into the Joyce Kilmer Slickrock Wilderness, a 17,000-acre area that straddles the high crest of the Unicoi Mountains. Sixty miles of trails here follow mountain streams and climb to spectacular viewpoints before heading into Tennessee.

After you have explored the Kilmer forest, return 0.5 mile to the main road from the forest parking lot. Go left on SR 1127, which is also known as Santeetlah Road. Gravel FR 416 turns off to the right almost immediately and leads in a short distance to Horse Cove Campground. Stay on the main paved road as it begins to climb toward Maple Springs Observation Point. SR 1127 is a well-built paved highway that goes only a few miles and ends at an overlook. The road climbs steadily, giving visitors views of Santeetlah Lake through gaps in the trees. You can view the entire Cheoah River valley and the distant Great Smoky Mountains; the vistas get better as you climb.

The road ends 4.5 miles from the Joyce Kilmer turnoff. At the Maple Springs Observation Point, a short, almost level boardwalk and paved trail offer barrier-free access and great views. If you want a real hike, walk back down the road about 0.1 mile. From its trailhead there, the Haoe Trail climbs high into the Joyce Kilmer Slickrock Wilderness. Note the large number of uprooted and broken-off trees in this area, signs of hurricane damage. North Carolina has been pounded in recent years by several ferocious storms.

From the observation point, backtrack past the Kilmer forest entrance and follow Santeetlah Road toward Robbinsville. In 0.3 mile you will cross the rushing waters of Big Santeetlah Creek. The road then climbs toward Santeetlah Gap, passing a nice picnic area with a view on the right. The road crests at Santeetlah Gap after 2.3 miles.

Turn right at the junction here and begin the long climb to the crest of the Unicoi Mountains. This highway, NC 143 (the Cherohala Skyway), was completed

Unicoi Mountains in mist, Nantahala National Forest

in 1996 and is not heavily traveled. Almost immediately after you start up the route, gravel FR 81 forks right and drops to Santeetlah Creek. It later rejoins NC 143 on the mountain crest. FR 81 is also a scenic route, but it is gravel-surfaced, steeper, and slower. Stick with NC 143 for now; you may wish to consider a return trip on FR 81.

At Santeetlah Gap the elevation is a respectable 2,660 feet, offering decent views. As the new highway climbs steadily, the views become spectacular. The road gains so much elevation that in early spring you may start in lush green forest and end at gray, leafless trees. In fall, colored leaves turn earlier up on the crest. The road finally levels out near the top of the Unicoi Mountains. It contours along the crest with mild ups and downs. Tennessee lies just over the other side of the ridgetop.

The road reaches Mud Gap, elevation 4,480 feet, about 14.3 miles from Santeetlah Gap. In another 1.8 miles it comes to the junction with the upper ends of FR 81 and FR 217. FR 217 leads down into the Cherokee National Forest in Tennessee. Stratton Meadows lie just beyond this junction at a big bridge. In another 1.3 miles, a nice overlook offers great views into Tennessee. The drive ends just beyond the overlook at the state line in Beech Gap.

From here, TN 165 descends steeply to the town of Tellico Plains. Like NC 143, TN 165 is a very scenic route with tremendous views of the lush mountains in the Cherokee National Forest. To return to Robbinsville, consider making a long loop into Tennessee and back via US 411 and US 129. Don't try taking FR 81 back down Big Santeetlah Creek if you have a trailer or large RV.

15

Mountain Waters Scenic Byway

Highlands to the Nantahala River Gorge

General description: A 61-mile paved route that winds through some of the most spectacular country in the Nantahala National Forest, including multiple waterfalls, a roaring whitewater river, and tremendous mountaintop views.

Special attractions: Nantahala National Forest, Nantahala River and Gorge, Cullasaja Gorge, Glen Falls, Bridal Veil Falls, Dry Falls, Cullasaja Falls, Camp Branch Falls, Wayah Bald Fire Tower, historic Wilson Lick Ranger Station, Nantahala Lake, Appalachian Trail, Bartram Trail, whitewater rafting and kayaking, hiking, fishing, boating, fall colors, scenic views.

Location: Southwestern North Carolina. The drive starts at the junction of US 64 and NC 106 in the resort town of Highlands.

Drive route name/numbers: US 64, Old Murphy Road, SR 1310/Wayah Road, US 19.

Travel season: Travel is best from spring through fall. Snow can close the road in winter, especially parts of SR 1310/Wayah Road.

Camping: The Nantahala National Forest has a campground along the route at Van Hook Glade. Other campgrounds are maintained in other nearby parts of the forest.

Services: All services are available in Highlands, Franklin, and in scattered locations in the Nantahala River Gorge.

Nearby attractions: Great Smoky Mountains National Park, other parts of the Nantahala National Forest, Joyce Kilmer Memorial Forest, Fontana Lake, Ellicott Rock Wilderness, Nantahala Wilderness, Whitewater Falls, Chattooga Wild and Scenic River, gemstone mines.

For more information: Nantahala National Forest (Wayah and Highlands Ranger Districts); Franklin, Highlands, and Swain County (Bryson City) Chambers of Commerce. See Appendix for addresses and phone numbers.

The Drive

This drive follows an official USDA Forest Service National Scenic Byway. Its name—the Mountain Waters Scenic Byway—is appropriate but understated. Few, if any, other routes in North Carolina go so close to as many large waterfalls and rushing whitewater rivers and streams. To add a little variety, this drive also climbs to the top of a high peak for excellent views of southwestern North Carolina. The drive includes parts of two state scenic byways, the Waterfall Byway and the Nantahala Byway. The main route is entirely paved and easy for most smaller vehicles. However, part of SR 1310 is steep, narrow, and winding; large RVs and trailers should avoid this section. A short segment of US 64 in the Cullasaja Gorge can also be tricky.

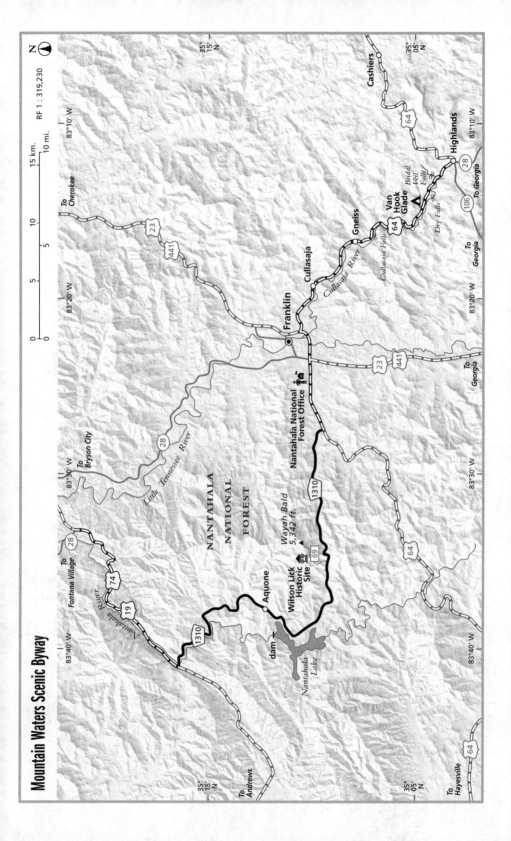

Mountain Waters Scenic Byway

The drive starts in the resort town of Highlands at the junction of US 64 and NC 106. Founded by developers, Highlands was a resort town from day one in 1875. Early promotional advertising was long on hype and short on substance. Nevertheless, the town *did* have a scenic setting and soon thrived. The mountain air, cool even in summer, drew many buyers from hot lowland areas. Even with modern air conditioning today, Highlands' population swells from about 900 year-round residents to summer highs of 10,000 to 20,000. At an elevation of 4,118 feet, Highlands was for many years the highest incorporated town in the eastern United States. Today it is exceeded only by Beech Mountain, a North Carolina ski town incorporated in 1981.

Although Highlands was never a mining or timber boomtown, it still managed to have a real gun battle in its early years. Four Billingsley brothers from nearby Georgia were notorious for their moonshining activities. When federal agents arrested two members of their enterprise, they held them under arrest at a hotel in Highlands because there was no local jail. Eighteen members of the Billingsley outfit came to town to free their accomplices. The federal agents holed up in the hotel while the Billingsley gang settled in across the street. Gunfire raged for three days until one of the outlaws was shot and killed. The moonshiners scuttled back to Georgia and blockaded the main road, threatening to kill anyone who attempted to run the blockade. The threat was empty, however; after one brave soul passed through unmolested, the Highlands "war" was over.

The area around Highlands is dotted with waterfalls. Macon, Jackson, and Transylvania Counties have the highest concentration of waterfalls in North Carolina and some of the best in the United States. Estimates of as many as 200 waterfalls, both big and small, have been made for the area. If you get tired of shopping in Highlands and need a little fresh air, consider visiting Glen Falls on the south side of town. Take NC 106 about 1.7 miles south from the middle of town. At a sign for Glen Falls, turn left onto a small side road (SR 1618). Follow it to its end in 1.1 miles at a parking area. A steep trail leads down to the falls' three major cascades.

If Glen Falls whetted your appetite for whitewater, you are ready to start the scenic drive. To do so, head west on US 64. You may wish to stop at the Nantahala National Forest Office before you go. In less than 2 miles past the edge of town, you will reach the small Lake Sequoyah Dam. From here the Cullasaja River begins its rapid drop. From the dam to the bottom of Cullasaja Falls, roughly 7 miles, the river loses about 1,400 feet in elevation. Not surprisingly, this steep gradient leads to a whole series of waterfalls and cascades. The first series of cascades, known as the Kalakaleskies, begins downstream from the dam. Some sources count eighteen cascades here, but in reality there are considerably fewer. The falls are difficult and dangerous to get to, however, so save your energy for bigger things to come.

In about 0.5 mile you will reach Bridal Veil Falls. This 60-foot waterfall doesn't require much energy to see—in fact, you could drive under it until recently. The old highway, now a parallel side loop of the main highway, runs under the overhang behind the falls. In December 2003 a large rock broke off the cliff, blocking the road. As of 2005 it still had not been removed. With only moderate water flow, Bridal Veil is not the most scenic feature in the area. But where else could you drive under a waterfall?

The next stop, Dry Falls, is on the left in about 0.9 mile. The large, busy parking area here is hard to miss. A short trail leads down to a dramatic 75-foot waterfall where the Cullasaja River roars over a large rock overhang. The name Dry Falls may seem like a misnomer, but it refers to the fact that you can walk behind these falls without getting wet. "Dry" is relative, however. If the river is flowing heavily, spray will drench you regardless.

The national forest campground in Van Hook Glade lies on the right side of the road about 0.8 mile from Dry Falls. Just beyond it is the side road to Cliffside Lake Recreation Area. This small lake offers picnicking, hiking, fishing, and swimming.

The main drive route now hugs the rushing river in an increasingly narrow and rugged gorge. In about 4 miles the river falls away, leaving the road perched on a narrow, manmade ledge high above the bottom of the gorge. The highway through here was not built until the 1930s. Not surprisingly, it was a difficult and expensive engineering feat. Surveyors, engineers, and laborers had to be virtual rock climbers.

Below and to the left, Cullasaja Falls roars down a cliff. This is a spectacular 250-foot series of large cascades. The small viewing pullout on the other side of the road is dangerous to get to because of blind curves and heavy traffic. Park farther down the highway and walk back, or turn around in a safe place down the road and come back to park here.

Below Cullasaja Falls, the gorge opens up and the highway leaves the national forest. It passes through the rural villages of Gneiss and Cullasaja before reaching the larger town of Franklin. Probably one of the most notable features of Franklin is the Nikwasi Indian Mound, a former village and sacred site of the Cherokee near the confluence of the Cullasaja and Little Tennessee Rivers.

If rockhounding interests you, consider a side trip north on NC 28. The Cowee Valley has long been famous for its rubies. Rubies are a type of corundum. Valuable in colored varieties (as ruby and sapphire gemstones), corundum is also important to many industrial processes. Because corundum is extremely hard and wear-resistant (only diamonds are harder), it is often used in grinding wheels, saw blades, abrasives, and similar products.

Red stones had been found in the creek gravel here for many years, but they were largely ignored until a jeweler from Tiffany's in New York realized their value in 1893. Mining efforts began after the discovery, but the mining company was

Fire lookout tower at Wayah Bald, Nantahala National Forest

unable to find the hard-rock source of the gems. Since only a small percentage of the stones found in creek gravels were of gem quality, the commercial mines eventually closed. Today the ruby mines mine tourists. For a fee, you can pan the creek gravels and get a shot at riches. Even if you don't find any rubies, there are worse things to do than muck around in a cool creek on a warm summer day.

At Franklin, stay on US 64 and pass the junctions where US 441/US 23 heads north and south. From the second US 441/US 23 junction, go 0.9 mile west to reach the Wayah District Office of the Nantahala National Forest; pick up maps and information here. Then backtrack to the junction and follow US 64 about 3.7 miles west to Old Murphy Road on the right. The road is marked with a sign for Wayah Bald. After only 0.3 mile on Old Murphy Road, turn left onto lightly traveled SR 1310/Wayah Road at a corner gas station.

SR 1310 travels through pastoral country as it approaches the Nantahala Mountains. *Nantahala* is a Cherokee word meaning "land of the noonday sun"; some of the mountain gorges here are so deep that the sun strikes the bottom only at midday. In 3.1 miles, you reach the shady Arrowwood Glade picnic area, marked by old stone gates on the right. Across the road is a Forest Service facility, the LBJ Civilian Conservation Center. Beyond the picnic area, the road passes through a stretch of private land with cabins, then enters undeveloped national forest land. Large hardwoods arch over the narrow, paved highway. The valley narrows and the mountains close in as you follow Wayah Creek upstream. The road soon begins to climb steeply, offering views of the mountains above and the valley below.

You reach Wayah Gap almost 13 miles from Franklin. *Wayah* is the Cherokee word for "wolf." The gap is a great place to pause in your journey, since the air is cooler here and the small Wayah Crest picnic area beckons hungry stomachs. The Appalachian Trail crosses the road here; by following this famous trail, you can hike to Georgia (not too bad) or Maine (a long haul).

Consider making a side trip from Wayah Gap up FR 69 to Wayah Bald. The steep but good gravel road leads in 3 miles to the bald's 5,342-foot summit. About 1.3 miles up FR 69, you pass the old Wilson Lick Ranger Station, built in 1913. The first ranger cabin in the Nantahala National Forest, this station is now maintained as a historic site. From the parking lot at the end of FR 69, a short paved trail leads to the stone lookout tower on the top of the mountain. Built by the Civilian Conservation Corps in the 1930s, the tower offers views of much of the Southern Appalachians.

After you take in the views, you can eat lunch or a snack at the picnic area on the summit. Even in summer it can be quite cool up here. The Appalachian Trail and another long trail, the Bartram Trail, cross the top of Wayah Bald. The 70-plus-mile Bartram Trail was named in honor of William Bartram, a botanist and scholar who wandered in western North Carolina from 1773 to 1777.

To continue the main scenic drive, return to Wayah Gap and head down the other side of the mountain. The road descends steeply but doesn't wind as much as it follows Jarrett Creek down to Nantahala Lake. This very pretty lake was created when the Nantahala River was dammed and filled a mountain valley. After passing the lake, the road enters the small community of Aquone. At a fork here, stay straight on SR 1310. The less-improved left fork follows the Nantahala River below the lake and rejoins SR 1310 downstream. The main road winds down another valley and rejoins the Nantahala River in about 5.5 miles.

Kayak in white water, Nantahala River

Both river and road now follow a narrow path carved into the mountains at the start of the Nantahala Gorge. Clear, rushing mountain water attracts lots of anglers seeking trout. Watch the far wall of the gorge as you drive, since 200-foot Camp Branch Falls pours into the river there at 1.4 miles. Because of masking vegetation and the waterfall's layout, it is difficult to see the entire series of cascades. Be careful where you park to get a view.

About 2 miles below the falls, the road leaves the national forest and the gorge widens abruptly. There is a small hydroelectric plant here, fed by an aqueduct and a long tunnel that carries water from Nantahala Lake. Just down the road, SR 1310 ends at its junction with US 19. Rafters and kayakers often use the river put-in access here. The Nantahala is one of the classic whitewater rivers of the eastern United States. On summer days, rafts and kayaks float the river in droves.

Turn right on US 19 and continue to follow the Nantahala River downstream. Though most of the busy route lies within lush undeveloped national forest, inholdings are filled with tourist-oriented businesses. Across the river lie the tracks of the Great Smoky Mountain Railroad, a tourist line that offers train trips through the gorge. As you journey down the gorge on US 19, numerous spots allow you to stop and watch boaters go by. At the Ferebee picnic area, you can eat lunch and watch the river parade. Probably the most exciting spot is just upstream from the Nantahala Outdoor Center where the river roars over Nantahala Falls, a roaring Class III rapid of foaming, swirling whitewater. Kayakers congregate here, charging into the rapid again and again.

Outfitters along the route offer guided whitewater trips and rent all manner of watercraft. Most of the river is not exceptionally difficult, but you should not try to float it without having some experience. The Nantahala Outdoor Center offers guided trips, paddling instruction, boat rentals, and other services. If you seek more excitement than the Nantahala can give, try nearby rivers such as the Ocoee, Chattooga, Nolichucky, and French Broad; some are considerably more difficult. For a trip with multiple kinds of transportation, drive to Bryson City, ride the train to the river put-in, and float back downriver.

Below the outdoor center, the highway leaves the river and passes about 4 miles of numerous commercial establishments, from outfitters to restaurants and motels. The scenic drive ends at the junction with NC 28, which is also the ending point of the Fontana Lake drive (Drive #13).

16

Whitewater Falls

Highlands to Rosman

General description: A 41-mile paved route through the resort towns of Highlands, Cashiers, and Lake Toxaway via Whitewater Falls, one of the highest waterfalls in the eastern United States.

Special attractions: Nantahala National Forest, Whitewater Falls, Toxaway Falls, Glen Falls, Whitesides Mountain, Ellicott Rock Wilderness, Horsepasture Wild and Scenic River, hiking, fishing, scenic views, fall colors, rock climbing.

Location: Southwestern North Carolina. The drive starts in Highlands at the junction of US 64 and NC 106.

Drive route numbers: US 64, NC 107, SC 107, SC 413, SC 130, NC 281, US 64.

Travel season: The best season is from spring through fall. Winter snow can make travel treacherous, if not impossible.

Camping: There are no public campgrounds directly on the route. However, the Nantahala National Forest manages Van Hook Glade Campground just west of Highlands.

Services: All services are available in Highlands, Cashiers, and Lake Toxaway.

Nearby attractions: Pisgah National Forest, other sections of Nantahala National Forest, Cullasaja Gorge, Dry Falls, Bridal Veil Falls, Cullasaja Falls, Wayah Bald, Chattooga Wild and Scenic River, Cradle of Forestry, Shining Rock Wilderness, Middle Prong Wilderness, Forest Heritage Scenic Byway.

For more information: Nantahala National Forest (Highlands Ranger District); Highlands, Cashiers, and Brevard Chambers of Commerce. See Appendix for addresses and phone numbers.

The Drive

From the town of Highlands (see Drive #15), this drive winds through what could be considered Waterfall Central in North Carolina and adjoining areas of South Carolina and Georgia. Transylvania, Macon, and Jackson Counties have the highest concentration of waterfalls in North Carolina, owing to a fortuitous combination of geology and climate. High mountain plateaus and good rainfall allow decent-size streams to build up here. Hard metamorphic and igneous rocks resist the leveling processes of erosion, and geologic folding and faulting have created steep escarpments. The combination of good-size streams, durable rock, and high escarpments leads to great waterfalls. One particularly good waterfall lies just beyond the scope of this drive on the south side of Highlands. Glen Falls has three major falls in rapid succession of about 15 feet, 60 feet, and 70 feet. To make a short detour to this impressive waterfall, see directions in Drive #15.

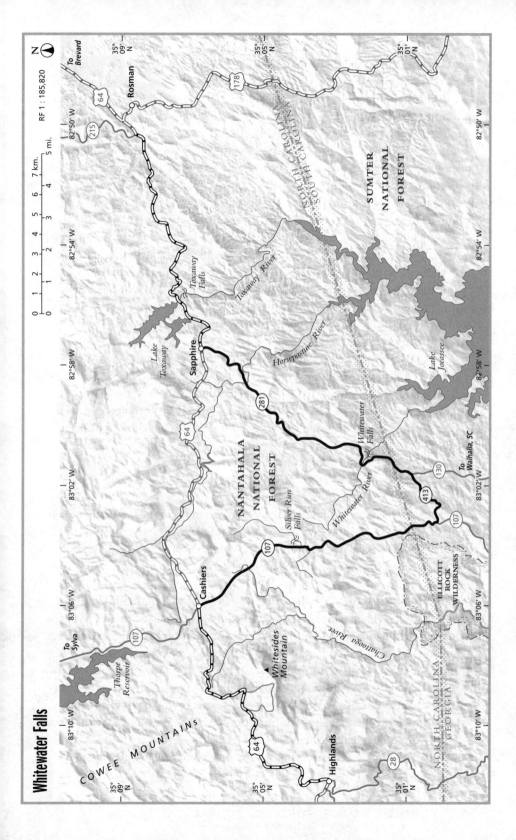

Whitewater Falls

N

RF 1 : 185,820

0 1 2 3 4 5 6 7 km.

0 1 2 3 4 5 mi.

Start the drive at the junction of US 64 and NC 106 in Highlands. Follow US 64 east from town past expensive homes, inns, and shops. Along the way you will pass the district office of the Nantahala National Forest; stop in if you need maps or information.

Just past the forest office, a side road leads to a great hike up Whitesides Mountain. About 6 miles from the start of the drive, turn right onto SR 1600. The junction is marked with a sign for Whitesides Mountain; start looking for it when you come to the local country club. Follow this road a little more than a mile to a parking area on the left. A moderate 2-mile round-trip hike up an old road takes you to the top of one of the most dramatic sites in the area.

Along the entire southeast side of the mountain, a rocky crest abruptly gives away to thin air. A massive band of cliffs from 400 to 750 feet high drops down to the Chattooga River. Rock climbers are drawn to the spot. You can do the trail as a slightly more strenuous loop if you don't want to go up and back on the same route. If you don't mind rising early and carrying a flashlight, this may be the best sunrise spot in the Nantahala National Forest—just don't get anywhere near the edge of the cliffs in the dark.

Beyond the turnoff to Whitesides Mountain, the highway offers a great view (sometimes called the "Big View") and then begins a steady descent off Highlands' high plateau. You lose more than 600 feet in elevation by the time you hit the vacation town of Cashiers, a smaller version of Highlands. Like its neighbor, Cashiers has long been frequented by summer people from the low, hot country near the Carolina coast.

One of the best-known early vacationers here was Colonel Wade Hampton II. After the Battle of New Orleans in 1814, General (and future president) Andrew Jackson charged Hampton with delivering news of the American victory to President James Madison in Washington. Legend says Hampton rode the 1,200 miles in ten days using only one horse. In later years he built an elaborate retreat in Cashiers Valley. His son Wade Hampton III commanded an important unit of the Confederate States Army and later became a governor and U.S. senator from South Carolina.

Turn right onto NC 107 in the center of Cashiers and head south past manicured golf courses lined with attractive homes. In about 4 miles, you will enter the Nantahala National Forest and begin a steady descent toward South Carolina. A pullout on the left at 4 miles has a short trail that leads to scenic Silver Run Falls. In another 3 miles, you will brush the edge of the Ellicott Rock Wilderness Area on the right. This undeveloped area, accessible by foot and horse, straddles the Chattooga Wild and Scenic River, which was made famous by the movie *Deliverance*.

Soon you cross the state line and enter South Carolina and the Sumter National Forest. The road becomes SC 107 here. Turn left in 1 mile onto SC 413, a paved road. After 0.8 mile, drivers pass a great viewpoint on the right that looks out over a broad sweep of mountain foothills and beyond to the Piedmont. Below you is 7,500-acre Lake Jocassee, one of South Carolina's best trout lakes. From the overlook, the road descends steadily, reaching SC 130 in 1.5 miles. Turn left here to reenter North Carolina and the Nantahala National Forest in 0.9 mile. The road becomes NC 281.

In only 0.2 mile, a well-marked spur road on the right leads to a parking lot for Whitewater Falls. This popular spot has a short paved trail to a great overlook of the falls, stairs leading to a lower overlook, picnic tables, and toilets. Some claim that Whitewater Falls is the highest waterfall in the eastern United States, though it is impossible to say with certainty which waterfall is highest. Do you count only free drops, or do you measure an entire series of cascades? Do you measure year-round flows? Some high falls, such as Glassmine Falls on the Blue Ridge Parkway, have a small flow and can go dry during dry spells. Even if 411-foot Whitewater Falls is not the highest in the East, it may well be the most impressive. In his book *North Carolina Waterfalls: A Hiking and Photography Guide,* Kevin Adams writes, "If you could see only one waterfall in North Carolina, Whitewater Falls would be a good candidate. To many people, it's the most spectacular waterfall in the East."

Now, opinions vary, but most people would agree that Whitewater Falls is worth a stop.

An easy, paved 0.2-mile trail leads from the parking lot to an overlook high above the falls. Steps to the right lead down to another lower overlook. A trail that was once an old road leads past the upper overlook to a crossing of the Whitewater River above the falls. Large rocks and pools make this area a great place for sunbathing, swimming, and wading, but don't get anywhere near the top of the falls. More people die here than at any other waterfall in the state. Rocks and cliffs near any waterfall are often wet, polished, and slick. If you are not convinced that this area is waterfall heaven, consider that 400-foot Lower Whitewater Falls lies just a short distance downstream in South Carolina. Across the gorge from the trail to Whitewater Falls is Laurel Falls, which is difficult to see through screening trees.

From Whitewater Falls, the highway climbs north. In 6.4 miles you cross the Horsepasture River. In 1984, a power company obtained permits to build a hydroelectric power plant here, creating an outcry among locals. A grassroots opposition campaign led to the demise of the power plant plan and the designation of this section of the Horsepasture as an official National Wild and Scenic River in 1986. The river earns the designation as it roars down a deep gorge over numerous cascades and large waterfalls. Hikers, swimmers, and anglers love this area, but don't park here. The no parking signs are strictly enforced.

If Whitewater Falls left you wanting more, consider hiking to some of these falls. To access the Horsepasture River falls, park at Gorges State Park's Grassy Ridge access area, located about a mile north on NC 281. See Kevin Adams's book for detailed directions. The state park is new, and access may change.

Whitewater Falls, Nantahala National Forest

Beyond the bridge area, drive about 2 miles north on NC 281 to the junction with busy US 64 in the village of Sapphire. This small community was named for a mining company that dug here for corundum, the mineral of which sapphires and rubies are composed, before the turn of the last century. There is a gas station at the junction. Turn right here and head toward Rosman and Brevard. You will pass an arm of small Lake Toxaway in 1.4 miles, and enter Lake Toxaway, another resort community.

The name *Toxaway* comes from a Cherokee leader. Developers began building the high-class resort here in the 1890s, starting with a dam that created 640-acre Lake Toxaway. In the beautiful setting of mountain and lake, the developers constructed an ornate five-story hotel with more than 500 rooms. With beautiful hardwood trim, electric lighting, steam heat, and elevators, the hotel was very refined for its time and place. With a ballroom, orchestra, and formal dining room, the hotel was the ultimate in luxury. The railroad arrived in 1903, and several trains brought guests here daily.

The resort's heyday was short-lived, however. A massive flood in July 1916 gravely damaged much of the area and led to the dam's failure that August. The ensuing flood caused major losses for miles downstream. Liability claims against the development company caused closure and abandonment of the property. In 1948 the once-luxurious hotel was demolished. The area was too beautiful for developers to resist, so in 1960 a new company began to revive the resort. A new dam was constructed, watering a golf course and new homes. The resort thrives today.

The busy road now crosses the top of Toxaway Falls on a new bridge just below the dam. This attractive waterfall has a main cascade of 125 feet, but the area is cluttered with encroaching condominiums and commercial development. Beyond Lake Toxaway, the road winds through woods scattered with occasional homes and developments. A sign marks the point where you cross the Eastern Continental Divide. Rivers on one side ultimately drain into the Atlantic; the other side drains into the Gulf of Mexico.

In a few miles, the drive ends at the junction with NC 215 on the west edge of Rosman. This small town lies at the point where four major tributaries of the French Broad River come together. The town was once a prosperous lumber and railroad community, but it is fairly quiet today. The French Broad is a major western North Carolina river popular with boaters, especially in its lower reaches. From here you can return to Highlands or take the Forest Heritage Scenic Byway (see Drive #10).

17

Crowders Mountain

Kings Mountain National Military Park, South Carolina, to Crowders Mountain

General description: A short, paved 10-mile route chock-full of interesting sights, including a Revolutionary War battlefield, two state parks, a living history farm just over the border in South Carolina, and prominent Piedmont peaks.

Special attractions: Kings Mountain National Military Park, Kings Mountain State Park, Crowders Mountain State Park, historic battlefield, Living History Farm, hiking, fishing, swimming, rock climbing, boating, fall colors, scenic views.

Location: South-central North Carolina and adjacent South Carolina. The drive starts in South Carolina at Kings Mountain National Military Park. Take Exit 2 from I-85 a little less than 40 miles west of Charlotte, and follow the signs on SC 216 about 4.5 miles to the military park visitor center.

Drive route name/numbers: SC 216, SR 1100/Battleground Road, SR 1102/Unity Church Road, SR 1126/Lewis Road, SR 1112/Lewis Road, SR 1125/Sparrow Springs Road, State Park Lane.

Travel season: All year. The drive is probably most pleasant in spring and fall.

Camping: Kings Mountain State Park has a large campground. Crowders Mountain State Park has primitive backpacking campsites only.

Services: All services are available in nearby Gastonia and Kings Mountain.

Nearby attractions: South Mountains State Park, James Polk Memorial State Historic Site, Reed Gold Mine State Historic Site, Duke Power State Park, Cowpens National Battlefield.

For more information: Kings Mountain National Military Park (South Carolina), Kings Mountain State Park (South Carolina), Crowders Mountain State Park, Gaston County Travel and Tourism. See Appendix for addresses and phone numbers.

The Drive

This short drive is notable for its connection to Revolutionary War history. Many people tend to think of places like Lexington, Concord, Philadelphia, Boston, or Yorktown when they think of the battle for American independence. However, battles in North and South Carolina were critical to the ultimate defeat of the British. The drive begins at Kings Mountain National Military Park, just across the South Carolina border. The park is an excellent launching point for a journey into the Carolina past.

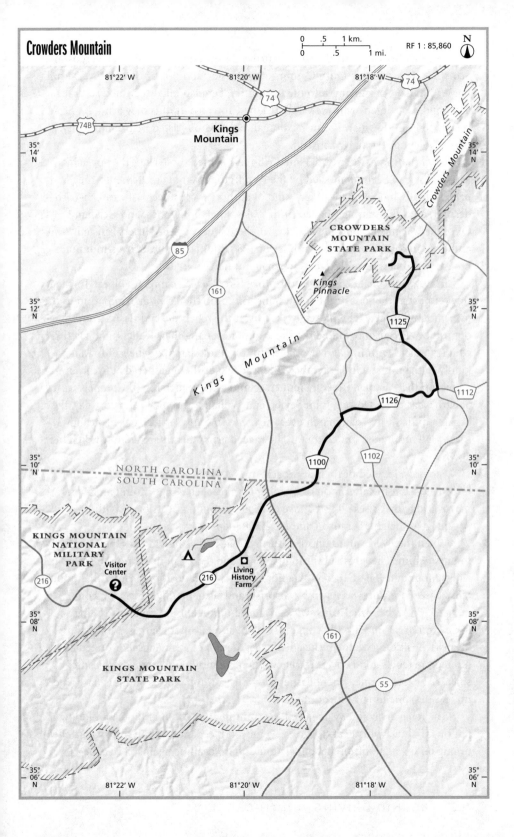

Crowders Mountain

RF 1 : 85,860

N

0   .5   1 km.
0   .5   1 mi.

81°22′ W   81°20′ W   81°18′ W

74

Kings
Mountain

74B

74

85

161

1125

CROWDERS
MOUNTAIN
STATE PARK

Kings
Pinnacle

Crowders Mountain

1126

1112

1100

1102

NORTH CAROLINA
SOUTH CAROLINA

KINGS MOUNTAIN
NATIONAL
MILITARY
PARK

Visitor
Center

216

216

Living
History
Farm

161

Kings   Mountain

KINGS MOUNTAIN
STATE PARK

55

35°
14′
N

35°
12′
N

35°
10′
N

35°
08′
N

35°
06′
N

35°
14′
N

35°
12′
N

35°
10′
N

35°
08′
N

35°
06′
N

In 1780, British general Charles Cornwallis ordered Major Patrick Ferguson, a Scotsman, to scour the South Carolina countryside and build a strong loyalist militia. Within days of moving into the upcountry, Ferguson had recruited several thousand Carolinians who were loyal to the Crown. With this new army, he proceeded to hunt down and punish colonial rebels who resisted British authority. A nasty, violent guerrilla war ensued.

Until that time, the frontiersmen who had settled these rugged Appalachian Mountains had been unaffected by the war. In their remote settlements, they had been virtually independent of any kind of authority. Most were of Scottish-Irish descent, but other families hailed from Wales, England, France, and Germany. Once the war moved into their backyard, these independent settlers resisted royal authority fiercely. During the summer of 1780, militias of these "over-mountain" men engaged Ferguson's loyalists in small but fierce battles.

In August of that year, Ferguson's Tory forces set up camp at Gilbert Town, a tiny outpost at the foot of the mountains. Ferguson then sent an ultimatum to the over-mountain men. The message was this: If the rebels did not desist from their opposition, Ferguson would cross the mountains, hang their leaders, and lay their country waste "with and sword." Naturally, these scrappy rebels didn't take kindly to the threat. On September 25, some 800 of them gathered at Sycamore Shoals on the Watauga River in Tennessee under the leadership of Colonels Isaac Shelby, Charles McDowell, John Sevier, and William Campbell. The next day, they began a difficult five-day march over the snowy mountains to Quaker Meadows, where 350 more men joined them. The ragged army then marched toward Gilbert Town.

Ferguson learned of their approach and retreated while he called for reinforcements. On the afternoon of October 6 he reached Kings Mountain, a long narrow ridge that rises 60 feet above the rolling country at its base. With the advantage of height, Ferguson and his 1,100 men set up camp.

When the over-mountain men learned that Ferguson had fled, they resolved to pursue him. They pushed through a night and day of pouring rain to arrive at Kings Mountain. There they took a horseshoe-shaped position around the mountain's base. Ferguson was taken by surprise, and sustained fighting soon commenced. The rebel Americans twice advanced up the mountain before being forced to retreat under withering musket fire and bayonet charges. Although the loyalists' position gave them the advantage, the slopes were densely wooded and offered the rebels good cover. To one soldier, the mountain seemed "volcanic" since, as he later wrote, "there flashed along its summit, and around its base, and up its sides, one long sulfurous blaze."

The rebel army finally achieved the summit after about an hour of bloody fighting. Using a whistle and a horse, Ferguson raced around the smoky battlefield urging on his men until rebel bullets found him. Leaning against a tree, he died;

his subordinate then raised a white flag to surrender. But the rebel leaders could not immediately gain control of their independent men, who continued to shoot down terrified loyalists. Ironically, the only British soldier to die here was Ferguson; all the other dead were loyalists or rebels from the colonies. The toll was high: 225 Carolina loyalists dead and 163 wounded; 28 over-mountain men slain and 62 wounded.

One soldier recalled the first night after the battle: "The groans of the wounded and dying on the mountain were truly affecting—begging piteously for a little water; but in the hurry, confusion, and exhaustion of the [rebels], these cries, when emanating from the Tories, were little heeded." The next day was little better for the loyalist captives. Those who had not died fighting were marched toward Hillsborough, North Carolina, and the American army there. On the journey, the rebels' fury led them to beat their charges and hack at them with swords. A week later, nine of the Tories were hanged after a wartime trial.

The over-mountain men drifted back to their villages and homesteads, but this Carolina battle greatly raised rebel spirits and hurt loyalist recruiting. Cornwallis retreated while the American Continental army gained strength. On January 17, 1781, the Americans defeated a superior force of regular British troops at Cowpens, about 30 miles west of Kings Mountain. On March 15, General Nathanael Greene led his American troops against Cornwallis's main army at Guilford Courthouse in North Carolina. Though Greene's troops were forced to withdraw, the Americans inflicted heavy losses on the British. Greene proceeded to retake South Carolina while Cornwallis spent the summer fighting a string of unproductive battles. The British leader finally surrendered at Yorktown, Virginia, on October 19, 1781. His surrender effectively ended the Revolutionary War.

Start your visit at Kings Mountain by viewing the interpretive exhibits in the visitor center, which give more details about the battle described above. Then take the paved trail that leads through the battlefield itself. Monuments and markers commemorate the crucial sites along the trail. Birds twittering in the trees give no hint of the bloodshed that occurred here more than 200 years ago. If you are interested in Revolutionary War history, be sure to visit Cowpens National Battlefield only about 30 miles west. Guilford Courthouse National Military Park is quite a bit farther away, on the edge of Greensboro, but it, too, is particularly worthwhile.

From the rich history at Kings Mountain National Military Park, the scenic drive heads southeast toward Kings Mountain State Park. After passing through lush woods, you enter the state park in 0.9 mile. Be sure to stop in at the Living History Farm on the right in another 1.7 miles. Park staff have reconstructed and restored a nineteenth-century farm, complete with houses, barns, corrals, and other structures. Workers reenact activities from those times, giving visitors a glimpse of pioneer life.

Just down the road is the main state park entrance, with access roads to many

Mountain laurel on Kings Pinnacle, Crowders Mountain State Park

of the park's facilities, including a large campground, a lake, a store, and a picnic area. You can hike, ride horses, fish, boat, camp, or even play miniature golf here. From the state park center, continue down the highway 0.9 mile to the park boundary at SC 161. Continue straight across the intersection on Battleground Road and enter North Carolina in 0.8 mile.

The road now becomes SR 1100/Battleground Road. Turn left in 1 mile on SR 1102/Unity Church Road, then almost immediately turn right onto SR 1126/Lewis Road. Follow Lewis Road 1.6 miles, then turn left onto SR 1125/Sparrow Springs Road. Turn left again in 2.3 miles onto State Park Lane, which enters Crowders Mountain State Park, the ending point of the drive. The *North Carolina Atlas & Gazetteer* can help you find your way through some of these back roads, but it names some of the roads incorrectly. The directions and road names in this book are accurate.

Two peaks in this state park, Crowders Mountain and Kings Pinnacle, are monadnocks or remnants of ancient mountain ranges that have eroded away. A mighty mountain range that was an outlier of the Appalachians once ran through here, but millions of years of erosion have made it disappear in most places. Only the durable quartzite-kyanite core of the range remains. The two peaks rise about 800 feet above the gently rolling Piedmont; Kings Pinnacle is the highest, reaching an elevation of 1,705 feet. Although Crowders Mountain is not quite as high, it has a more impressive band of cliffs.

Crowders Mountain was named for Ulrich Crowder, a German who purchased land here in 1789. Gold was discovered east of Charlotte in 1799, leading to a minor gold rush in the area. Many mines and claims were developed over the following years. In 1970, miners hoped to strip-mine Crowders Mountain for kyanite. The Gaston County Conservation Society was established to push for protection of this important local landmark as a state park. After much negotiation and many complicated transactions to acquire more than one hundred parcels of land, the state park opened in 1974.

To really see Crowders Mountain State Park, you have to get out of your car and don your hiking boots. Moderately strenuous trails lead to the summits of both mountains, giving you eyeball-to-eyeball looks at vultures riding the thermals over the peaks. The lush, green Piedmont stretches out in all directions below, marked with highways, homes, and factories. Not surprisingly, the park's cliffs of durable rock attract climbers. The park allows climbing in certain areas only; be sure to check in at the park office before heading for the cliffs.

Although the peak trails are relatively strenuous, the trail that circles the park lake is quite easy. If climbing and hiking sound a little too adventurous, you can always cast a line for bass in the lake, or relax and grill a steak at the picnic area to end your drive.

18

Hanging Rock
Pilot Mountain to Hanging Rock

General description: A 24-mile paved road between two prominent remnants of the ancient Sauratown Mountains, often called "the mountains away from the mountains" because of their isolation from the Blue Ridge.

Special attractions: Hanging Rock State Park, Pilot Mountain State Park, hiking, rock climbing, equestrian trails, fishing, swimming, boating, scenic views, fall colors, waterfalls.

Location: North-central North Carolina. The drive starts at Pilot Mountain State Park, about 22 miles northwest of Winston-Salem.

Drive route name/numbers: SR 2053/Pilot Knob Park Road, SR 1151/Pilot Knob Park Road, SR 1152/Old Winston Road, SR 1855/Highway 52 Bypass (Old US 52), NC 268, SR 1504/Lynchburg Road, NC 89, SR 1001/Hanging Rock Park Road.

Travel season: All year. Winters can be cold and gray. Occasional snow can make travel difficult, especially in the two parks.

Camping: Both Hanging Rock and Pilot Mountain State Parks have campgrounds. Pilot Mountain's is closed in winter.

Services: Danbury and Pilot Mountain have food and gas. All services are available in nearby Mount Airy and Winston-Salem.

Nearby attractions: Blue Ridge Parkway, Stone Mountain State Park, Guilford Courthouse National Military Park.

For more information: Hanging Rock State Park, Pilot Mountain State Park, Horne Creek Living Historical Farm, Mount Airy and Winston-Salem Chambers of Commerce. See Appendix for addresses and phone numbers.

The Drive

This drive connects two prominent Piedmont mountains, Pilot Mountain and Hanging Rock. These two peaks are remnants of the ancient Sauratown Mountains, which rose in this area many millions of years ago. The ancient mountains have eroded steadily over time, and only a few peaks of durable quartzite remain. Isolated, remnant peaks such as these are known as monadnocks.

Start the drive at Pilot Mountain State Park. The park is easily accessible from an exit on US 52, about 22 miles northwest of Winston-Salem. If you drive to the park via US 52, the distinctive summit of Pilot Mountain will be visible long before you reach the exit. To visit the mountaintop, drive up the winding paved road (pass on this option if you have a large RV or trailer). Driving up is the easy way to get there. If you're up for a greater challenge or want to get some exercise, hike to the top on the Grindstone Trail, which starts at the park campground. Either way, the views are spectacular.

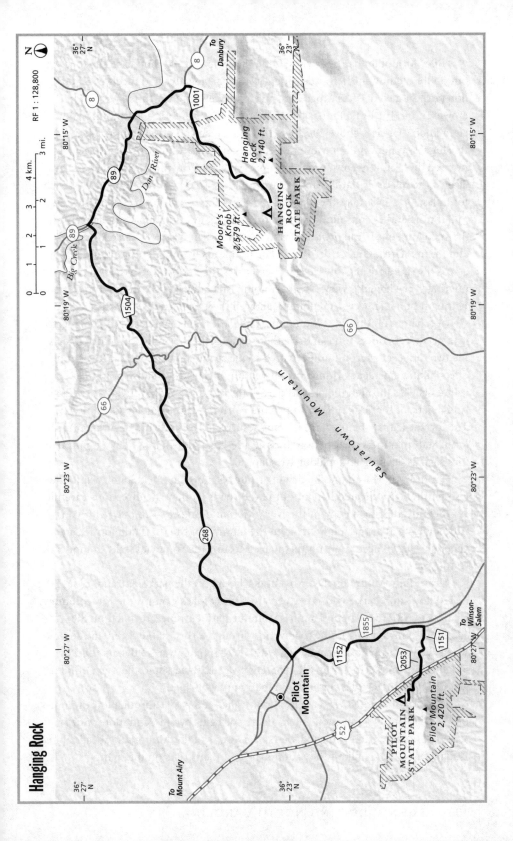

Hanging Rock

Pilot Mountain has two peaks, Little Pinnacle and Big Pinnacle. The road tops out on the slightly shorter Little Pinnacle at a parking area. On nice weekends, don't expect a wilderness experience here. The views are worth the weekend crowds. From the Little Pinnacle Overlook, visitors can look across to Big Pinnacle, a knob that rises above 200-foot cliffs to a green cap of vegetation. Although this highest point on Pilot Mountain reaches an elevation of only 2,420 feet (it's not exactly Mount Everest, or even Mount Mitchell), the mountain looks striking against the relatively flat Piedmont surroundings. In every direction, views stretch for miles. On a clear day, the Blue Ridge Mountains are visible to the northwest.

If time and energy allow, take another short jaunt on the park's relatively easy 0.8-mile Jomeokee Trail. *Jomeokee* is the Saura Indian name for Pilot Mountain and means "Great Guide," or "Pilot." The trail leads from the summit parking lot across the saddle to Big Pinnacle. It then circles the knob at the base of the cliffs, offering ever-changing views. Rock climbing isn't allowed here in order to protect nesting raptors. However, climbing is allowed in other sections of the park.

A separate unit of Pilot Mountain State Park lies a few miles south, connected by a narrow corridor. You can drive there or walk the 5.5-mile trail that connects the two units. The second unit lies on a scenic segment of the Yadkin River and offers hiking, horseback riding, primitive camping, wading, and swimming. Canoeists pass through the park as part of the 165-mile Yadkin River Canoe Trail. A highlight of the Yadkin River unit is the Horne Creek Living Historical Farm. The former Hauser family farm is being resurrected as a late nineteenth-century farm. Staff members wear period dress and re-create life in those days, doing activities such as farming and making lye soap.

From Pilot Mountain, the driving route to Hanging Rock State Park follows a somewhat complicated network of paved roads. Follow the directions carefully. It is helpful to bring a copy of the *North Carolina Atlas & Gazetteer* with you. Although the atlas has a few errors in the naming of the roads, the routes are generally shown accurately on the maps. Most of the route has light to moderate traffic.

Leave Pilot Mountain and cross under US 52 on the park's entrance road, SR 2053/Pilot Knob Park Road. After you cross into Stokes County, the route number changes to SR 1151. About 1.3 miles from the park entrance, turn left on SR 1152/Old Winston Road. The road winds through a rural subdivision and some woods before it reaches the junction with SR 1855/Highway 52 Bypass (Old US 52) after 3.1 miles. Go left on SR 1855/Highway 52 Bypass into the town of Pilot Mountain. There are gas stations and food purveyors here.

Turn right onto NC 268 after 0.3 mile. The road passes through lots of homes on the edge of town but soon enters an area of fields, woods, and more widely scattered homes. There are good views back toward Pilot Mountain. Ahead looms Hanging Rock; the bulk of the Sauratown Mountains rises on the right.

You pass a gas station in 4.3 miles down NC 268.

In another 4 miles, you will come to the junction with NC 66. Continue straight ahead here, on SR 1504/Lynchburg Road. The countryside now gets considerably more hilly, wooded, and undeveloped along SR 1504. Right after crossing Big Creek, SR 1504 ends at the junction with NC 89. Turn right onto NC 89 and immediately cross the Dan River, another good canoe route. You are now following part of an official state scenic route, the Hanging Rock Scenic Byway.

You then cross the river again. Turn right 1.4 miles after the second river crossing onto SR 1001/Hanging Rock Park Road. This junction is very obvious, with state park signs and a hospital on one corner. You will reach the entrance to Hanging Rock State Park in 1.6 miles. From there, the road climbs steadily. In 1.7 miles, turn left to reach the visitor center and the end of this drive. Popular 6,192-acre Hanging Rock State Park has enough appeal to satisfy everybody.

Like Pilot Mountain, Hanging Rock is a remnant of the ancient Sauratown Mountains. It is slightly higher than Pilot Mountain and has multiple summits, the highest being Moore's Knob at 2,579 feet. Several of the peaks have bare, rocky summits and sheer cliffs, offering unobstructed views across the Piedmont. The summits encircle a small jewel of a lake cupped in a high bowl. Hanging Rock is not especially high in an absolute sense, but it does tower over the surrounding Piedmont. It's also high enough for the climate to be a little cooler here. In early spring, when the Piedmont is quite green, the mountain's trees are only starting to leaf out.

Hanging Rock State Park was formed in 1936 when 3,096 acres were donated to the state by the Stokes County Committee for Hanging Rock and the Winston-Salem Foundation. Over the following years, quite a lot more land was added to the park. Many of the facilities here, including the lake, road, and trails, were built by the Civilian Conservation Corps during the Great Depression.

Hanging Rock is made for hikers. Trails lead to its many summits and cliffs, and also to several waterfalls. Probably the most popular trail is the steep, rocky 1.2-mile trail up to Hanging Rock itself. On the west end of this landmark, a huge beak of bare stone protrudes over the forest below, giving hikers great views and vertigo. The best time for a quiet hike on this broad, busy route is on weekdays or in winter and early spring. A more strenuous and less busy hike is the 4.2-mile Moore's Loop Trail. It climbs near the cliffs of Moore's Wall to Moore's Knob and the observation tower that crowns its summit. For good views with the least crowds, take the trail out to Cook's Wall and House Rock. Truly serious hikers can take the 30-mile Sauratown Trail, which connects Hanging Rock to Pilot Mountain.

The park's large cliffs of solid, durable rock have made it a popular destination for rock climbers. Climbing is allowed at Moore's Wall and Cook's Wall. Be sure to register first at the visitor center.

Hanging Rock

If you're worn out on views, consider a walk to one of the park waterfalls. Probably the most scenic of the falls is the Lower Cascades, accessed off SR 2012/Hall Road on the north side of the park. The creek plunges 25 feet over a rocky ledge into a pool overhung by a massive cliff. A short, easy trail leads to the top of the cliff and a view of the falls below. Use care near the edge; it's a long way down.

If you're hot and sweaty from all the hiking and climbing, consider a dip in the 12-acre park lake. You can also wet a line or rent a canoe there. The park includes an access point on the Dan River if more serious canoeing strikes your fancy. It's one of several public access points for the Dan River Canoe Trail.

Although this scenic drive itself may take only thirty to forty minutes, most visitors could easily spend several days thoroughly exploring these two state parks.

19

Reed Gold Mine

Morrow Mountain State Park to Reed Gold Mine State Historic Site

General description: A 32-mile paved drive from the wooded hills of Morrow Mountain State Park to the exhibits and musty tunnels of Reed Gold Mine State Historic Site.

Special attractions: Morrow Mountain State Park, Reed Gold Mine State Historic Site, Lake Tillery, hiking, fishing, boating, fall colors, scenic views, horse trails, gold panning.

Location: South-central North Carolina. The drive starts at the entrance of Morrow Mountain State Park, located a few miles east of Albemarle.

Drive route name/numbers: SR 1798/Morrow Mountain Road, SR 1720/Valley Drive, SR 1720/Stony Gap Road, US 52, SR 1906/Southside Road, NC 138, SR 1984/Union Grove Road, SR 1960/Mabry Road, SR 1956/Old Aquadale Road, SR 1956/Reap Road, SR 1968/Hartsell Road, SR 1968/St. Martin Road, SR 1970/Hazard Road, SR 1221/Frog Pond Road, NC 24/27, SR 1100/Reed Gold Mine Road.

Travel season: All year. Spring and fall are probably the most pleasant. Winters can be cold and gray with occasional snow.

Camping: Morrow Mountain State Park has camping.

Services: Albemarle has all services. Locust has food and gas. Limited food and gas are scattered in a few sites along the route.

Nearby attractions: Uwharrie National Forest, Birkhead Mountain Wilderness, Town Creek Indian Mound State Historic Site, Spencer Shops State Historic Site, Boone's Cave State Park.

For more information: Morrow Mountain State Park, Reed Gold Mine State Historic Site, Stanly County Chamber of Commerce. See Appendix for addresses and phone numbers.

The Drive

This drive is both very scenic and historic. It starts in Morrow Mountain State Park, located in the low Uwharrie Mountains, and travels through rolling, pastoral Piedmont country to Reed Gold Mine, the first gold mine in the United States. The driving route follows a complicated network of paved roads between the two sites. Follow the directions carefully. It is helpful to have a copy of the *North Carolina Atlas & Gazetteer*, although it has a few errors in the naming of the roads. Most of the route is lightly traveled.

Start at Morrow Mountain State Park, an area that can fill at least an entire day. The park lies in the Uwharrie Mountains, which are the weathered remnants

Reed Gold Mine

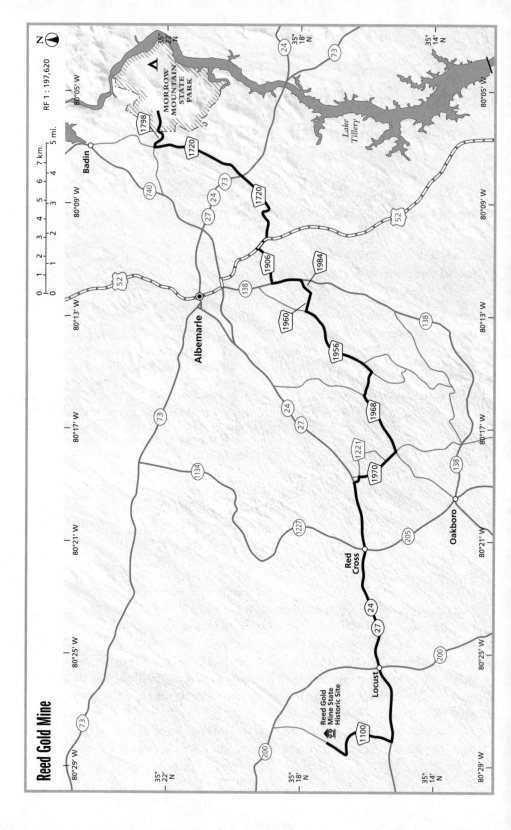

of one of the oldest mountain ranges in North America. The range's long history began about 500 million years ago with volcanic eruptions on the floor of a shallow sea. In succeeding millennia, more eruptions, folding, and faulting built the Uwharries into a mighty range. Millions of years of erosion then wore the range down to the peaks you see here today, topping out at only about 1,000 feet. Although these peaks and ridges are not particularly high in absolute terms, they stand in prominent contrast to the rolling Piedmont country that surrounds them. Morrow Mountain is the highest summit here and rises to 936 feet, about 700 feet above Lake Tillery at its base.

Various Native American tribes lived in this area for thousands of years. The first recorded European visitor to the Uwharrie Mountains was John Lederer, a German doctor and trader who arrived in 1673. Settlement of the area occurred in the mid-1700s, primarily along the Yadkin and Pee Dee Rivers and Mountain Creek. A ferry operated across the Pee Dee River in about 1780; it was the only means of crossing in this area until a bridge was built downstream in the 1920s.

Francis Kron immigrated to the United States in 1823 from Prussia and settled in what would later become Morrow Mountain State Park in 1834. Kron is believed to have been the first doctor to practice medicine in this part of North Carolina. He traveled widely to serve his patients and practiced until he was more than eighty years old. He lived in what is now the park until he died in 1883. His property was later sold and acquired by James McKnight Morrow, donor of much of the park's land. Dr. Kron's house, infirmary, and greenhouse are now part of the park's exhibits; they have been reconstructed to match their appearance in 1870, offering a glimpse of life here more than a hundred years ago.

Interest in creating a state park at Morrow Mountain developed in the 1930s. Much of the land was donated to the park by local citizens such as James Morrow. Many of the facilities were constructed by the Civilian Conservation Corps and the Works Projects Administration, organizations established during the Great Depression to employ young men and create public works. Today the state park encompasses a sizable 4,693 acres.

Any visit to the park should include a drive or hike to the summit of Morrow Mountain. Views range from the Uwharrie Mountains to the east to Charlotte to the west. Seventeen miles of hiking trails lead through mixed pine and hardwood forest to the summits of Sugarloaf, Hattaway, and Fall Mountains, Lake Tillery, and other destinations. Although the park is very popular, many of its trails are often quiet and deserted. Mountain laurel grows thickly along these paths and can be spectacular when it blooms in late April and early May. For horse fans, the park offers 16 miles of equestrian trails. If the trails are not enough to occupy you, there are also a nature museum, picnic area, rental cabins, campground, a swimming pool, boat rentals on Lake Tillery, and fishing for largemouth bass, striped bass, catfish, crappie, and other species.

Historic Kron House, Morrow Mountain State Park

After Morrow Mountain State Park wears you out, head west toward Reed Gold Mine. Most of this scenic drive follows quiet rural roads rather than busy highways. From the park entrance gate, drive 1.4 miles from the mountains across Little Mountain Creek and turn left on SR 1720/Valley Drive. Follow it through lush woods for 3.3 miles to a junction with NC 24/27/73. From here we take the scenic route. Cross NC 24/27/73 and stay on SR 1720 (the name changes to Stony Gap Road). A seafood restaurant, Jays, seems out of place along this rural road.

Turn right on busy US 52 after 2.8 miles. Follow it only 0.4 mile, then turn left on SR 1906/Southside Road. Be careful as you drive here. SR 1906 is a narrow road with an unmarked railroad crossing in 0.4 mile—stop, look, and listen here since there are no warning lights or gates. The road passes through a countryside of fields, woods, and scattered homes.

After another 0.9 mile, go left on NC 138, a moderately busy highway. In just 1 mile, turn right onto SR 1984/Union Grove Road across from the brick Union Grove Baptist Church. Turn right yet again on SR 1960/Mabry Road in 0.6 mile. In another 0.6 mile, go left on SR 1956/Old Aquadale Road. Enjoy the countryside, even if you get lost. You'll eventually find your way.

Follow SR 1956 for 2.9 miles to a fork. Bear right onto SR 1956/Reap Road (the number stays the same, although the name changes). Turn right again on SR

1968/Hartsell Road in 0.4 mile. There is a narrow one-lane bridge over Long Creek in 0.4 mile. Turn left at a stop sign onto SR 1968/St. Martin Road about 0.5 mile past the bridge. The junction is poorly signed.

SR 1968 crosses Big Bear Creek in 1.6 miles. Turn right on SR 1970/Hazard Road about 0.6 mile past the creek. Turn left onto SR 1221/Frog Pond Road at a stop sign in 1.6 miles (the junction is unsigned) and stay on the more major road. In only 0.3 mile you reach busy NC 24/27 near an auto repair shop in the village of Frog Pond. Pat yourself on the back if you have reached this point without getting lost.

Now turn left on NC 24/27. The next 9 miles of the route follow NC 24/27. It is busier and less scenic than the back roads, but at least it's easier to find your way. Gas and snacks are available in 1.8 miles. The interesting Red Cross Store occupies a corner at the junction with NC 205. This rustic brick building is covered with antique signs and heaps of old equipment.

The terrain flattens as you continue west. The town of Locust lies about 6 miles away along NC 24/27. Locust has food, gas, and a big lumber mill, among other things. Beyond the town, NC 24/27 becomes a four-lane highway. Turn right onto SR 1100/Reed Gold Mine Road soon after NC 24/27 becomes four-lane (about 2.6 miles from the junction with NC 200 in the center of Locust). The narrow paved road winds north 3 miles to the entrance to Reed Gold Mine State Historic Site on the right. There is a one-lane bridge across Little Meadow Creek along the way.

Reed Gold Mine was the site of the first documented gold find in the United States. John Reed was a Hessian soldier who left the British army near the end of the Revolutionary War and settled near other Germans in the southern Piedmont of North Carolina. Most of these immigrants made their living with small farms. Like them, Reed would have faded into history had his son Conrad not found a large, heavy, yellow rock in Little Meadow Creek on a Sunday in 1799. Reed did not realize the rock's value and used it as a doorstop for three years.

A jeweler in Fayetteville identified the rock as a seventeen-pound gold nugget in 1802 and purchased it for Reed's asking price of $3.50, even though it was worth about $3,600. The jeweler tried to buy more such rocks from the Reed family, but the Reeds soon learned their value. In 1803, Reed formed a mining partnership with three area men. His partners contributed equipment and laborers while Reed supplied the mine site. Profits were to be divided equally.

In the early years, the miners only used placer methods. These involved digging up sediment along the creek and using pans, sluices, and rockers to wash out the gold. Although farming was most important to these part-time miners, they recorded a good first year—in part because a slave owned by Reed and his partners found a twenty-eight-pound nugget. As word spread of the gold discovery, other farmers did some prospecting and mining in the area. Local workers were joined by outsiders, including skilled miners from Cornwall, England. By 1824, the Reed Mine had produced more than $100,000 in gold and was one of three major mines in North Carolina.

In 1825, area miners learned that more gold existed in the area's quartz lodes, leading to more capital- and labor-intensive underground mining. Underground work began at the Reed Mine in 1831, but ended four years later after a family squabble ended up in court. For ten years the mine was inactive, although others in the area continued operating. John Reed died wealthy in 1845. The mine was sold at a public auction after John Reed's death and changed owners many times.

By 1854, there were fifteen separate shafts and many tunnels at the mine. In deeper areas, water had to be pumped out to prevent the mine from flooding. Miners loosened ore from the walls with picks, shovels, drills, dynamite, and back-breaking labor. They hauled out ore and waste rock using iron buckets and ore carts. Initially, large grinding stones crushed the ore; later, a stamp mill that used large steel hammers was built. The mine's last large nugget, a twenty-three-pound stone, was found by placer miners in 1896. Underground mining efforts stopped in 1912. The stamp mill at the Reed Mine today is similar to the one actually used there in the late 1800s. It is the only stamp mill left east of the Mississippi.

Reed Gold Mine can keep you busy for several hours. The historic site has extensive exhibits, underground mine tours, picnic areas, trails, and historic struc-tures. Watch the short interpretive movie for general information about the area. Tours of some of the tunnels are particularly interesting. Be sure to take a sweater or light jacket since the mine is cool and damp. Trails on the surface lead to the ruins of the old engine house, mine shafts, the stamp mill, and other sites. If that's not enough, try your luck panning for gold. Maybe you'll find a nugget large enough to pay for more scenic drives. At the very least, you'll gain an appreciation of the hard work required of miners in years past.

Until the California Gold Rush of 1849, North Carolina led the United States in gold production. Enough gold was produced here to allow the federal govern-ment to open a mint in nearby Charlotte. During the Reed Mine's heyday, mining was the area's second-largest employer after agriculture. Gold mining in North Carolina has steadily tapered off over the years; in recent years mining has been sporadic and of only minor importance.

If you have time, consider visiting the Bost Grist Mill just northwest of the mine on NC 200 near its junction with US 601. The operating mill dates to around 1810 and is open Sunday afternoons spring through fall.

20

Uwharrie Mountains
Uwharrie National Forest

General description: A 34-mile paved and gravel route that winds through the ancient Uwharrie Mountains and the Uwharrie National Forest, past rivers, a lake, a covered bridge, and many hiking opportunities.

Special attractions: Uwharrie National Forest, Uwharrie Mountains, Pisgah Covered Bridge, Birkhead Mountain Wilderness, Badin Lake, hiking, fishing, boating, scenic views, fall colors.

Location: South-central North Carolina. The drive starts at the junction of NC 47 and NC 49 about 16 miles southwest of Asheboro.

Drive route name/numbers: SR 1178/Bombay School Road, SR 1181/New Hope Road, SR 1143/High Pine Church Road, SR 1112/Lanier Road, SR 1114/Pisgah Covered Bridge Road, SR 1111/Mount Lebanon Road, SR 1110/Randall Hurley Road, SR 1307/Horseshoe Bend Road, SR 1306/Flint Hill Road, SR 1134/Robinson Road, SR 1301/Low Water Bridge Road, SR 1302/Coggins Mine Road, NC 109, SR 1153/Reservation Road, FR 576, FR 544, FR 554, FR 597, FR 597A.

Travel season: All year. Spring and fall are the most pleasant seasons. Summer can be hot and humid, and winter is cold and gray. In winter, snow can make travel difficult, especially on some of the gravel sections toward the end of the drive.

Camping: The Uwharrie National Forest manages a campground along the route at Badin Lake.

Services: All services are available in nearby Asheboro. Food and gas are available in Troy. Gas is available along NC 109 south of Eldorado.

Nearby attractions: Morrow Mountain State Park, Reed Gold Mine State Historic Site, North Carolina Zoological Park, Town Creek Indian Mound State Historic Site.

For more information: Uwharrie National Forest, Asheboro Chamber of Commerce. See Appendix for addresses and phone numbers.

The Drive

This drive winds through the northern part of the Uwharrie Mountains past fields, farms, woods, and a covered bridge to an idyllic campground on the shore of Badin Lake. Most of the route is paved, although a few segments near the end are gravel. In general, the entire route is suitable for everything but very large trailers or RVs. Although the gravel surfaces seem quite good, use care when they are wet.

The Piedmont is crisscrossed with numerous roads, and this area is no different. Therefore, like several other drives in this guide, the drive route is complicated. Follow the directions carefully. The roads are better marked in the first half

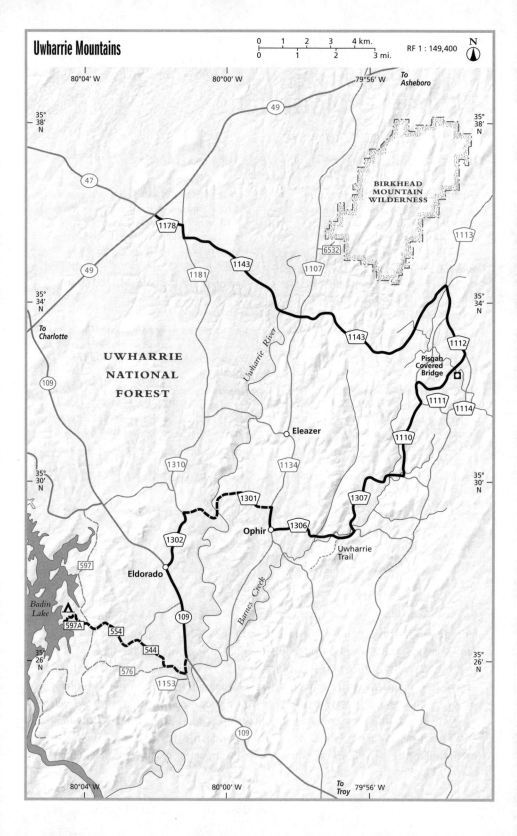

of the drive (in Randolph County) than in the second half (Montgomery County). It is helpful to have a copy of the *North Carolina Atlas & Gazetteer,* although it has a few errors in the naming of the roads. The first section of the route partly follows an official North Carolina Scenic Byway called the Birkhead Wilderness Route. The scenic byway signs will help you find your way along that part of the drive.

Start at the junction of NC 49, NC 47, and SR 1178/Bombay School Road near Asheboro. Follow SR 1178/Bombay School Road east for 0.8 mile, then turn right onto SR 1181/New Hope Road. In only 0.3 mile, go left onto SR 1143/High Pine Church Road. An old country store building marks the corner; the store has long since closed. This is the start of the official North Carolina Scenic Byway.

SR 1143/High Pine Church Road crosses many fields as it approaches the low, wooded ridges of the Uwharrie Mountains. The Uwharries were a major mountain range many millions of years ago, but have long since eroded into a series of hills and ridges. Some geologists believe that the range is one of the oldest in North America. Parts of these mountains make up the 47,000-acre Uwharrie National Forest. The forest is not large compared to other national forests, but it does offer plenty of recreational opportunities. Although the federal government began acquiring land here in the 1930s, the forest was not formally designated until 1961 by President John F. Kennedy.

Some of the ridges visible to the left are part of the Birkhead Mountain Wilderness. This 5,000-acre area in the Uwharrie National Forest holds some good hiking trails. The Birkhead is the only designated wilderness on the Piedmont. If you are interested in hiking there, take a short side trip to the best trailhead by turning left on SR 1107/Lassiter Mill Road. Follow the road about 2 miles north to a marked side road on the right (FR 6532). FR 6532 leads a short distance to the trailhead.

Back on the main scenic drive, continue to follow SR 1143/High Pine Church Road. Turn sharply right onto SR 1112/Lanier Road about 9.2 miles from the earlier junction with SR 1181/New Hope Road. You leave the state scenic byway here. Turn right again in 1.9 miles, at a stop sign, onto SR 1114/Pisgah Covered Bridge Road. A marked side road in 0.5 mile leads 50 yards to the site of the old covered bridge, which used to parallel the newer highway bridge as both crossed the West Fork of the Little River. The bridge was washed away in recent floods, but efforts are under way to rebuild it.

Turn left in 1.2 miles onto SR 1111/Mount Lebanon Road at the Mount Lebanon Baptist Church. Then turn right onto SR 1110/Randall Hurley Road in 0.6 mile. In another 2 miles, turn right onto SR 1307/Horseshoe Bend Road. The terrain gets quite hilly and thickly wooded. Turn right again in 2.6 miles onto SR 1306/Flint Hill Road. The road enters a beautiful section of undeveloped national forest blanketed with a mixed hardwood-pine forest. In a 0.5 mile you cross the

Pisgah covered bridge, Uwharrie County

rushing, clear mountain waters of Barnes Creek. Right afterward is a large parking area on the left for the Uwharrie Trail, a National Recreation Trail. The 20.5-mile trail crosses a large expanse of the Uwharrie Mountains and stays almost entirely within the national forest. Day hikes and backpacking trips of various lengths begin here.

In a short distance, turn right toward Eleazer onto SR 1134/Robinson Road in the hamlet of Ophir. In less than a mile, turn left onto SR 1301/Low Water Bridge Road. After another mile the pavement ends and a good gravel surface starts. The road now enters lush forest that is heavily posted with ugly TRESPASSING FORBIDDEN signs. The owner definitely gets the point across. The road hits the Low Water Bridge over the Uwharrie River after about 0.9 mile of gravel. If water is flowing over the road surface here, go around on an alternate route to continue the drive. Downstream, the Uwharrie River joins the Yadkin River at Lake Tillery to form the Pee Dee River.

Once you are on the other side of the bridge, climb out of the river valley and go 1.1 miles to a junction with paved SR 1302/Coggins Mine Road. Go left here.

The abandoned Coggins Mine is hidden in the forest on the left. The mine was one of the largest gold mines in North Carolina; it was developed early in the nineteenth century after gold was discovered at the Reed Gold Mine near Charlotte. Follow SR 1302 1.6 miles south, past some interesting old buildings on the right, to the village of Eldorado.

In town, go left on busier NC 109. You'll pass a gas station on the left in 1.5 miles. The countryside is a little flatter here and more open. Turn right 2.3 miles from the SR 1302 junction onto SR 1153/Reservation Road. Uwharrie National Forest and Badin Lake signs mark the junction. Go 0.5 mile past the Uwharrie Hunt Camp picnic area, and turn right on gravel FR 576, a scenic road that dead ends in about 7 miles above Badin Lake and the Pee Dee River.

After 0.6 mile, turn right onto FR 544. Follow this road about 0.8 mile to the start of pavement. Continue about another 0.2 mile to the junction with FR 554. Go left here toward Badin Lake. In 1.7 miles, the pavement ends at the junction with FR 597. Turn right on this road and follow it 0.2 mile to FR 597A, the Badin Lake Campground entrance road. Follow FR 597A about a mile to the two campground loops on the lakeshore and the end of the drive. If you have managed to reach the lake without getting lost, it's time to stretch your legs. Pitch a tent, take a walk, have a picnic, or go for a swim here before heading back down the road.

21

Town Creek Indian Mound

Ellerbe to Town Creek Indian Mound

General description: A 16-mile paved route through hilly Piedmont countryside to a historic mound built by Creek Indians.

Special attractions: Town Creek Indian Mound State Historic Site, Rankin Museum of American Heritage, hiking, fall colors.

Location: South-central North Carolina. The drive starts in the tiny town of Ellerbe, about 9 miles north of Rockingham and 47 miles south of Asheboro.

Drive route name/numbers: US 220, NC 73, SR 1160/Indian Mound Road, SR 1542/Indian Mound Road.

Travel season: All year. It can be cold and gray in winter and hot and humid in summer.

Camping: There is no public camping along the route. The nearest public campgrounds lie in nearby Morrow Mountain State Park and the Uwharrie National Forest.

Services: Food and gas are available in Ellerbe and nearby Mount Gilead. More extensive services are in Albemarle and Rockingham.

Nearby attractions: Morrow Mountain State Park, Uwharrie National Forest, Reed Gold Mine State Historic Site, Weymouth Woods Sandhills Nature Preserve.

For more information: Town Creek Indian Mound State Historic Site, Richmond County and Stanly County Chambers of Commerce. See Appendix for addresses and phone numbers.

The Drive

This drive is a short and easy but scenic route through a very lightly settled section of the Piedmont. The route follows most of a 1996 addition to the state system of designated scenic byways called the Indian Heritage Trail. The byway signs are posted along the drive.

The drive starts in Ellerbe on US 220, the main north-south route through the village. Although the town is tiny, it is home to the Rankin Museum of American Heritage, one of North Carolina's most extensive collections of Indian artifacts.

Head north from Ellerbe on busy US 220 for about a mile and turn left onto NC 73. An attractive, shady rest area marks the junction. The road heads northwest along the edge of the low Uwharrie Mountains. These mountains are part of an ancient range that has eroded to a chain of hills. They may be some of the oldest mountains in America, and are not connected to the more extensive Appalachians many miles to the west.

Highway NC 73 is a lightly traveled and quiet route through undeveloped, scenic countryside. It crosses a series of creeks and wooded hills, beginning with

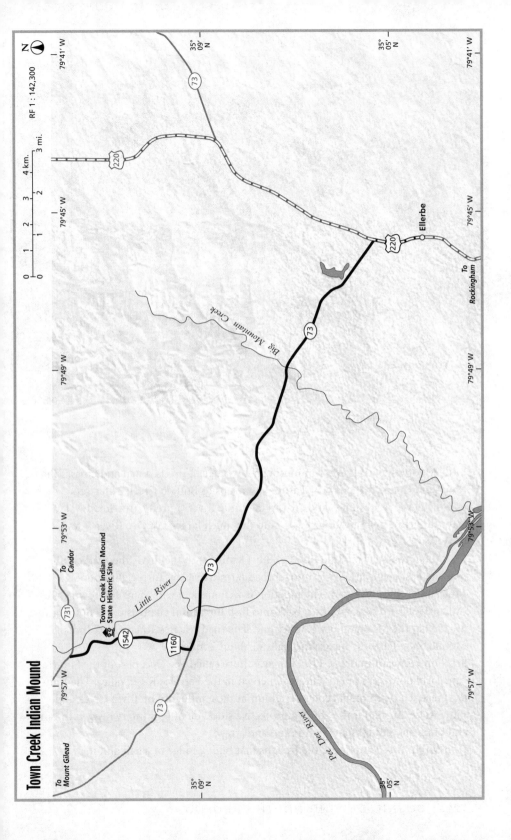

Town Creek Indian Mound

Town Creek Indian Mound State Historic Site

Little Mountain Creek. After mounting a low ridge, it drops down and crosses Big Mountain Creek. It then climbs again and drops to Buffalo Creek. After yet another climb, it descends and crosses the Little River, a pretty, tree-lined water-way. All these creeks and rivers flow into the much larger Pee Dee River, a few miles south.

After crossing the Little River, about 11 miles into the drive, the road climbs over one last ridge and drops into a broad farming valley. Turn right onto SR 1160/Indian Mound Road. The junction is well marked with signs for Town Creek Indian Mound. The road heads back into lush forest and changes route number to SR 1542 at the Montgomery County line. The road reaches Town Creek Indian Mound State Historic Site on the right in about 2 miles.

Sometime around A.D. 1100, a new culture called Pee Dee, part of the South Appalachian Mississippian culture, emerged in the Pee Dee River valley. The Indians created a ceremonial center on a bluff at the confluence of Town Creek and Little River. Around it they built a protective stockade of logs interwoven with cane and branches and plastered with mud and straw.

Within this compound, the Indians first built a lodge of earth and thatch supported by logs. The earthen lodge eventually collapsed. The Indians buried their old meeting place under a mound of earth, then constructed another temple atop the new mound. When it burned, another mantle of earth was laid over the remains. A final temple was built on top the others, using wooden supports, a thatched roof, and walls plastered with clay.

Archaeologists have reconstructed the old stockade, temple, burial hut, and priests' dwelling. From evidence excavated at the site and historic documents, researchers have developed theories about the site's use by Indians of the Pee Dee culture. They believe that the site served as a fortified refuge and gathering place for feasts and major religious ceremonies. Only priest caretakers lived here, though different clans gathered here for political meetings, social events, and religious ceremonies. Indians of social importance were buried here, and enemies were put to death after victories on the field of battle. Games were staged between warriors of different villages, crimes were forgiven, and grievances settled.

The Indians occupied the area around the Town Creek Indian Mound for about 200 years. Today you can visit the reconstructed mound. A short nature trail goes to an overlook of the Little River. Shady picnic tables near the parking area make a good lunch spot. The state historic site is open year-round Tuesday through Sunday. Call ahead for the exact schedule.

The drive continues only 1 mile farther, heading north to the junction with NC 731. Turn right to go back east to the town of Candor on US 220 or left to reach Mount Gilead.

22

Meteor Lakes
Spivey's Corner to Elizabethtown

General description: A 39-mile paved drive across a section of the coastal plain past several natural lakes of mysterious origin and a state forest.

Special attractions: Jones Lake State Park, Bladen Lakes State Forest, Tory Hole Park, hiking, boating, fishing.

Location: Southeast North Carolina. The drive starts at the junction of US 421 and NC 242 about 4 miles southeast of Spivey's Corner (about 30 miles east of Fayetteville).

Drive route number: NC 242.

Travel season: All year, but spring and fall are the best seasons. Winters can be cold and gray and summers hot and humid.

Camping: Jones Lake State Park has a campground open all year.

Services: All services are available in Elizabethtown. Food and gas are available in Salemburg and Roseboro. Gas is available in Ammon.

Nearby attractions: Singletary Lake State Park, Cliffs of the Neuse State Park, Bentonville Battlefield State Historic Site, Lake Waccamaw State Park.

For more information: Jones Lake State Park, Bladen Lakes State Forest, Elizabethtown's White Lake Area Chamber of Commerce. See Appendix for addresses and phone numbers.

The Drive

This scenic drive crosses a stretch of flat country with a mix of farms, forest, and small towns. The drive goes by cypress-lined Jones Lake and near several other natural lakes that were formed by uncertain means. The drive is an official North Carolina Scenic Byway—Meteor Lakes Byway—and is marked with byway signs.

The drive starts at the junction of US 421 and NC 242 about 4 miles southeast of Spivey's Corner, the self-proclaimed "Hollerin' Capital of the World." This wide spot in the road is well known for its annual Hollerin' Contest. During the affair, people come from far and wide to test their skills at yodeling, animal calling, and any other conceivable type of hooting and hollering.

Taking NC 242, head south beyond Spivey's Corner through attractive Sampson County, named for John Sampson, a member of the House of Commons under North Carolina's royal governors during British rule. Traffic here is light to moderate. A prominent church and graveyard is about all there is of the small crossroads hamlet of Piney Green, 4 miles into the drive. Salemburg, reached in another 5 miles, is a neat and clean small town. The North Carolina Justice Academy offers advanced law enforcement training here.

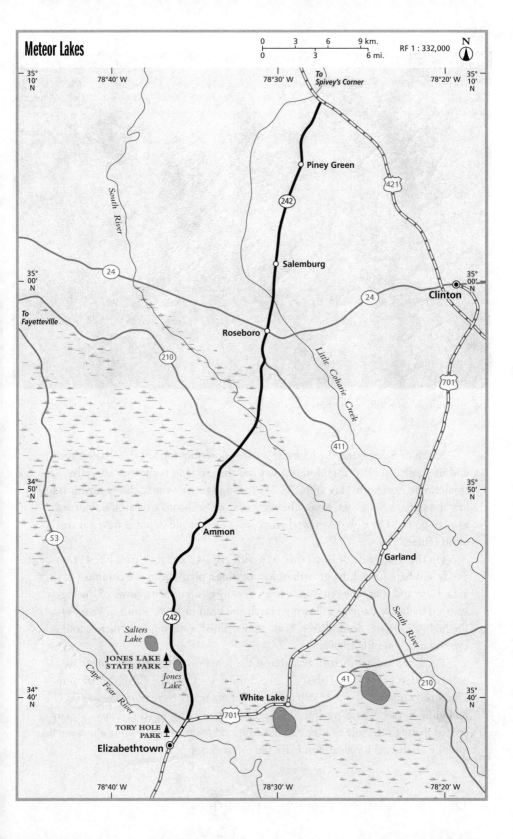

Fishermen in the South River, Sampson County

South of Salemburg, the highway crosses slow-moving Little Coharie Creek and its scenic, wooded corridor. Just beyond the crossing is another attractive small town, Roseboro. Stay with NC 242 through town—the highway turns, so follow the signs. You can see where the tracks of the Seaboard Coast Line Railroad used to go right by downtown and cross NC 242. The old depot is now a recreation center.

On the south side of Roseboro, stay with NC 242 at a fork with NC 411. Sandy soil here fosters the growth of lots of pines; plantations are common in the area. Here and there the pines have been heavily clearcut, with some of the logging spurred by heavy damage following Hurricane Fran in 1996. South of Roseboro, the highway crosses South River. This cypress-lined waterway is attractive to the eye and a magnet for anglers.

Food and gas are usually available at the junction with NC 210. The drive enters Bladen Lakes State Forest about 5.5 miles south of the village of Ammon. The forest contains about 32,000 acres and offers many recreational activities, including horseback riding, hunting, and primitive camping. It is financially supported through the sale of pine needles collected from its forest floor. Pines such as loblolly, slash, and longleaf dominate the forest canopy.

In less than 3 miles, visitors will find it difficult to miss the tall Jones Lake Lookout Tower. The tower rises high above the forest canopy next to the road. Lookouts such as this one were once commonly used to spot and locate forest fires throughout the United States. The towers are used less today because planes have largely replaced them. The Jones Lake Tower is still being used, however. Below the tower are the offices of the North Carolina Forest Service. Stop here to get information about the Bladen Lakes State Forest.

Jones Lake becomes visible through the trees on the right just past the forest offices. The entrance to Jones Lake State Park is on the right just a short distance farther. The park preserves this lake and nearby Salters Lake. The lakes fill shallow depressions that are often found on the coastal plain. These dips in the land's surface are called bays after the red, sweet, and loblolly bay plants that grow around them. About 500,000 such bays lie on the coastal plain of the southeastern United States, but most are less than 500 feet in diameter.

Scientists are not in complete agreement about what causes the bay depressions. Some people have suggested that meteor showers caused the holes in the ground, although little or no evidence supports this theory. Other theories include ground subsidence after dissolution of subsurface minerals, underground springs, and whale wallows created when sea levels were higher. Probably the most accepted theory attributes formation of the depressions to wind and wave action at higher sea levels.

Although some of the bay lakes are sizable, they are all shallow. Even though Jones Lake is more than a mile across, it is only 8.7 feet deep. Like most bays, Jones and Salters Lakes eventually will fill with debris and become swamps rather than lakes. Because the lakes are shallow and not fed by streams or springs, their water tends to become quite acidic from decaying plant matter. The tannin-laden water at Jones Lake resembles a clear tea. Its acidity limits fish species to catfish, yellow perch, chain pickerel, and a few others.

The area around Jones Lake was settled during colonial times. Farming and the production of lumber, pitch, and turpentine from the pine forests created the basis for the economy. During the Great Depression, when times were hard, the federal government created conservation-oriented job programs that benefited the area. Recreational facilities were established at Jones Lake, and the state park opened in 1939.

Be sure to walk along the shore of Jones Lake. Bald cypresses grow out into the lake's waters, creating a primeval atmosphere. A 3-mile trail completely circles the lake, offering numerous lake views and dense forest; another shorter trail is a self-guiding nature trail. The lake itself offers a sandy swimming beach, fishing, and boating in small watercraft such as canoes. Salters Lake is undeveloped, and you must obtain permission from park staff for access. The new visitor center offers museum exhibits, plus there is a new concession area open in summer.

Bald cypresses and misty lake in Jones Lake State Park

Continue the scenic drive past Jones Lake. After leaving the state forest in 1.3 miles, you will reach a stop sign at the junction with NC 53. Go left here, staying on NC 242. You'll immediately hit the junction with US 701. Go right on combined US 701/NC 242 toward Elizabethtown. US 701 is a four-lane divided highway and very busy. The highway crosses the large Cape Fear River in about a mile.

In 1781, a Revolutionary War battle was fought here. The rebels defeated the Tories (British loyalists) by driving them into a ravine on the banks of the Cape Fear River. The ravine became known as Tory Hole. To see Tory Hole and the river up close, turn right after crossing the bridge and drop to Tory Hole Park, under the highway. The pleasant park has boat access, picnicking, hiking trails, a physical fitness trail, and a nature trail.

Across the river, the highway reaches Elizabethtown and the end of the scenic drive. This Carolina town was founded in 1773, before the American Revolution, and was probably named for Queen Elizabeth I.

Bentonville Battlefield

Cliffs of the Neuse State Park to Bentonville Battlefield

General description: A 33-mile paved route from a state park with cliffs (surprising for the coastal plain) to Bentonville Battlefield the site of the last major Confederate offensive of the Civil War.

Special attractions: Cliffs of the Neuse State Park, Bentonville Battlefield State Historic Site, hiking, fishing, boating.

Location: East-central North Carolina. The drive starts at Cliffs of the Neuse State Park, a few miles south of Goldsboro on NC 111.

Drive route name/numbers: SR 1743/Park Entrance Road, NC 111, SR 1744/Indian Springs Road, SR 1933/Eagle Nest Road, SR 1120/Sleepy Creek Road, SR 1120/O'Berry Road, SR 1006/Grantham School Road, US 13, SR 1205/Bentonville Road, SR 1196/St. John's Church Road, SR 1008/Harper House Road.

Travel season: All year, but spring and fall are best. Summers can be hot and sticky; winters cold and gray.

Camping: Cliffs of the Neuse State Park has camping.

Services: Some gas and snacks are available along the route. All services can be found in nearby Goldsboro.

Nearby attractions: CSS Neuse State Historic Site, Governor Richard Caswell Memorial, Charles Aycock Birthplace State Historic Site, Waynesborough State Park.

For more information: Bentonville Battlefield State Historic Site, Cliffs of the Neuse State Park, Goldsboro Chamber of Commerce. See Appendix for addresses and phone numbers.

The Drive

This drive connects two interesting sites on the coastal plain south of Goldsboro. Cliffs of the Neuse State Park has surprisingly high cliffs along the Neuse River; the high rocks are oddities on the otherwise flat coastal plain. Bentonville Battlefield, at the end of the drive, marks the site of the last Confederate offensive in the waning days of the Civil War.

The drive starts at Cliffs of the Neuse State Park just off of NC 111 only a few miles south of Goldsboro. The park protects a section of high cliffs along the Neuse River, plus some surrounding country. Over time, the slow-moving Neuse has slowly cut these 90-foot cliffs into the area's low hills on its journey to the sea. The cliffs are cut into relatively soft layers of sediment. They continue to erode as the river cuts away at their base.

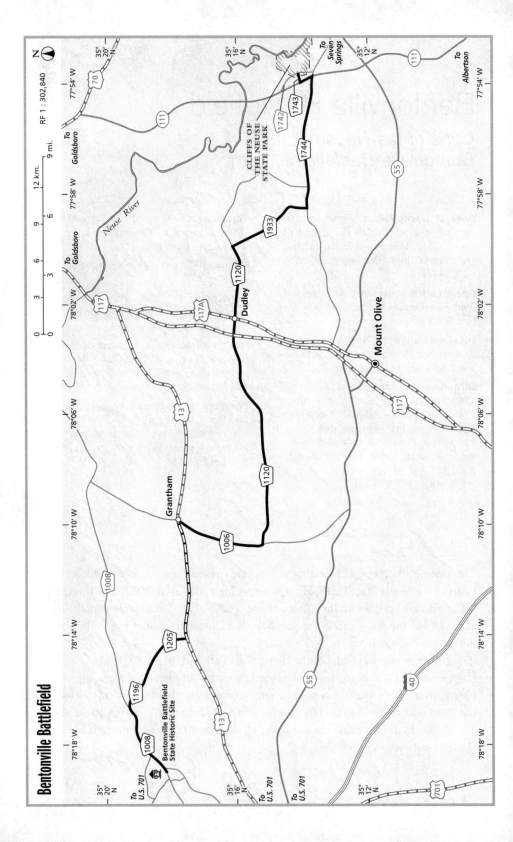

Bentonville Battlefield

RF 1 : 302,840

Within the state park, sandy hills, bottomlands, and high shady cliffs hold a broad variety of plant habitats. Visitors can see bald cypresses along the river or walk in a Piedmont oak-hickory forest. Several hiking trails wander through the park along creeks and down to the river. One trail follows the clifftop, giving hikers views of the river below. A small lake offers swimming and rental boats. Anglers can test their skills from the riverbanks.

A navigable river, the Neuse was an important travel route during the early days of North Carolina's settlement. Nearby Seven Springs (once called Whitehall) may have been the earliest English settlement in the region. The CSS *Neuse*, an ironclad ship, was built in Seven Springs by the Confederates to oppose Northern control of the North Carolina coast. When the ship ran aground in the river, the Confederates destroyed it to prevent its capture by the Union. The old vessel was excavated in the 1960s and is now displayed in a museum near Kinston, North Carolina (about 25 miles east of the park).

Around the turn of the century, the town of Seven Springs became a tourist mecca. People came to drink the mineral water that flowed from its seven natural springs, which lay in close vicinity to each other. Supposedly each spring had a different mineral content; a dose of the water was said to cure a host of ills. If the water didn't cure people, the locally made whiskey helped visitors forget about their aches and pains.

The route from Cliffs of the Neuse State Park to the end of this scenic drive is fairly complicated because it follows so many roads. Follow the directions carefully. You may wish to refer to a copy of the *North Carolina Atlas & Gazetteer* as you drive. Most of the route follows an official North Carolina Scenic Byway called Sherman's Run. Scenic byway signs will help you find your way. The route is lightly traveled for the most part.

From the state park entrance at the junction of SR 1743 and SR 1742, follow SR 1743 Park Entrance Road to NC 111 less than 0.5 mile away. Much of the surrounding flat country has been cleared for farmland, unlike the heavily wooded park. Go left on NC 111 for 0.4 mile and turn right on SR 1744/Indian Springs Road. A school is on the corner here. Beyond this intersection, the drive passes farmland, scattered homes, and patches of woods.

Turn right in another 4.5 miles onto SR 1933/Eagles Nest Road (marked with a state scenic byway sign). The *North Carolina Atlas & Gazetteer* shows this road incorrectly as Camp Tuscora Road. The road dips where it crosses Burnt Mill and Sleepy Creeks. After 3.1 miles turn left onto SR 1120/Sleepy Creek Road (shown mistakenly in the *Atlas* as Dudley and Eagle Nest Roads). This road passes through the center of the small town of Dudley in 2.5 miles. A handy gas station and a big Georgia-Pacific mill are here.

Continue along SR 1120, crossing US 117A and US 117. Note the odd design of the Presbyterian church on the right near the US 117 junction. After you cross

US 117, SR 1120 becomes O'Berry Road. Here and there, tiny family cemeteries form islands in the middle of plowed fields. Erosion of these fields has caused many of the cemeteries to sit higher than the surrounding land.

About 7.5 miles from the US 117 junction, turn right on SR 1006/Grantham School Road. Head north on SR 1006 and go 3.1 miles to the village of Grantham. You can gas up here. From Grantham, turn left on US 13 and follow it 4.1 miles west. Then turn right on SR 1205/Bentonville Road. After 3.1 miles, this road becomes SR 1196/St. John's Church Road where it enters Johnston County. St. John's Church itself waits on your left.

In just 0.3 mile, turn left onto SR 1008/Harper House Road. (The *North Carolina Atlas Gazetteer* shows this as Cox Mill Road and incorrectly locates Bentonville Battlefield about 2 miles north of its actual location.) The state scenic byway turns right in only 0.1 mile; instead of turning, follow signs for Bentonville Battlefield State Historic Site and stay on SR 1008 to reach the battleground. Historic markers along the way tell of Civil War events.

You'll soon hit a Confederate cemetery and, just beyond it, the center of Bentonville Battlefield State Historic Site. The visitor center here has exhibits describing the Civil War battle of March 19–21, 1865. At that time, the South's future looked grim. Here, at Bentonville, the Confederacy was able to mount one last large offensive.

The battle held at this site was the South's only serious attempt to stop General William T. Sherman's march north after he had crossed Georgia. After Sherman left Savannah in January 1865, he met little resistance as his troops marched north through South Carolina, leaving a swath of destruction. With only North Carolina lying between Sherman's troops and Grant's army in Virginia, Confederates made a last-ditch attempt to prevent the two armies from uniting. Since the South's forces were widely scattered and in disarray in the Carolinas, General Joseph E. Johnston was ordered to organize them and halt Sherman's northward march. Because Johnston could summon only about 20,000 men to contest Sherman's 60,000, he knew that his only hope was to find a site where Sherman's forces would be split into more than one group.

When Johnston learned that road conditions had forced Sherman to split his army into two sections separated by a half-day's march, he moved his men into position. Here, near the village of Bentonville, he attacked one of Sherman's two wings. Johnston arranged his men in a curving line along the Goldsboro Road on the evening of March 18 and waited for Sherman's troops. The Union army marched into the trap. Though Johnston's army overran the enemy troops, one Union division managed to hold on. Unfortunately for Johnston, the second wing of Sherman's army arrived the next day.

Bitter fighting continued until March 21. Union general J.A. Mower then outflanked the Confederates and advanced to within 200 yards of the Southerners'

Harper House at Bentonville Battlefield State Historic Site

headquarters. With defeat imminent, Johnston's forces retreated toward Smithfield that evening, ending the largest battle ever to occur in North Carolina. Sherman did not pursue them, but marched on to Goldsboro to resupply. Johnston surrendered near Durham on April 26, ending the war in North Carolina. The battle at Bentonville didn't change the course of the war, but it exacted a heavy toll. More than 4,000 men died, were wounded, or were missing in action here.

A nearby farmhouse, that of farmer John Harper, was taken over by the Union army and used as a hospital for wounded troops. Be sure to take a tour of the Harper House, outfitted as it was in those days when it was used as a hospital. Because there was no way to treat infections or gangrene back then, amputation was the only way to save soldiers' lives. The primitive hospital rooms are somewhat gruesome, with simple wood tables, saws, and sawdust on the floor to absorb blood. With little sterilization and no antibiotics, it is miraculous that amputees had an 83 percent survival rate. The hospital treated 500 Federal and 45 Confederate soldiers. Colonel William Hamilton of the Ninth Ohio Cavalry described the scene in his memoir, *Remembrances of a Field Hospital at Bentonville*:

> A dozen surgeons and attendants in their shirtsleeves stood at rude
> benches cutting off arms and legs and throwing them out of the win-

dows, where they lay scattered on the grass. The legs of infantrymen could be distinguished from those of the cavalry by the size of their calves, as the march of 1000 miles had increased the size of one and diminished the size of the other.

Once you recover from seeing the primitive hospital in the Harper House, get some fresh air by taking the easy 0.25-mile walk that starts near the Confederate cemetery and takes you to some of the trenches dug by the Union troops. Only the overgrown trenches tell of the terrible violence that occurred here more than 140 years ago when 80,000 men met on the field of battle.

Green Swamp
Clarkton to Supply

General description: A 44-mile drive across a very lightly developed area of the coastal plain, past the interesting Green Swamp.

Special attractions: Green Swamp, Lake Waccamaw State Park, carnivorous plants, hiking, boating, swimming, fishing.

Location: Southeastern North Carolina. The drive starts at the junction of US 701 Bypass and NC 211 in Clarkton, a small town about 10 miles south of Elizabethtown.

Drive route number: NC 211.

Travel season: All year. Summers can be hot and humid.

Camping: There are no public campgrounds along the route. Jones Lake State Park has the closest campground.

Services: Clarkton and the nearby town of Supply have gas and food. Full services are available in Elizabethtown and the beach towns in the Southport area.

Nearby attractions: Jones Lake State Park, Singletary Lake State Park, Southport area beaches.

For more information: The Nature Conservancy (Wilmington), and Elizabethtown's White Lake and Southport Oak Island Chambers of Commerce. See Appendix for addresses and phone numbers.

The Drive

This is a low-key trip across a very lightly developed section of the coastal plain. Traffic is usually quiet. The route crosses the extensive Green Swamp, a low-lying marshy area heavily planted with pines. The Nature Conservancy owns a part of the swamp; trails on the Conservancy preserve lead through restored natural forest and let visitors observe odd meat-eating plants. The drive follows most of the state's Green Swamp Scenic Byway.

Start the drive in Clarkton, a small, somewhat depressed-looking town. Clarkton was incorporated in 1901; prior to that time, it had been called Brown Marsh Station and Dalton. Take NC 211 southeast from town toward Bolton and Supply. In 2 miles you cross the lush woods of Brown Marsh Swamp. Fields, woods, and occasional farms follow. Plantations of pines raised for wood and pulp take up some of the land here. Like most of the coastal plain, this country is very flat. Drainage tends to be poor, and this combined with good annual rainfall creates plenty of marshy areas.

After about 19 miles, the route crosses busy US 74/US 76 at the edge of the village of Bolton. A gas station waits at the junction of NC 214 in Bolton. Take a

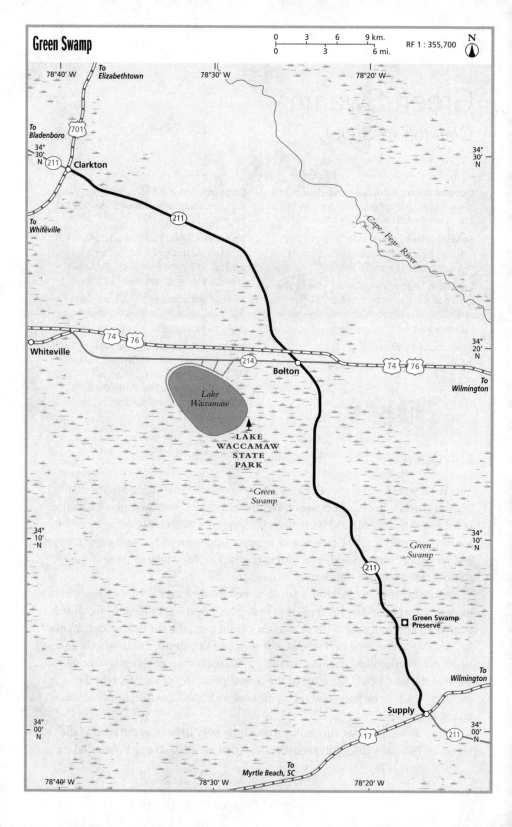

side trip by heading right here to Lake Waccamaw State Park. Follow NC 214 a few miles west to the lake. About 75 percent of the lake's shoreline is developed; the state park protects the rest and allows public access. Activities at the park include boating, hiking, fishing, picnicking, and swimming.

Lake Waccamaw is a Carolina bay, a natural lake in a depression that was formed by somewhat uncertain means. Romantics believe that the many bay lakes of the coastal plain (named for the bay plants that grow on their shores) were created by a meteor shower. Others suspect they fill the holes left by whale wallows made when the sea level was higher. More likely, the depressions were formed by wind and wave action.

Like all the bay lakes, Lake Waccamaw is very shallow. Even though it covers 8,938 acres, its deepest point is only 10.8 feet. Most bay lakes have limited or no drainage through them and tend to have dark, acidic, tea-colored water from decaying vegetation. Waccamaw, however, has better flow-through and acid-neutralizing limestone outcrops along its northeast shore. Hence, its water is clear and conducive to fish and underwater flora. Because it is so shallow, Waccamaw will eventually fill in with debris and vegetation and become a marsh.

Return to Bolton to continue the drive. The route soon enters the Green Swamp, a vast area that once covered some 140 square miles of the coastal plain. Some areas of the swamp have been drained for farmland; most of the rest is timberland owned by large paper companies. Bald cypresses were once heavily logged here and along the shores of Lake Waccamaw. Cypress wood was nearly waterproof, and it made good shingles. Cutting of this area's virgin timber began in earnest in 1904. Loggers' work was often wet and insect-ridden. In places, railroad tracks were laid out into the swamp to aid in the harvest; the ties were placed very close together to be able to support the weight of work trains. Today most of the Green Swamp is still used as timberland, and many of its acres are planted with pines. You will drive past clearcuts from recent logging.

For the next 20 to 25 miles, the scenic drive goes through the swamp, crossing occasional sluggish and winding creeks. Except after heavy rains, most of the area does not appear to be all that wet. However, much of the swamp can be quite muddy and mucky. Its wetness and high groundwater level have inhibited development to this day. A fire tower looks out over the swamp about 10.5 miles south of Bolton.

A small, subtle sign on the left about 18 miles south of Bolton marks the edge of The Nature Conservancy's Green Swamp Preserve. In another 0.9 mile, look for a parking area on the left by a small pond, allowing public access. The Nature Conservancy is a nationwide organization that works to protect vital ecosystems by purchasing land or conservation easements. Without politicking or lobbying, and with no taxpayer funds, the organization just buys and maintains natural areas using individual member and corporate donations.

Carnivorous pitcher plants at Green Swamp Preserve (The Nature Conservancy)

The original 13,000 acres of the Green Swamp Preserve were donated to the Conservancy by the Federal Paper Board Company in 1977. Later additions, including another 2,577 acres donated by the same company, created a preserve of 15,907 acres today. To maintain this large preserve, Conservancy members use carefully prescribed burns. Fire is necessary in a swamp; without it, plants such as longleaf and pond pines can't germinate and thrive.

Fourteen species of carnivorous plants—plants that eat meat, usually insects—live in the Green Swamp. The swamp hosts extensive populations of Venus flytrap and four different species of pitcher plants, among others. Carnivorous plants often grow in areas where the soil lacks enough nutrients to feed vegetation; here the soil is sandy and constantly leached by heavy rainfall. To adapt, the plants supplement their diet by eating insects. Pitcher plants grow in clumps of tall yellow-green stalks. The stalks are actually tubes that emit the scent of nectar to attract insects. When insects crawl into the tubes, downward pointing hairs prevent them from climbing back out. At the bottom, they meet their fate in a pool of digestive juices. In spring, another type of pitcher plant can be found by looking for tall, round, dark red flowers. The flowers are obvious, but the rest of the plant is usually hidden in the grass.

The swamp also hosts substantial wildlife populations. The alligator and the red-cockaded woodpecker are two of its most interesting residents. The alligator population has recovered remarkably from lows earlier in this century. The woodpecker, on the other hand, is still rare, due in part to its finicky nesting criteria. It favors nests in old-growth pines with red heart disease. The disease softens the core of the tree enough for the birds to dig nesting cavities. To protect itself from disease, the tree secretes sticky resin around the wound created by the pecking birds. The resin then helps to protect the birds' eggs and young by keeping out ants, squirrels, and snakes. With little old-growth forest left, the woodpeckers have a limited habitat.

Easy hiking trails lead out into the swamp at The Nature Conservancy access area. Spring and fall are the best times to come here; summers are hot and steamy. Be sure to use insect repellent if you leave your car, since mosquitoes, ticks, and chiggers can be found here at various times of the year. One trail leads to a good spot to find carnivorous plants. From the Conservancy parking area, follow the trail along the edge of the pond to a fork on the other side. Go right on the more obvious trail. The trail passes through a beautiful pine savannah for about 0.25

A slash pine forest at Green Swamp Preserve (The Nature Conservancy)

mile, then heads through a dense, marshy thicket on a narrow boardwalk and goes back into open forest with bigger pines. Where the trail starts getting muddy in another 0.25 mile, start looking for pitcher plants and orchids. Please stay on the trail, even if it means getting your feet wet. Doing so means you will save the unique plants here from being trampled. Be sure to stop hiking where a sign indicates the end of public access, just before the trail passes into another swampy thicket. Please do not disturb or remove any of the carnivorous plants.

Continue down the road from the preserve parking area. You'll leave the Green Swamp in about 3.4 miles. The drive ends after another 2.3 miles in the small town of Supply at the junction with US 17. You can fill both your tank and stomach here before venturing onward.

Mackay Island National Wildlife Refuge

Virginia state line to Bodie Island

General description: A 43-mile drive that starts on Knotts Island at the Virginia state line, passes through a large wildlife refuge, crosses Currituck Sound on a car ferry, and continues south along the Currituck Peninsula. The drive eventually crosses a causeway to Currituck Banks and Bodie Island, part of the Outer Banks.

Special attractions: Mackay Island National Wildlife Refuge, Currituck–Knotts Island ferry, Currituck County Courthouse, hiking, fishing, boating, wildlife.

Location: Upper North Carolina coast. The drive starts at the north end of NC 615 at the Virginia state line. It can be reached by taking the Currituck–Knotts Island ferry over to Knotts Island and driving north on NC 615. To avoid retracing your steps, go north to Virginia Beach, Virginia, and drive south.

Drive route numbers: NC 615, NC 168, US 158.

Travel season: All year. Summers can be hot, and they are the busiest time on the coast. Spring and fall are less crowded, and temperatures are usually pleasant.

Camping: There are no public campgrounds along this route.

Services: You can gas up on Knotts Island. Gas and food can be found at scattered locations along the Currituck Peninsula. More extensive services are available in nearby Camden, Elizabeth City, and on the Outer Banks in Kitty Hawk and other towns.

Nearby attractions: Wright Brothers National Memorial, Fort Raleigh National Historic Site, Cape Hatteras National Seashore, *Elizabeth II*, Jockey's Ridge State Park, Bodie Island and Currituck Beach lighthouses.

For more information: Mackay Island National Wildlife Refuge, North Carolina Ferry System, Outer Banks, Currituck, and Elizabeth City Chambers of Commerce. See Appendix for addresses and phone numbers.

The Drive

Starting at one of the more remote parts of the North Carolina coast, on Knotts Island, this scenic route passes through the Mackay Island National Wildlife Refuge, a large area of marsh and forest heavily used by wildlife, particularly the greater snow goose. The drive then requires a ferry crossing of beautiful Currituck Sound to the mainland. Traveling south down the Currituck Peninsula, it ends after crossing a bridge to the Outer Banks.

From the Virginia state line, head south on NC 615 through farmland and scattered homes. You will soon enter the Mackay Island National Wildlife Refuge.

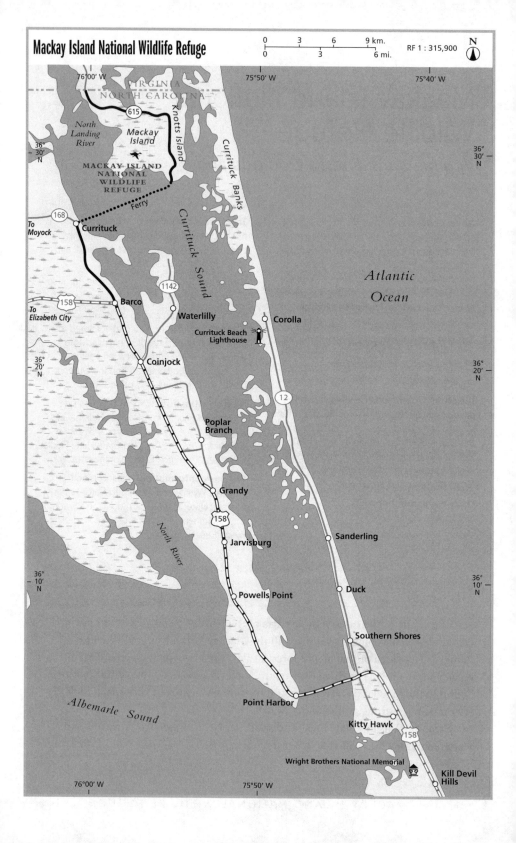

The refuge office is on a gravel road that heads right only about a mile after the start of the drive. Be sure to stop in at this office when it's open for maps and other information. The refuge was acquired by the U.S. Fish and Wildlife Service in 1961. The heart of the refuge is Mackay Island, a low-lying island connected to Knotts Island by marshes and built-up dike roads. The island was named for its first-known European settler, John Mackie. In 1761, he purchased what was then known as Orphan's Island from John Jones. Apparently Mackie lived on the island until his death in 1823. Legend says that he was buried here in an upright position so that he could watch over his fields.

The island changed ownership several times over the following years until it was purchased in 1918 by Joseph P. Knapp, a New York printing magnate and philanthropist. Among other accomplishments, Knapp was instrumental in the development of color printing. He first saw the area on a hunting trip and fell in love with it. He built a private resort on the island with a mansion, swimming pool, golf course, boating facilities, and other amenities. As a duck hunter, Knapp experimented with new game practices, such as managing marsh water levels to encourage production of waterfowl and other wildlife. He then founded the More Game Birds in America Foundation in 1930. He and fellow luminaries such as banker J. Pierpont Morgan and political cartoonist J. N. "Ding" Darling served as directors of the organization. It later became Ducks Unlimited.

Knapp did more than help found modern game management. He adopted Currituck County as his own and donated considerable sums to the public schools. With his help, its education system changed from one of the poorest in the state to one of the strongest. The county was the first in North Carolina to provide free textbooks and lunches to its students. Knapp brought in experts to help local farmers become more productive, and he aided the organization of a regional hospital in Elizabeth City. He also gave money to the University of North Carolina for fisheries research and other projects.

After Knapp's death in 1951, Mackay Island was sold. The island was logged and the estate fell into disrepair. Knapp's old home was torn down in the 1960s, and his golf course was planted with corn and wheat for use by wintering waterfowl. Even the swimming pool has found a new use as a pond for wood ducks. Although the federal government now owns Knapp's holdings on Mackay Island, a foundation established by Knapp has donated sizable parcels of land to what is now Mackay Island National Wildlife Refuge.

Today the wildlife refuge consists of almost 8,500 acres of marsh, upland forest, islands, and open water. Most of it lies in North Carolina, but about 800 acres extend into Virginia. It is managed primarily to benefit migratory birds. Many ducks and swans winter here, along with as many as 40,000 snow geese. The refuge is an important breeding area for wood ducks and ospreys; nesting boxes and platforms are scattered throughout the refuge.

Marsh and pines at Mackay Island National Wildlife Refuge

After you stop at the refuge office, continue south through the refuge on NC 615. The road crosses the Great Marsh, several miles of open marsh that connect Knotts Island to the mainland. The Great Marsh is wet and low-lying—if it got any wetter, it would be part of the bays that flank it. If you stop along the road in the marsh here, you will see many different kinds of birds, from waterfowl to wading birds. A small bridge crosses Corey's Ditch, a manmade waterway that connects Barleys Bay with North Landing River. The bridge is popular with anglers.

The road continues beyond the bridge to Knotts Island, where the land gets a little higher and pines and other trees appear again. On the right is a pullout for a hiking path known as the Great Marsh Trail. This easy, 0.3-mile loop follows the edge of the Great Marsh and circles around a pine-shaded pond. Water moccasins are common here, so watch where you put your feet. The highway leaves the wildlife refuge about 0.3 mile past the Great Marsh Trail. At a junction here, stay right on NC 615. A historic marker notes that the Virginia and North Carolina border was first staked out 3 miles northeast of here on March 18, 1728.

At another junction, in about 0.5 mile, stay right again on NC 615. A store and gas station at this junction are about the only significant commercial businesses on the isolated island. The highway continues south for another mile past farms and scattered homes to another Mackay Island National Wildlife Refuge entrance on the right. Be sure to stop here at an information kiosk if the refuge office you passed earlier was closed. A gravel road leads into the refuge, through lush forest and then into marshland. The roads are closed from October 15 to March 15 to protect wintering waterfowl.

To continue the drive, stay with NC 615 all the way to the ferry. The road is narrow and winds some, so take your time. The highway ends at the Currituck–Knotts Island ferry dock. Until the ferry began service in 1962, the residents of Knotts Island were quite isolated from the rest of Currituck County and had to make a long drive around Currituck Sound through Virginia to reach the mainland. It was particularly grueling for high school students who had to commute daily to the mainland.

Be sure to check the ferry schedule ahead of time to avoid long waits (call 1–800–293–3779). It runs six times a day at two- to three-hour intervals. Cars cross here at no charge; the ferry run takes about forty-five minutes. It's an easy, relaxing way to see the broad expanse of Currituck Sound from the water.

The sound stretches north-south for about 30 miles and is usually less than 4 miles wide. Like the other North Carolina sounds, it separates the mainland from the barrier islands and peninsulas that line the Atlantic shore. These sandy barriers help protect the sounds and the mainland from the fury of hurricanes and other ocean storms.

Until 1828, Currituck Sound was a saltwater body open to the ocean through several inlets. When currents and storms closed off the inlets, freshwater inflow slowly pushed out the salt water. With the influx of fresh water, the plants and animals of the sound changed. Bass began to swim in the waters and ducks and geese began to winter in its marshes. When locks were removed on the Intracoastal Waterway on the north end of the sound at the end of World War I, local patron Joseph Knapp paid to have them reinstalled to prevent the influx of saltwater and pollution from the north.

The ferry ends on the other side of the sound at the county seat of Currituck. Park in the public parking lot and stroll past some of Currituck's historic buildings. Currituck was once a bustling port. Established as the county seat in 1722, the town has a county jail that is believed to have been built as far back as 1786; it's the oldest jail in North Carolina. The courthouse next door dates back to 1842, although it has seen considerable changes and additions since that time. Unlike many county seats, this village has not turned into a large commercial center.

From the ferry dock, turn left and follow a short spur road to NC 168. Turn left and follow NC 168 south. You'll pass through farmland dotted with homes and hit US 158 in about 5 miles near the tiny settlement of Barco. Turn left onto US 158 and continue south. This busy four-lane road is a popular route to the Outer Banks. Unlike Knotts Island, outlets for gas and food are plentiful here.

Pond and pines at Mackay Island National Wildlife Refuge

In about 3.5 miles, the highway crosses a high bridge over the Atlantic Intra-coastal Waterway. The waterway was built in sections over the course of many years. It offers ships and barges a route through which they can move goods up and down the Atlantic coast without having to venture into the open ocean. As time has passed, it has also become very popular with recreational boat traffic. In effect, the waterway turns the Currituck Peninsula into an island. A small town at the bridge, Coinjock, has long served boat traffic. The ditch that cuts across the peninsula here was built in the mid-1800s as part of a canal system that connected Albemarle Sound and Chesapeake Bay.

Continue the scenic drive by crossing the waterway bridge. If time allows, take a short side trip on SR 1142 to Church Island. This "island" is really a marshy peninsula that pokes a finger far into Currituck Sound. The road passes through the village of Waterlily, offering good views. It ends at the tip of the peninsula at a private campground with fishing piers and other facilities.

From Coinjock, US 158 continues south through farmland and scattered small villages. It follows the higher ground near the center of the peninsula rather than dropping into the swamps that line its shores. Various side roads lead to the water on both sides. Fruit stands dot US 158, taking advantage of heavy beach traffic in summer. Historic homes and buildings can be found in many of the peninsula villages. The area was settled by the British as early as the mid-1600s.

The peninsula ends at the town of Point Harbor, where the waters of Currituck and Albemarle Sounds come together. The highway continues, however, across the mouth of Currituck Sound on the almost 3-mile-long Wright Memorial Bridge. In 1930, a toll bridge constructed here was the first span to connect the mainland with Currituck Banks and Bodie Island. Since then the bridge has been enlarged and updated. On the other side of the sound, the highway enters Kitty Hawk and Dare County. In 1.6 miles, the scenic drive ends at NC 12. Currituck Banks, Bodie Island, and the Outer Banks are covered in Drives #26–29.

26

The Wright Brothers and Man's First Flight

Corolla to Oregon Inlet

General description: A 47-mile paved drive across Currituck Banks and Bodie Island, past the Wright Brothers National Memorial, two historic lighthouses, and part of Cape Hatteras National Seashore.

Special attractions: Wright Brothers National Memorial, Cape Hatteras National Seashore, Currituck Beach Lighthouse, Bodie Island Lighthouse, Nags Head Woods Preserve, Jockey's Ridge State Park, beaches, hang gliding, fishing, swimming, hiking, bicycling.

Location: Upper North Carolina coast. The drive starts in the small town of Corolla, about 20 miles north of Southern Shores and Kitty Hawk on Currituck Banks.

Drive route numbers: NC 12, US 158.

Travel season: All year. Summer is hot but ideal for beach activities. Spring and fall are less crowded, with cooler temperatures. Winter can be chilly and stormy.

Camping: Cape Hatteras National Seashore manages a public campground by Oregon Inlet near the south end of Bodie Island.

Services: Services are plentiful throughout most of the drive. Lodging can be tight in summer, especially on weekends, even with a huge supply of motel rooms, rental houses, and cottages.

Nearby attractions: Other parts of Cape Hatteras National Seashore, Cape Lookout National Seashore, Cape Hatteras Lighthouse, Pea Island National Wildlife Refuge, Fort Raleigh National Historic Site, Elizabethan Gardens, *Elizabeth II,* Alligator River National Wildlife Refuge.

For more information: Cape Hatteras National Seashore (National Park Service), Wright Brothers National Memorial (National Park Service), Jockey's Ridge State Park, Nags Head Woods Preserve (the Nature Conservancy), Outer Banks Chamber of Commerce, Outer Banks Visitors Bureau, Currituck Chamber of Commerce. See Appendix for addresses and phone numbers.

The Drive

This drive traverses most of two islands of the Outer Banks. There are nine main islands, or banks, that stretch from the Virginia state line to past Cape Lookout. These sand islands were built up over time through the actions of wind and wave, along with changes in sea level caused by the coming and going of ice ages. The islands are very young geologically and change constantly. They act as barriers that protect the sounds and mainland from the worst ocean storms. Hurricanes and large storms can change the islands overnight, opening and closing inlets that con-

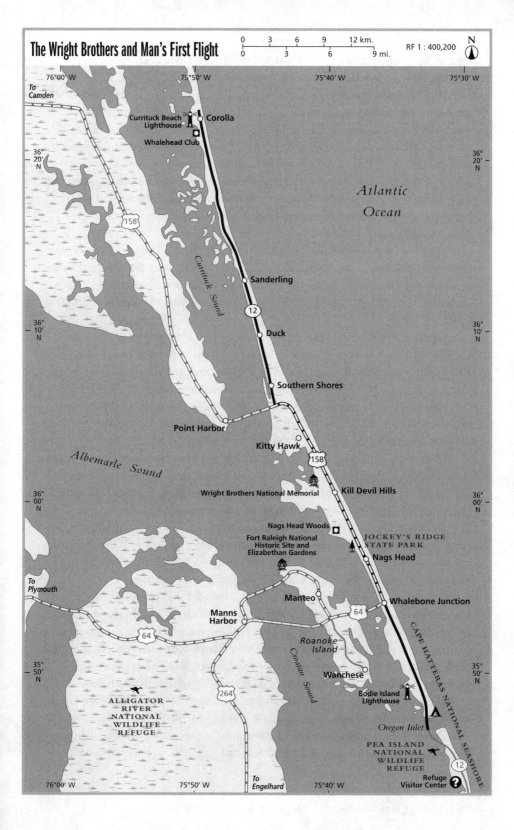

The Wright Brothers and Man's First Flight

RF 1 : 400,200

N

0   3   6   9   12 km.
0   3   6   9 mi.

76°00' W   75°50' W   75°40' W   75°30' W

To
Camden

36°
20'
N

Currituck Beach
Lighthouse
Corolla

Whalehead Club

Atlantic

Ocean

36°
20'
N

158

Currituck Sound

Sanderling

36°
10'
N

12

Duck

36°
10'
N

Southern Shores

Point Harbor

Albemarle Sound

Kitty Hawk

158

Wright Brothers National Memorial

Kill Devil Hills

36°
00'
N

36°
00'
N

Nags Head Woods

Fort Raleigh National
Historic Site and
Elizabethan Gardens

JOCKEY'S RIDGE
STATE PARK

Nags Head

To
Plymouth

Manteo

64

Whalebone Junction

Manns
Harbor

64

*Roanoke
Island*

Croatan Sound

35°
50'
N

264

Wanchese

Bodie Island
Lighthouse

35°
50'
N

CAPE HATTERAS NATIONAL SEASHORE

ALLIGATOR
RIVER
NATIONAL
WILDLIFE
REFUGE

Oregon Inlet

PEA ISLAND
NATIONAL
WILDLIFE
REFUGE

To
Engelhard

76°00' W   75°50' W   75°40' W

Refuge
Visitor Center

12

?

nect to the Atlantic. Today, Bodie Island and Currituck Banks are connected because the inlet that once separated them closed in the 1930s.

The section of the Outer Banks covered in this drive is the busiest and most developed part of the banks. Much of the drive passes through commercialized areas and is not particularly scenic. In recent years, even the once-peaceful area north of Duck has become highly developed. However, there are many scenic and historic sites along this route, so ignore the development and enjoy the ride. Although this drive is relatively short, you could easily spend several days here visiting all the area's attractions. If you are not interested in swimming and other beach activities, come in fall, winter, or spring. The area is much less crowded then, and lodging is cheaper.

The drive starts in Corolla, just past the end of NC 12. The state highway officially ends in Corolla, but it actually runs north a short distance to where the pavement ends at the beach. Unlike the area through which you have passed to reach the end of the road, the land north and west along the beach is mostly undeveloped.

Significant sections of beach here have been protected as part of the North Carolina National Estuarine Research Reserve and the Currituck National Wildlife Refuge. The reserve land was acquired in 1985 through the efforts of The Nature Conservancy and Monkey Island Investment Associates. It encompasses areas of beach, dunes, marsh, and maritime forest. If you have a four-wheel-drive vehicle, you can drive north along the beach and explore these areas. Unless you enjoy digging out stuck vehicles, don't try it without four-wheel drive.

From the beach, head south on NC 12. You will immediately enter a new, relatively expensive subdivision, one of many that have sprung up north of Duck in the last fifteen years. In a little over a mile, you will reach the center of the once-tiny village of Corolla. Unlike most old Outer Banks towns, Corolla was not directly dependent on fishing. Instead its residents were employed at lifesaving stations along the coast, or at the lighthouse and various hunt clubs in the area. You can gas up here. Gas, food, and lodging are plentiful throughout this drive— although lodging can be tight in summer, especially on weekends.

Because of accidents, the horses that once roamed the streets of Corolla have been moved north of town and fenced out. The remaining herd roams the reserve and wildlife refuge north of Corolla. The "Banker ponies" of Corolla are remnants of herds that once roamed all across the Outer Banks. Historians believe that these herds grew from horses left by Sir Walter Raleigh's expeditions or early Spanish explorers. The horses are thought to be of original Spanish mustang lineage.

In about 1.5 miles you'll see the obvious landmark of Currituck Beach Lighthouse on the right. Be sure to stop here. If you feel energetic, pay the small admission charge and climb to the top of the tower. It is open seasonally. The lighthouse was necessary in an area where a regrettable number of ships have wrecked. The

Outer Banks of North Carolina are notorious among sailors since they protrude far out into the Atlantic and present a navigational hazard. Early ships had the habit of hugging the shoreline to take advantage of favorable currents, and storms often forced these ships to run aground. More than 600 ships have been lost in the treacherous waters of the Outer Banks.

The particularly gruesome epic of the *Tyrrel*, a merchant brig, led to the construction of lighthouses along the coast. In June 1759, the *Tyrrel* set sail for Antigua, closely following the North Carolina shore as it traveled south. Near Cape Hatteras, it ran into a deadly squall at night. To escape the storm's escalating violence, the captain tried to run the ship through Hatteras Inlet into Pamlico Sound. But wind rolled the ship over as it turned. Crew members battled for their lives, some fighting their way out from belowdecks in the raging gale. With great effort, several crew members managed to right and bail out the ship's boat. Seventeen sailors dragged themselves aboard the tiny craft. In the dark, with a raging storm obscuring the sky and no working compass, the men had no clue in what direction lay the land. Tragically, they began rowing east, away from the cape.

At dawn they realized their mistake, but a new storm carried them farther out into the Atlantic. With no fresh drinking water, the situation became desperate. One by one, as the days went by, the men began to die. For the last week, only the first mate survived, lost in a thick fog. More than three weeks after the wreck of the *Tyrrel*, this lone surviving sailor was rescued by another merchant ship. His miraculous survival and the loss of all the other men led to an outcry for a lighthouse on Cape Hatteras.

Then, as today, the wheels of government moved slowly. Few in Britain felt like spending the necessary funds to construct a lighthouse in the remote American colonies. Even after the American Revolution, progress was slow; construction did not begin until 1799. The first (but only marginally adequate) lighthouse on Cape Hatteras began operating in 1803, more than forty years after the *Tyrrel* wrecked.

The Currituck Beach Lighthouse began service in 1875. It was the last of a series of three lighthouses built between 1870 and 1875; the other two are the present lighthouses at Cape Hatteras and Bodie Island. It provided a light on one of the longest dark stretches of Outer Banks shoreline. Many ships had been wrecked on the coast between the lighthouses at Bodie Island and Cape Henry in Virginia. Located on a low hill some distance in from the beach, the light at Currituck Beach sits at 158 feet and can be seen about 19 miles out to sea. It is still used as a navigation aid.

To keep mariners from confusing it with other Outer Banks lighthouses, the Currituck lighthouse was not painted and has a natural redbrick exterior. With a solid foundation and heavy 1.5-million-brick structure, the lighthouse has withstood numerous storms. Except during winter and early spring, the tower is open to visitors with healthy hearts and strong knees. The view from its tower encompasses the Atlantic Ocean and Currituck Sound along with much of the island. If you like lighthouse souvenirs, be sure to visit the gift store here. It has everything from lighthouse postcards to ceramic lighthouse replicas to lighthouse Christmas ornaments. A nicely restored Queen Anne–style keeper's house also occupies the grounds.

If you walk just west of the lighthouse parking lot, you will see a boardwalk disappearing into the woods. This long elevated platform leads through the woods, across marshes, and extends into the sound. It's a great, easy walk that allows you to view wildlife and fish the sound's waters near the picturesque redbrick tower of the lighthouse.

Right next door to the lighthouse, and easily visible from both the boardwalk and tower, lies the Whalehead Club. A large nearby dune once rose high over the area and gave the club its name. The elaborate mansion lies on land that was originally part of the Lighthouse Club, one of many hunt clubs on the Outer Banks. When a wealthy Philadelphia businessman named Edward Knight became a member of the club, he asked that his second wife also be made a member. Mrs. Knight was denied access since the club did not allow female members. When the property went up for sale in 1922, Knight purchased it so he could bring his wife to the island to hunt. His purchase included the building and almost 8,000 acres. He ordered the old clubhouse to be demolished and began constructing an elaborate mansion.

The showplace took three years to build and cost several hundred thousand dollars. Knight brought in a dredge to build the promontory upon which he would place his new mansion. Workers constructed a 20,000-square-foot home with three stories and a full basement. The mansion has a green copper roof and five brick chimneys—one more than the original Lighthouse Club. Large picture windows on the first floor and multiple dormer windows on the second story offer excellent views of the sound. In the Knights' mansion twelve bathrooms had solid brass plumbing that flowed both fresh and salt water to their tubs. Elaborate wooden doors, paneling, and trim complemented antique furnishings, Tiffany lamps, and many original oil paintings. An elevator eased travel between the floors and a staff of twelve servants tried to keep up with it all.

After the Knights' deaths in 1936, the mansion remained empty for four years. Its next owner proceeded to sell off many of its furnishings, then leased the huge home to the U.S. Coast Guard as a training facility during World War II. Over the following years, the mansion changed hands several times. Among other things, it was used as a boys' summer school and a rocket-testing site. Finally Currituck County purchased the property in 1991 to preserve the historic home and the surrounding marshes. The structure has been restored and is now open as a museum. It is closed in winter except at Christmas. The North Carolina Wildlife Resources

Commission is building the Outer Banks Center for Wildlife Education on the grounds. The North Carolina Department of Transportation plans new ferry service from here to the mainland.

From the Whalehead Club, head south on NC 12. The road passes through more ritzy subdivisions and resorts in an area that was once known for its peace and solitude. Here, what were once distinct communities now flow together; in the future, a bridge may connect this part of Currituck Banks with the mainland.

Several sections of NC 12 from Corolla to Duck are lined with walking and cycling trails that offer a great way to see the countryside at a more leisurely pace. The lifesaving station of Poyners Hill once lay near the resort development of Ocean Sands, a few miles south of Corolla. A famous shipwreck on January 31, 1878, led to its construction. The 198-foot *Metropolis,* a former navy ship converted to civilian use, ran aground and broke up just offshore, killing 102 people. About 7 miles south of Corolla, the large planned development of Pine Island boasts a seemingly endless quantity of virtual mansions. Much of the year they lie empty, used largely as seasonal vacation homes and rentals.

South of Pine Island is an Audubon sanctuary, a small patch of open land surrounded by new developments. Vegetation varies at this and other sites, depending on the width of the island and the protection from salt spray. Sometimes there are little more that dunes partly covered with sea oats and other hardy plants. In other places there is a scrub forest of live oak, cedar, and wax myrtle. In some places pines dominate, and near Duck a lush maritime forest of tall pines and hardwoods grows.

After leaving Currituck County and entering Dare County, the road passes through Sanderling, another large new resort development. A former military reservation lies about 3 miles south of Sanderling; the U.S. Army Corps of Engineers researches the erosional forces affecting beaches here. The reservation is obvious; signs warning of unexploded ammunition line the highway.

The highway then enters Duck, a small village bustling with the tourist trade. Beyond Duck, the road passes into Southern Shores, one of the oldest developments on the Outer Banks. The Southern Shores date back to the years after the end of World War II. Here many of the homes are more modest and older than those farther north. After about 22 miles, NC 12 intersects busy four-lane US 158. Turn left onto US 158 and join the traffic. NC 12 doesn't end here, but instead parallels US 158 closer to the beach.

US 158 was originally built as a bypass to relieve congestion on NC 12 as it passed through Kitty Hawk, Kill Devil Hills, and Nags Head, but rampant development has rendered it even busier than NC 12. If you need travel information or maps about the Outer Banks, look for the handy visitor center and rest area at the junction of NC 12 and US 158. As you drive south along US 158, you will notice mile marker signs. These are often used as directions for finding shops, businesses, and other establishments along the highway.

The three main settlements along US 158—Kitty Hawk, Kill Devil Hills, and Nags Head—all blend together. Development has become continuous along this part of the Outer Banks. Don't let it deter you; there are some very worthwhile places to visit here. As you start down US 158, you'll first enter Kitty Hawk. If you want to see some of the old village, turn right on Kitty Hawk Road. It's tucked into woods on the sound side of the island. The first monument to the Wright brothers' achievements lies in the village. On the right side of US 158 in about 6 miles is the Wright Brothers National Memorial, managed by the National Park Service. This monument commemorates the site of man's first sustained and controlled powered flight.

Wilbur and Orville Wright were blessed with a natural mechanical ability, strong intelligence, and tremendous perseverance. In 1892, they opened a bicycle shop in Dayton, Ohio, which thrived. But the brothers were restless. In 1899, Wilbur wrote to the Smithsonian Institution for information on the study of flight. After seeing the available literature, he and his brother Orville were dismayed at the lack of progress in aeronautics. They dedicated the next four years toward realizing mankind's dream of flight.

The Wrights determined that the solutions to a wing design that would provide lift and a method of propulsion were already partly solved and only needed refining. Their biggest problem was finding a way to control an aircraft in flight. Wilbur came up with the idea of warping the wings to steer the craft. The brothers chose Kitty Hawk for their tests because of the almost constant winds here and the open sandy terrain that would make testing easier and safer. In 1900 they built a glider to test their new control ideas, but the wings generated less lift than they had hoped, so they went home to Ohio disappointed. The next year they built a larger glider and experimented with the wings' camber to try to improve lift.

At their new Kill Devil Hills camp, they found that the wing change made the craft uncontrollable. They returned to the earlier camber and managed a 335-foot glide, but control was still a problem. When the pilot warped the wings upward on the right side, expecting to turn left, the plane tended to slip back to the right, a problem known as adverse yaw. Frustrated, the Wrights almost quit trying, but they returned to Ohio and built a wind tunnel to test their own wing designs.

In 1902, the brothers returned yet again to the Outer Banks with a new design based on their research. The changes were moderately successful, and the pair accomplished about 400 glides. However, they still suffered control problems. Orville came up with the idea of making the tail movable, and Wilbur thought to tie the tail movements to the warping of the wings. Eureka! After 600 successful glides, the Wrights proved that they had developed the first working aircraft.

The Wrights had one more hurdle to overcome: propulsion. They were unable to find an appropriate, lightweight gasoline engine, so they designed their own. Because no one had developed an efficient propeller, they went back to their wind

Wright Brothers National Memorial

tunnel and created their own model of that, too. Returning once more to Kill Devil Hills in 1903, they installed their engine on a new 40-foot craft called the *Flyer*.

The plane's engine turned two propellers using bicycle chains and steel shafts. To make the propellers spin in opposite directions to prevent the craft from twisting in flight, they crossed one of the chains. Troubles with their cranky engine and weak propeller shafts slowed their progress. On December 14 they were ready to try. The *Flyer* was set on a wooden track to prevent it from bogging down in the sand. Orville lost the coin toss, so Wilbur climbed aboard. He lay down prone on the lower wing where the controls were located, mere inches from spinning propellers and bicycle chains. To keep the wingtip from tilting into the sand on takeoff, Orville ran alongside the craft holding it level as it started down the track. Unfortunately, Wilbur oversteered and the plane climbed too steeply, stalled, and crashed.

They hastily repaired the craft and were ready for another try on December 17, 1903. The weather was deteriorating, with winds of 27 miles per hour, but the brothers could not wait for better conditions since they needed to return home to Dayton. Hoping for success, they donned coats and ties for the occasion and recruited volunteers from the local lifesaving station. Orville climbed into the craft for his turn. The engine was started and the *Flyer* started down the track with Wilbur running alongside to steady the wingtip. The aircraft lifted off as John Daniels, one of the lifesaving crew, hit the shutter of a preset camera. For twelve seconds, Orville kept the unruly *Flyer* aloft, touching down 120 feet from the track. Man had flown in a powered aircraft for the first time. The brothers made three more flights that day, the last covering 852 feet in fifty-nine seconds. They had conquered the skies.

"They have done it! Damned if they ain't flew!" said a witness to the first flight. The public was skeptical, having heard many such claims before, but the brothers were undaunted. They continued to refine their design and skills and by 1905 made routine flights that lasted as long as thirty-eight minutes. The world would never be the same. Even today, planes use the same principles discovered by the Wright brothers.

The centerpiece of the Wright Brothers Memorial is a large, 60-foot monument on the summit of 90-foot Kill Devil Hill. This granite marker not only commemorates the Wright brothers' accomplishment, but also offers great views of the island, the Atlantic Ocean, and the sound. At night, floodlights make the monument an impressive sight. The visitor center here has exhibits on the first flight and a replica of the *Flyer;* the original rests in a place of honor at the Smithsonian. Replicas of the brothers' camp buildings have been built on their original sites, and a stone monument marks the spot where the first airplane left the ground. Four other numbered markers show the distance of each of the four flights of December

17, 1903. A life-size replica of the first flight was erected to match the famous photo during the centennial celebration in 2003.

After you have stopped at the Wright Brothers Memorial, consider taking a break from all the man-made hubbub along US 158 by visiting Nags Head Woods. Continue south on US 158 about 1.7 miles to a stoplight at Ocean Acres Drive by a McDonald's restaurant. Small brown signs for The Nature Conservancy also mark the junction. Turn right onto Ocean Acres Drive and follow it west about a mile through a subdivision; the pavement gives way to a good dirt surface. You'll soon reach the well-marked entrance to Nags Head Woods Preserve on the left.

The preserve protects a 1,400-acre tract of maritime forest, an uncommon ecosystem that survives in patches on the Outer Banks. The lush woods of oak, hickory, beech, pine, and other trees are a surprise on the narrow, windswept, sandy islands of the North Carolina coast. Survival is difficult for such forests. Wind, salt spray, lack of fresh water, and poor, sandy soils make life difficult for plants. At Nags Head Woods, a series of dune ridges helps protect the forest from salt spray and wind.

The woods were threatened with development in the 1970s. Local residents, The Nature Conservancy, and other organizations fought the trend, raising money to buy part of the forest. Donations and purchases in succeeding years have since protected the bulk of the woods. Stop in at the visitor center to register and learn more about the preserve. More than 5 miles of hiking trails wind through these woods, passing several ponds and visiting the shore of Roanoke Sound. Before making a trip to the woods, you may want to call ahead to check the hours, especially in the off-season (see Appendix for the address and phone number). Take mosquito repellent in the warm months.

A short distance south of the turnoff to Nags Head Woods, US 158 enters Nags Head. The town is the granddad of North Carolina resort towns, born as the result of mosquito-borne diseases on the coastal lowlands. Plantation owners, their families and slaves, and other residents often died from fever, believed to be caused by vapors or miasmas given off by nearby swamps. Physicians thought that breathing salt air would prevent such afflictions, so they prescribed summers on the coast. In the 1830s, planter Francis Nixon decided to take his doctor's advice and scouted the Outer Banks for a good site for a summer home. He liked the large dunes near Nags Head and ended up purchasing 200 acres fronting Roanoke Sound.

Nixon built a house here and invited friends and neighbors to join his family after the crops were harvested. The planters found swimming, boating, and other recreational pursuits here to their liking. Other affluent people joined them, building their own summer homes. The community grew and prospered until the Civil War. After the war, Nags Head made a slow recovery. When the bridge from the mainland arrived at Kitty Hawk in 1930, the stage was set for accelerated growth, interrupted only by the Great Depression and World War II.

You will pass Jockey's Ridge State Park on the right about 2 miles after entering Nags Head. It's hard to miss; the bare sand of 100-foot-high Jockey's Ridge looms over the highway. It's the largest of several prominent dunes in the area—in fact, it's the largest coastal dune anywhere along the Atlantic or Gulf coasts. The dunes are formed by sand carried ashore onto beaches by storms and ocean currents. This particular dune might not have gotten so large if it weren't for early settlers' cutting and overgrazing of erosion-resistant ground cover.

Many legends try to explain the Jockey's Ridge's name. The most popular one points to early residents' habit of capturing wild Banker ponies and racing them near the base of the massive dune. The ridge's steep slope made ideal bleachers for spectators. Like Nags Head Woods, the state park was formed when the area was threatened with development. In 1973, Carolista Baum woke to the sound of heavy construction. Horrified at seeing developers near the base of the massive dune, she placed herself in the path of a bulldozer, forcing its operator to shut down. The ensuing fuss led the North Carolina General Assembly to appropriate funds to create the park in 1975. Matching federal funds allowed the state to purchase 152 acres; The Nature Conservancy bought and added another 115 acres. Today the park covers 420 acres that include Jockey's Ridge, other dunes, scrubby maritime forest, and frontage on Roanoke Sound.

Park activities include picnicking, hiking the nature trails, and playing on the sandy slopes. The Wright brothers weren't the only people to take advantage of the Outer Banks' sandy landing sites and steady winds. Jockey's Ridge is famous as a premier hang-gliding and kite-flying site. The center for such activity is Kitty Hawk Kites, a training and supply center for hang-glider pilots that sits just across US 158.

Continuing the drive, you will hit a large highway intersection about 4.5 miles south of Jockey's Ridge State Park on US 158. This is Whalebone Junction. Turn left here, heading back on NC 12 toward Cape Hatteras National Seashore. The road narrows to two lanes as you enter the national seashore. An information center on the right offers details about the national seashore and other area attractions. An official North Carolina Scenic Byway—the Outer Banks Scenic Byway—starts here.

The scenery changes radically from this point south, leaving behind the long commercial strip along the shore. Cape Hatteras National Seashore preserves the natural beauty and historic sites of a large portion of the Outer Banks. The highway passes through wild marshes and scrub forest as it proceeds south. Some development is occasionally visible to the east along the beach for a few miles, but it eventually disappears. There are several marsh overlooks and blinds along the right side of the road.

Be sure to pause at a junction after driving about 6 miles. The road to the left leads to Coquina Beach, a beautiful sandy beach backed by sea oat–covered dunes.

It's popular with swimmers, fishermen, sunbathers, and beachcombers. The remnants of the shipwrecked *Linda A. Barnes,* another maritime victim of the Graveyard of the Atlantic, rest here behind the dunes. Back at the intersection, the turnoff to the right leads a short distance to the Bodie Island Lighthouse and Visitor Center. This active 156-foot lighthouse, painted with horizontal black and white bands, has stood guard over the Outer Banks since 1872. Like the light at Currituck Beach, it lies some distance back from the ocean, surrounded by freshwater marshes and a grove of pines.

The site was first proposed for a light in 1837. In that year, because of continuing shipwrecks off the Outer Banks, Lieutenant Napoleon Coste was sent by the government to scout the coast for lighthouse sites. He recommended constructing a light on or near Bodie Island by which southbound ships could fix their location before navigating the treacherous Cape Hatteras. His report stated that "more vessels are lost [here] than on any other part of our coast." Congress appropriated the funds that year, but then the process was bogged down by land ownership complications. Construction finally began in 1847.

Along with building came problems. Seasoned engineer Francis Gibbons was commissioned to design the lighthouse, but the project's chief was former customs official Thomas Blount, who had no lighthouse experience whatsoever. Over Gibbons's objections, Blount ordered an unsupported brick foundation for the tower. Within two years of its completion, the 54-foot tower began to lean. Numerous expensive repairs failed to fix the problem, so the lighthouse was abandoned in 1859. A replacement tower was built nearby, but it too was short-lived. It succumbed to the Civil War, blown up in 1861 by retreating Confederate troops who feared that the Union would use it as an observation post.

After the war, the Lighthouse Board was not disposed toward building a third lighthouse at Bodie Island. However, pressure from the shipping and insurance industries eventually changed the board's position. Oddly enough, the first two "Bodie Island" lights were actually built just across Oregon Inlet on Pea Island. This time a site was selected that actually lay on Bodie Island. Crews, equipment, and materials were moved north from the newly completed Cape Hatteras Lighthouse, and construction began in 1871. On October 1, 1872, the new lighthouse shined its light for the first time. The beam was magnified by a powerful first-order Fresnel lens. A month after its lighting, a flock of geese flew into the tower, seriously damaging the lens. The problem was remedied by draping the outside of the lantern with heavy wire netting. The light still shines today and is visible from 19 miles out at sea.

Although the tower is closed to visitors, the keeper's quarters have been restored and serve as a visitor center with exhibits and an information desk. If you feel like stretching your legs, take the short nature trail that starts right behind the lighthouse and leads to a boardwalk, pier, and observation platform along a fresh-

Bodie Island Lighthouse, Cape Hatteras National Seashore

water marsh. The marsh is popular with waterfowl and shorebirds—and often mosquitoes. A longer trail starts behind a gate at the back of the parking lot. It follows a short gravel road toward a small boat dock, then splits off to the left at a small bridge. It winds through shady pines, then heads across marshes all the way to NC 12. Along the way are good views of the lighthouse and all kinds of birds and other wildlife.

After the turnoffs for Bodie Island Lighthouse and Coquina Beach, the highway continues south another 2 miles to Oregon Inlet Campground on the left. It's open during the warmer months of the year. Call the national seashore for opening and closing dates. A short distance past the campground is a marina, boat ramp, and a U.S. Coast Guard office on the right. Just beyond, the highway crosses Oregon Inlet, a channel opened by an 1846 hurricane.

Until the long Bonner Bridge opened in 1963, this inlet had to be crossed by boat. Enjoy the water views as you drive onto the bridge to reach Pea Island. The Atlantic, with its pounding surf, lies to the east, and the shallow, calmer waters of Pamlico Sound lie to the west. This scenic drive ends at the high point of the bridge, but the route is continued in the Cape Hatteras National Seashore Drive (Drive #28).

27

Lost Colony of Roanoke
Nags Head to Bath

General description: A 118-mile paved drive past numerous worthwhile attractions on historic Roanoke Island and several wildlife refuges to Bath, the oldest town in North Carolina.

Special attractions: Fort Raleigh National Historic Site, Elizabeth II State Historic Site, Elizabethan Gardens, North Carolina Aquarium, Alligator River National Wildlife Refuge, Mattamuskeet National Wildlife Refuge, Bath State Historic Site, fishing, boating, cycling, wildlife.

Location: Upper North Carolina coast. The drive begins on the Outer Banks at the junction of US 158, NC 12, US 64, and US 264 at the south end of Nags Head.

Drive route numbers: US 64/264, US 264, NC 99, NC 92.

Travel season: All year. Summer is hot but ideal for water activities. Spring and fall are less crowded, with cooler temperatures. Winter can be chilly and stormy.

Camping: There are no public campgrounds along this route. Goose Creek State Park, west of Bath, offers some primitive campsites.

Services: All services are plentiful in Nags Head and on Roanoke Island. Most of the larger towns along the mainland part have food and gas. There is limited lodging in Engelhard, Belhaven, Swan Quarter, and Bath.

Nearby attractions: Wright Brothers National Memorial, Cape Hatteras National Seashore, Currituck Beach Lighthouse, Bodie Island Lighthouse, Nags Head Woods, Jockey's Ridge State Park, Swan Quarter National Wildlife Refuge, Pocosin Lakes National Wildlife Refuge, Goose Creek State Park.

For more information: Fort Raleigh National Historic Site (National Park Service), Elizabethan Gardens, North Carolina Aquarium, Alligator River National Wildlife Refuge, Mattamuskeet National Wildlife Refuge, Bath State Historic Site, Outer Banks Chamber of Commerce, Outer Banks Visitors Bureau. See Appendix for addresses and phone numbers.

The Drive

This drive travels from the Outer Banks to Roanoke Island, one of the most historically important places in the United States. Roanoke Island was the site of the first English settlement in the New World; its colonists disappeared without a trace. The drive also crosses a large section of the coastal mainland, passing Alligator River National Wildlife Refuge, home of wild, endangered red wolves, and ends at Bath, the oldest incorporated town in North Carolina. It's a long drive with plenty of historic and scenic attractions. If possible, try to spend at least two days doing it.

Lost Colony of Roanoke

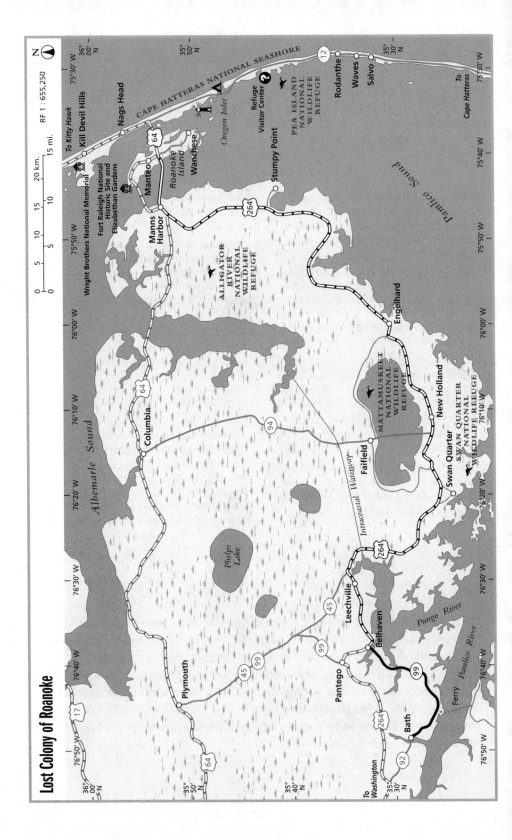

The drive starts on Bodie Island at the junction of US 64/US 264, US 158, and NC 12 at the south end of Nags Head, and heads west across Roanoke Sound on US 64/US 264 on a causeway. After crossing the shining blue waters of the sound, you arrive on Roanoke Island. The island lies in open water between the Outer Banks and the mainland. Because it is not as exposed to the salt spray and the ocean's power as the Outer Banks, it is heavily wooded. NC 345 turns off to the left soon after you reach the island. This road goes to Wanchese, an old fishing village that doesn't really cater to tourists. If you continue straight, you will drive onto the new Virginia Dare Bridge, the longest bridge in North Carolina, and cross to the mainland. To continue the drive, turn right and follow the business route of US 64/264 into Manteo.

In the middle of the town of Manteo, turn right where signs indicate the *Elizabeth II* and head downtown. Unlike the commercial strip along US 64/264, Manteo's downtown area is quite charming, with historic buildings, small inns, and numerous shops. Park near the waterfront and walk around some of the old structures and into the little park. The *Elizabeth II* lies across a small bay. It's a replica of the type of ship used by England in the late 1500s to transport colonists to Roanoke Island. To get to it, walk across the bridge that spans the bay. The ship was built with private funds and given to the state to commemorate America's 400th birthday at Roanoke. It is now the centerpiece of a state historic site. Exhibits there tell of the English settlement of the New World and the colonists' lives on Roanoke Island.

Be sure to take a tour of this ship, which was built to be as authentic as possible. It was named after the *Elizabeth,* one of the ships in the 1585 English fleet. Try to imagine crossing the Atlantic Ocean in this tiny ship, dependent on the wind to push you. No satellites could show hurricanes then, and no radios could be used to call for rescue. All the people, food, supplies, and livestock to start a new colony in a wild, untamed land were crammed into small ships such as this one, yet somehow our forefathers persevered. It makes you think twice before whining about modern irritants.

Return to the main road and continue north up the island. In about 2 miles, signs mark the turnoff on the left for the North Carolina Aquarium. This aquarium, one of three in the state, offers exhibits about North Carolina's underwater life and related coastal human and natural history. A series of aquariums, including two large ones that feature sharks and red drum, the state fish, are the highlight of the facility.

Beyond the aquarium turnoff, US 264 continues through a tunnel carved through tall forest and beautifully landscaped with crape myrtle trees and grass. These beautiful flowering trees were planted here in 1984 to celebrate the founding of the colony at Roanoke. A walking/cycling path parallels the highway here.

If you make no other stop on this drive, be sure to turn right into Fort Raleigh National Historic Site and the Elizabethan Gardens about a mile past the aquar-

Elizabeth II *ship replica in Manteo*

ium turnoff. Here lies one of the most crucial sites in American history. Park at the historic site visitor center and enter the National Park Service building to start your tour.

The history of Roanoke Island starts in England with the reign of Queen Mary I. Under the Catholic queen's rule, the country had been somewhat stagnant, its people suffering from religious persecution and the covetous eye of other European countries. When Mary's sister Elizabeth began her reign in 1558, the country welcomed its new intelligent, strong-willed ruler. Unlike Mary, Elizabeth ruled with a form of benevolent authoritarianism. English society became more open, and living standards improved. Its feudal system was fading and a new middle class began to appear.

With new confidence and strength, England began to turn outward and challenge the power of its rivals, Spain and Portugal. Merchant ships called privateers were authorized to raid the ships of England's enemies in a form of politically sanctioned piracy. Successful privateer captains found Elizabeth's favor. Sir Francis

Drake, who circumnavigated the world from 1577 to 1580, raided Spanish ships as he went. Drake's exploits revealed the weakness of Spanish control of the New World, and England quickly entered the race for control of the Americas.

After obtaining a charter from his queen, Sir Humphrey Gilbert made the first English effort toward New World colonization with two attempts to reach New-foundland. He died on the second trip, and his half brother, Sir Walter Raleigh, took up the cause. Raleigh's first expedition, in 1584, returned to England with reports of "a most pleasant and fertile ground." Raleigh had little difficulty getting the queen and other investors to back a proposed colony. In the spring of 1585, 500 men (including 108 colonists) set sail for Virginia in seven ships commanded by Sir Richard Grenville, Raleigh's cousin. One of Raleigh's inspired moves was to include scientist Thomas Hariot and surveyor-artist John White. Between them, they would create an excellent portrait of the New World through collecting, observation, drawings, and mapmaking. After weeks of privateering and searching the coast, the colonists found a defensible, fertile spot on Roanoke Island.

Ralph Lane was appointed governor, and the settlers immediately began building a fort to protect themselves from the Spanish. They established a trading relationship with the Indians, but were ill-prepared for winter because one of their supply ships had run aground. Without the ability to raise crops, they soon became dependent on the Indians for food. But in the depths of winter, and a seri-ous drought, as recent research indicates, the Indians may have had little to spare. When measles and smallpox began to sicken their Indian supporters, disillusion-ment set in for the colonists. By spring, the settlers became anxious to relocate. Relations with the Indians deteriorated to open warfare.

Sir Francis Drake's privateering fleet appeared at Roanoke just when the colonists were at their lowest. Grenville had not returned to bring supplies to the colony, and Lane had lost hope that he might show up. Drake offered the ship *Francis* to help the colonists return to England. Before they could get aboard, how-ever, a storm forced the ship to leave Roanoke with much of their supplies. The demoralized colonists left Roanoke with Drake's fleet. Ironically, a supply ship sent by Raleigh arrived two days later to find the settlement abandoned; Grenville's ship arrived in two weeks. Not knowing the fate of the colonists, Grenville searched the island, then left fifteen men to guard the colony while he recruited new settlers.

Although his first attempt at colonization had failed, Raleigh was soon ready to try again. The second American colony would be more agrarian and less mili-taristic. Seventeen women and nine children would be included among the 110 colonists. To encourage the settlers' commitment, each person would be deeded 500 acres. John White was appointed governor. Because Lane reported a good har-bor and friendly Indians there, the colony would be located on Chesapeake Bay.

Three ships sailed in May 1587, planning to stop just briefly at Roanoke to resupply Grenville's group before continuing to the Chesapeake. However, when the ship arrived at Roanoke in July, the Portuguese pilot claimed that the season was late and refused to continue to Chesapeake Bay. Reluctantly, the new colonists settled for Roanoke Island. Like the first group, they got off to a poor start. They had not stopped for fruit and salt in Haiti as planned, and the local Indians were still hostile. They had attacked Grenville's men and all had disappeared; White found nothing more than the bones of one of them. Relations remained uneasy.

In August, White's daughter gave birth to Virginia Dare, the first English child born in the New World. A week later, White left for England to order desperately needed supplies. There the governor's ship was pressed into service against Spain. All White could do was petition the queen for a ship through Sir Walter Raleigh. After three long years, he finally got passage on a privateer in 1590. Upon the ship's arrival at Roanoke, no colonists greeted the sailors; silence reigned.

The Roanoke settlers left few clues as to their fate. The letters "CRO" were carved on a tree at the shore, and the houses had been taken down and a stockade built. "CROATOAN," the name of a nearby island, had been carved on a post. The colonists had agreed to leave such a message if they had to leave Roanoke, but there was no carved Maltese cross, the symbol that meant trouble had caused the departure. White wanted to sail to Croatoan Island, but the privateers were low on supplies and suffering losses from a storm. They refused. Raleigh made several attempts to locate the lost colonists between 1590 and 1592, but no trace of them was ever found. Today, the disappearance remains one of the great mysteries of American history. The colonists may have been attacked by Indians or assimilated into the tribes, but we may never know for sure.

Although Raleigh's colony at Roanoke Island failed, the importance of his undertaking cannot be overestimated. Although seventeen years would pass before a permanent colony was established at Jamestown, Virginia, his colonists had set the stage for English settlement of America. Today we speak English and have an Anglo-based culture in large part because of these colonization attempts.

The Fort Raleigh Visitor Center has exhibits, artifacts, talks by park rangers, and an interesting video reenacting the settlement of Roanoke. Behind the visitor center is a reconstructed earthen fort, built after intensive archaeological study to resemble one constructed by the colonists. It is the only structure here for which the original site has been exactly located. A short nature trail, named for Thomas Hariot, winds through the woods near the fort. In summer, a live drama, *The Lost Colony,* plays in the evening at an outdoor theater overlooking the sound. With drama, music, and dance, it tells the story of the doomed colony. The play has run continuously since 1937. Almost 3 million people have viewed it over the years.

From the visitor center, it's only a short walk next door to the Elizabethan Gardens. These beautiful gardens combine the natural beauty of the North Carolina woods with formal British gardens. The Garden Club of North Carolina built in 1951 in memory of the English colonists who came to Roanoke Island. You

Elizabethan Gardens on Roanoke Island

enter the gardens through a formal gatehouse, which was once part of the French Embassy in Washington. Portraits of Queen Elizabeth I and Sir Walter Raleigh hang on the walls, their stern visages emblematic of the drive necessary to begin colonies in the New World.

Paths wind through shady woods of live oak and pine to the centerpiece of the gardens, the Sunken Garden. Manicured hedges and trees surround an antique stone fountain donated by John Hay Whitney, a former American ambassador to Great Britain. Old marble statues and ornaments decorate other parts of the garden. One sculpture, a marble statue of an adult Virginia Dare, adds a note of sadness. In all likelihood, the child never reached maturity. After strolling through the gardens, relax in the thatched gazebo overlooking the sound. On a quiet day, you can almost hear the slap of oars in the water and the faint voices of the colonists as they came ashore here.

From Fort Raleigh National Historic Site, head west on the highway toward the mainland. This is the starting point of an official North Carolina Scenic Byway, the Alligator River Route. Be sure to check your gas tank, since fuel isn't available for the next 45 miles or so except in Manns Harbor. In about a mile, you will pass a rest area on the left, then start across the bridge that connects the island with the mainland. This busy, 2.7-mile bridge replaced a ferry in 1957. It offers a great view of Croatan Sound and the land that lines its shores.

The highway next passes through the small fishing village of Manns Harbor, named for a German fishing captain who sheltered here during a storm. Here the highway rejoins the new highway that crosses the new Virginia Dare Bridge. On the other side of the town, it enters the marshes of the Alligator River National Wildlife Refuge. This 152,000-acre refuge was created in 1984 when the Prudential Insurance Company donated 118,000 acres to the U.S. Fish and Wildlife Service. Much of the refuge consists of marshes that were once thought to be wastelands. This is pocosin habitat, pocosin being an Indian word meaning "swamp in a hill." Pocosin wetlands are marshy areas with thick peat deposits. When wet, the sponge-like deposits hold large amounts of water; when dry, they burn easily. For many years, coastal pocosin areas were logged, drained, and farmed. In more recent years, biologists realized that these "wastelands" were vital to wildlife, and efforts were made to protect some of the remaining areas.

More than 200 bird species have been sighted at the refuge. Alligator River is true to its name; the massive reptiles thrive in the refuge at about the northern limit of their range. However, the most famous resident of the refuge is the red wolf. Historically, it lived in bottomlands all over the Southeast, including North Carolina. Loss of habitat and extermination efforts by humans nearly led to the wolf's demise. By the 1970s only a handful survived, roaming the swampy low-lands on the Texas-Louisiana border. The few purebred wolves remaining were captured by 1980. From a mere fourteen animals, the present population of around forty red wolves was founded. A small number of wolves were successfully reintroduced to Cape Romain National Wildlife Refuge in South Carolina. In 1987, biologists released more wolves into the new Alligator River refuge. Although there have been losses from cars and other causes, the population has bred successfully and expanded. As you drive through the refuge, especially at night, watch closely for the wolves. Maybe you will be fortunate enough to see one.

Soon after entering the refuge, US 64 and US 264 split. Go left on US 264. Traffic is relatively light here since most vehicles take US 64. The Alligator River Route continues west on US 64, but another state scenic byway, the Pamlico Scenic Byway, starts at the junction and follows US 264. The highway passes through miles of undeveloped woods and marsh, part of the refuge. After about 13 miles, it brings you to Stumpy Point Bay, a tiny harbor, and a North Carolina Forest Service office with a tall fire lookout tower. A short side road leads to the small fishing village of Stumpy Point. The refuge continues for about another 15 miles after the bay.

Leaving the refuge, you pass timber clearcuts and large farm fields. The first town you reach is Engelhard, about 37 miles from the US 64–US 264 junction. This small town lies on Far Creek on the edge of Pamlico Sound. From here, the highway passes numerous farms and scattered homes as it travels west. Quite a few of the farm buildings are historic. Watch particularly for the eight-sided Octagon House, sometimes called the Ink Bottle House. You may catch a glimpse of Lake Mattamuskeet on the right.

After about 13 miles, you enter the hamlet of New Holland. Like all the towns of Hyde County, this one is quite small. Settled in 1910, it was named for a development company that tried to drain Lake Mattamuskeet. Though the lake was drained several times in the 1920s, allowing farm crops to be planted in its basin, the project eventually failed.

The junction of NC 94 lies about 2 miles past New Holland. For an interesting side trip, consider driving a short distance north on NC 94 to Lake Mattamuskeet National Wildlife Refuge. One interpretation of the lake's name says that it is derived from an Indian word for "moving swamp" or "shallow lake." This seems appropriate, since the lake has an average depth of about 2.5 feet. Another interpretation says that the name comes from an Algonquian Indian word for "dry dust." Mattamuskeet is the largest natural lake in the state and was once the center of an Indian reservation established in 1715.

Highway NC 94 crosses the vast lake on a causeway, giving drivers a great view of its waters. Bald cypresses and marshes line the lake's shores. The lake has been a national wildlife refuge since 1934; it attracts as many as 100,000 waterfowl during winter days, accompanied by hunters and birders. Roads surround the lake, offering many possible viewpoints. The massive old building that housed the pumps that drained the lake in the late 1920s can be seen on the shore.

From Lake Mattamuskeet, return to US 264 and continue west from the junction with NC 94. In a few miles, a side road leads to Swan Quarter on the shores of an arm of Pamlico Sound. This small fishing town has been the county seat of Hyde County for more than 150 years. Its waterfront is quite picturesque. The town is better known than it might otherwise be because it is the mainland terminus of the Ocracoke–Swan Quarter ferry. The ferry makes several daily runs lasting two and a half hours each, carrying people and their vehicles back and forth between Swan Quarter and the Outer Banks.

The section of the drive from Swan Quarter to the Intracoastal Waterway is quite scenic. Tall trees and thick forest line the highway; in some places trees arch over the road. A few miles past town, you will pass a marked side road on the left that leads to Swan Quarter National Wildlife Refuge. Like the refuge at Lake Mattamuskeet, Swan Quarter's primary mission is to provide wintering grounds for waterfowl. It lies on Pamlico Sound and consists of marshes and woods on both the mainland and islands. Part of the refuge is wilderness, much of it is accessible only by boat.

The hamlet of Rose Bay is a short distance past Swan Quarter National Wildlife Refuge on US 264. In another 9 miles you cross a high bridge over the Intracoastal Waterway by a tall fire lookout tower. The waterway provides a storm-protected inland channel for both commercial shipping and recreational boating all along the Atlantic coast. About 3.5 miles past the waterway, NC 45 turns off to the right. Follow it if you wish to visit yet another national wildlife refuge, Pocosin Lakes. Otherwise, continue west on US 264.

Just past the junction with NC 45, the highway crosses the Pungo River, the dividing line between Hyde and Beaufort Counties. Right after the river is the village of Leechville, which is not as bad a place as its name suggests. From here, continue along US 264 to the relatively new town of Belhaven. The town was settled in about 1890 when the business interests of a former Union army officer and a former Confederate captain coincided. Bounded on one side by the Pungo River and on the other by Pantego Creek, it became a lumber, railroad, and port town and now boasts an attractive harbor on the Intracoastal Waterway.

John Wilkinson opened a lumber mill in Belhaven at the turn of the century and built an impressive mansion, River Forest Manor. It's worth a short side trip into town to see this large, elegant house that is now run as a hotel, restaurant, and marina. Another interesting sight here is the Belhaven Memorial Museum on the second floor of the old city hall. It has one of the oddest collections of artifacts, curiosities, and knickknacks found anywhere.

In Belhaven, US 264 turns right at a highway junction. Leave it here and continue straight onto NC 99. The road soon crosses a large bridge over Pantego Creek, giving drivers a nice view of the Belhaven waterfront. In about 4 miles, it crosses two small arms of the Pungo River. The road winds through woods and fields to a short spur road that leads to the Bayview–Aurora ferry. This ferry carries people and vehicles across the Pamlico River in thirty-minute trips. The highway number changes at the ferry's spur road; NC 99 becomes NC 92.

After about 5 miles on NC 92, the highway crosses Back Creek, a small arm of Bath Creek, and enters the historic town of Bath. Europeans first started settling the Pamlico River area in the 1690s; the first settlers here were French Protestants from Virginia. The town was laid out by John Lawson, surveyor general of the British Crown. In 1701, a library sent to the St. Thomas Parish church became North Carolina's first public library. Bath also had North Carolina's first public school. Trade in pine pitch, turpentine, tobacco, and furs caused the town to develop into North Carolina's first port. Successful because of its location, Bath was incorporated in 1705. A gristmill and the colony's first shipyard were built here in 1707. By the next year, Bath had a population of about fifty, and twelve houses.

The fledgling town also had its problems. It suffered hostilities with Indians, an epidemic of yellow fever in 1711, and piracy in its early years. Much of the town's fame has come from part-time resident Edward Teach, the pirate better known as Blackbeard, who lived on nearby Plum Point. Blackbeard first came to Bath as early as 1712. He had started his career as an honest sailor for England in Queen Anne's War, during which he had served on a privateer ship that conducted raids on the ships of enemy countries. By the time the war ended, Blackbeard had tasted easy riches, and he didn't stop his pirating activities. Blackbeard's reputation quickly grew because of his tremendous success, his cruelty, and his fearsome appearance.

In 1717, Blackbeard settled into life in Bath, claiming that he had changed and that his pirate days were over. He married a young Bath girl—not telling her that she was only one of his many (probably fourteen) wives scattered across the colony. It's hard to teach an old dog new tricks. Blackbeard's men continued to raid ships on Pamlico Sound. When he threw lavish parties for local planters at his home, his crew would slip out and loot his guests' houses while he entertained them. Soon this sport wasn't enough for him. He outfitted his ship and began pirating anew.

Receiving no help from colonial officials in North Carolina, worried citizens appealed to the governor of Virginia. He sent two small British warships in pursuit of Blackbeard. They found his ship, the *Adventure,* in its usual hideout near Ocracoke Island. A bloody battle ensued in which the feared pirate was slain. His reign of terror was over, but his treasure was never found. Drive #29 tells more about Blackbeard.

The best way to see Bath is on foot. Start with the exhibits and a film in the Bath Historic Site Visitor Center. Walk to the many historic structures that still remain in the sleepy little village, including the 1744 Palmer-Marsh House, the 1790 Van Der Veer House, and the 1830 Bonner House. The Van Der Veer House is open year-round. The St. Thomas Church, established in 1734, is the oldest existing church in North Carolina. End this drive and your tour of town on the shore of Bath Creek in front of the Bonner House. Tall pines and hardwoods shade a grassy picnic area that looks out over the sparkling blue water of the creek.

28

Cape Hatteras National Seashore

Pea Island National Wildlife Refuge to Hatteras

General description: A 48-mile drive past the seemingly endless beaches and dunes of Cape Hatteras National Seashore, with a visit to a wildlife refuge and what is probably the best-known lighthouse in America.

Special attractions: Cape Hatteras National Seashore, Cape Hatteras Lighthouse, Pea Island National Wildlife Refuge, Buxton Woods, Hatteras–Ocracoke ferry, beaches, boating, fishing, surfing, swimming, hiking, wildlife.

Location: Upper North Carolina coast. The drive lies on the Outer Banks and starts at the bridge that connects Bodie Island to Pea Island, a short distance south of Nags Head.

Drive route number: NC 12.

Travel season: All year. Summer is hot but ideal for beach activities. Spring and fall are less crowded, with cooler temperatures. Winter can be chilly and stormy.

Camping: Cape Hatteras National Seashore manages public campgrounds at Frisco, by the Cape Hatteras Lighthouse, and just north of the drive by Oregon Inlet at the south end of Bodie Island.

Services: Most services are available at Avon, Salvo, Waves, Rodanthe, and Frisco. They are most plentiful in Buxton and Hatteras. Lodging can be tight in summer, especially on weekends, even with a large supply of motel rooms, rental houses, and cottages.

Nearby attractions: Other parts of Cape Hatteras National Seashore, Cape Lookout National Seashore, Fort Raleigh National Historic Site, Elizabethan Gardens, *Elizabeth II,* North Carolina Aquarium, Alligator River National Wildlife Refuge, Wright Brothers National Memorial, Bodie Island Lighthouse, Currituck Beach Lighthouse, Nags Head Woods, Jockey's Ridge State Park.

For more information: Cape Hatteras National Seashore (National Park Service), Pea Island National Wildlife Refuge, North Carolina Ferry System, Outer Banks Chamber of Commerce, Outer Banks Visitors Bureau. See Appendix for addresses and phone numbers.

The Drive

This drive travels the length of Pea and Hatteras Islands and includes much of Cape Hatteras National Seashore. Unlike the stretch of the Outer Banks from Nags Head to Corolla, most of this drive passes through undeveloped country. It offers extensive opportunities for swimming, fishing, beachcombing, sunbathing, hiking, and wildlife observation. One of the most noteworthy landmarks of the Atlantic coast, the Cape Hatteras Lighthouse, looms over the southern part of this drive.

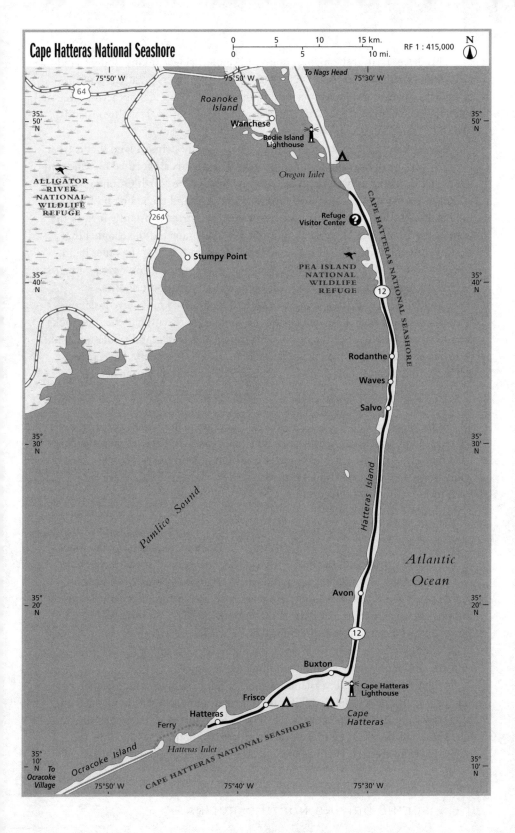

Cape Hatteras National Seashore

RF 1 : 415,000

N

| 0 | 5 | 10 | 15 km. |
| 0 | 5 | | 10 mi. |

75°50' W   75°50' W   To Nags Head   75°30' W

Roanoke Island

Wanchese

Bodie Island Lighthouse

35° 50' N

Oregon Inlet

CAPE HATTERAS NATIONAL SEASHORE

Refuge Visitor Center

35° 50' N

64

ALLIGATOR RIVER NATIONAL WILDLIFE REFUGE

264

Stumpy Point

PEA ISLAND NATIONAL WILDLIFE REFUGE

12

35° 40' N

35° 40' N

Rodanthe

Waves

Salvo

35° 30' N

35° 30' N

Pamlico Sound

Hatteras Island

Atlantic Ocean

35° 20' N

Avon

35° 20' N

12

Buxton

Cape Hatteras Lighthouse

Frisco

Hatteras

Ferry

Cape Hatteras

Ocracoke Island

Hatteras Inlet

CAPE HATTERAS NATIONAL SEASHORE

35° 10' N

To Ocracoke Village

35° 10' N

75°50' W   75°40' W   75°30' W

This drive starts at the highest point of Bonner Bridge, linking Bodie Island to Pea Island (see the end of Drive #26). This long bridge offers great views of the Atlantic to the east and Pamlico Sound to the west. It snakes its way across Oregon Inlet, the ocean channel that separates Pea and Bodie Islands. These two islands, like all the other islands of the Outer Banks, are barrier islands.

Barrier islands are little more than low-lying, sandy strips of land that exist at the mercy of the ocean and its violent storms. The islands are formed by wind and waves and are constantly changed by the same forces. The North Carolina barrier islands are important because they protect the sounds and the mainland from the full brunt of Atlantic Ocean storms. However, these storms constantly rework the islands. Pea Island and Hatteras Island were once separate, but the channel that separated them sanded closed many years ago. Oregon Inlet, on the other hand, was opened by a hurricane in 1846. It took its name from the ship *Oregon,* the first to pass through it. Since then, the inlet has moved south almost 3 miles.

Until fairly recently the people of Hatteras Island lived in relative isolation. Ferry service operated by private entities began in 1924. Eventually the state took over its operation. In 1963, the Bonner Bridge opened. The island's isolation could return at any time, since the bridge is nearing the end of its useful life. Corrosive salt water and the constant pounding of storms take a toll on any structure. Replacement is problematic because of the great expense, the constant migration of the inlet, and environmental concerns.

At the south end of the bridge, on Pea Island, there is a parking area on the left side of the road used by fishermen and beachgoers. To help stabilize Oregon Inlet for navigation, a controversial jetty was built here in the early 1990s. Time will tell whether it helps. A short side road a short distance south along NC 12 leads to the abandoned Oregon Inlet Coast Guard Station.

Continue to follow NC 12 south. To your left, tall dunes rise between the beach and the road. These dunes were built and planted with vegetation by the Civilian Conservation Corps (CCC) during the 1930s to help stabilize the island. As you would expect with the ocean so near, storms regularly break through the dunes and send waves washing across the drive route. Additionally, wind constantly blows sand from the dunes across the road. Repairing such damage makes this an expensive road to maintain. It's tempting to pull off onto the sandy roadside so that you can hop over the dunes to the beach, but wait until you get to one of the many paved parking areas along the highway. The sand at the roadside is soft, and pulling off here is an invitation to getting stuck.

When you get to the Pea Island National Wildlife Refuge Visitor Center, be sure to stop. It offers refuge exhibits and information; it also sells items such as bird books and mosquito repellent. The refuge was created in 1938 consisting of 5,915 acres of the island and 25,700 acres of Pamlico Sound. At one time, the majority of the Western Hemisphere's greater snow goose population wintered here. The geese foraged in the dunes looking for the nutritious "dune peas" that gave the island its name.

Although the refuge was established primarily as a sanctuary for geese and other waterfowl, it lies on the Atlantic flyway and is a haven for many other kinds of birds. More than 300 species have been reported here. Other creatures, such as the river otter, raccoon, mink, and opossum, thrive in the wild environment. The beaches of the refuge are crucial nesting sites of endangered sea turtles, including the loggerhead. The nest temperature of the loggerhead turtle determines its sex. Because of the sand's coolness here at the northern edge of their nesting range, most young hatched here are male. These nests may produce many of the entire turtle population's males.

Be sure to take the easy hiking trail that starts at the refuge visitor center. It starts as a boardwalk over a small freshwater pond. Look for turtles sunning on logs here. It then follows a dike out across large freshwater ponds to several wooden observation platforms. If you feel energetic, you can loop all the way around North Pond from the end of the dike trail, returning to your car by walking the last section along NC 12. Be sure to take insect repellent in summer.

About 3 miles farther down the drive, you will pass the New Inlet boat launch on the right. Until storms closed the inlet in 1945, it separated Pea and Hatteras Islands. Continue on the drive by following NC 12 south to the boundary of the refuge at the village of Rodanthe. This town is the first significant development you will have encountered since the start of the drive. Unlike the mega-tourist towns on the northern part of the Outer Banks, the communities of Rodanthe, Waves, Salvo, and Avon are much more modest. There isn't much neon or plastic in these towns, and national restaurant and motel chains are almost nonexistent. Cape Hatteras National Seashore starts here, on the beach side of town. The National Park Service has a fishing pier concession here.

Before you leave Rodanthe, be sure to visit the Chicamacomico U.S. Life Saving Service Station. Dating to 1874, this station was one of the first built on the Outer Banks. Crews posted at these stations saved countless lives when ships wrecked on the treacherous shores of the islands. Since Europeans began sailing these shores in the 1500s, at least 600 ships and maybe more than 2,000 have wrecked along the banks. The area has become known as the Graveyard of the Atlantic. Cape Hatteras's reputation for wrecks was thus established early in American history; the graveyard nickname was coined by Alexander Hamilton after a traumatic passage around the cape as a boy.

To reduce the loss of life, lifesaving stations were built all along the coast. Heroic rescues were common, as the men of these stations braved howling winds and raging surf to rescue sailors and passengers from foundering ships. Many medals have been awarded for the valor displayed by the lifesaving crews. One prominent longtime Outer Banks family, the Midgetts, had more than 150 of its members serve in the Life Saving Service over the years. Their extensive service was commemorated when a new U.S. Coast Guard ship was named the *Midgett*.

As engines replaced sails, shipwrecks declined on the Outer Banks. World War II temporarily halted the decline. German U-boats took up stations off the North Carolina coast in early 1942, sinking so many ships that the area became known as Torpedo Junction. The lifesavers were kept busy until an effective defense was mounted. Today, sunken U-boats and other ships are popular destinations of recreational divers. After the war, improved navigation systems and weather forecasting again decreased the number of wrecks, and the need for the lifesaving stations declined. The Chicamacomico station was closed in 1954 but has been restored as a museum in recent years.

The towns of Rodanthe, Waves, and Salvo run together, forming a relatively continuous stretch of development about 5 miles long. Beyond Salvo, the drive enters an 11-mile stretch of undeveloped national seashore. Dunes, marshes, and scrub forests of pine and other trees line the highway. The road then enters Avon, a growing beach resort town with larger, more expensive homes. There is another ocean fishing pier here. From Avon, at the widest part of Pamlico Sound, the sound appears as large as a sea. The mainland lies far out of sight, 30 miles west. At no other place in the United States are barrier islands so far offshore.

After Avon, the highway reenters the undeveloped land of the national seashore. The road passes a popular windsurfing area on the sound a little south of town. Hatteras Island becomes very narrow here and highly vulnerable to ocean storms. Recent hurricanes have cut inlets through the island here that have filled back in. Regular repairs have to be performed to maintain the protective beachside dunes and the highway. In 1962 a ferocious storm completely cut through the island along here, requiring a massive repair effort. The road soon enters Buxton, site of the Cape Hatteras Lighthouse. A marked side road leads a short distance to this famous landmark. The 200-foot brick tower is the tallest lighthouse in the United States.

Because Cape Hatteras protrudes far out into the Atlantic, it creates a navigation hazard. However, that is only the start of the area's shipping problems. A barely submerged finger of sand called Diamond Shoals juts more than 10 miles out into the ocean from the cape, just begging for ships to run aground. Sailors have long used ocean currents that flow offshore of the Outer Banks to speed their travel. A short distance offshore, the warm Gulf Stream flows north at 4 knots and veers eastward. Northbound ships followed this current to shorten their trips. Between the Gulf Stream and the coast, a colder counter-current, the Virginia Coastal Drift, flows south. Not surprisingly, southbound ships followed this current south. Unfortunately, the Gulf Stream pinches this current into a very narrow channel at Cape Hatteras, forcing ships to sail very close to Diamond Shoals. Storms or slight errors in navigation set the stage for many shipwrecks here over the years.

Pushed in part by Alexander Hamilton, Congress authorized a lighthouse at the cape in 1794. However, the first tower was not completed until 1803. The 90-foot tower was small and had a weak light; it suffered frequent outages during storms, just when it was most needed. Ship captains complained vociferously. "As usual no light is to be seen from the lighthouse," one stated in 1837 after rounding the cape. After the national Lighthouse Board was created in 1852, the tower was raised to more than 150 feet and an efficient Fresnel lens was installed to brighten the light. Unfortunately, this new, much-improved tower suffered serious damage during the Civil War.

The taller brick tower that stands here today was begun in 1869 and completed the following year. Its distinctive spiral striping was added to serve as a useful daytime navigation aid—in other words, to help sailors distinguish this lighthouse from others along the Outer Banks. Automatic electric lights have long since replaced the original oil lamp. In clear weather, its beam can be seen 20 miles out to sea and sometimes even farther.

In warm months, the lighthouse tower is open to visitors willing to climb the 257 steps to its top. It offers a panoramic view of Cape Hatteras, the ocean, and the sound. The former keeper's quarters house a visitor center with exhibits on the lighthouse, shipwrecks, and nearby lifesaving stations. Another building houses a good bookstore carrying many titles on lighthouses, the Outer Banks, and related subjects. The beach near the lighthouse is one of the Atlantic coast's surfing hotspots.

Until recently, the lighthouse stood very close to the breaking waves of the Atlantic. When it was completed, it was 1,500 feet from the ocean. Since that time, currents and storms have eroded the cape. By 1935, waves washed around the base of the tower and it was abandoned. However, changes in the currents and beach erosion control work by the CCC temporarily reversed the erosion in the late 1930s, and the lighthouse was recommissioned in 1950. Unfortunately, erosion patterns changed again and the sea again encroached on the tower, coming within 100 feet. Erosion control efforts were made, but the ocean was relentless.

To save the lighthouse, the National Park Service moved it 2,900 feet, well back from the shore, in 1999. Not surprisingly, moving a 200-foot-tall tower built of 1.25 million bricks was an extremely expensive undertaking—it cost about $12 million. In a major feet of engineering, the entire tower was moved in one piece, with no damage.

Before you return to the highway, follow the park road toward the campground to the Buxton Woods Nature Trail, located at a roadside picnic area. This 0.75-mile-long trail loops through lush forest, part of Buxton (Cape Hatteras) Woods. The island at the cape is wide enough to allow the largest tract of maritime forest in North Carolina to survive. A combination of dunes that protect the forest from salt spray, a great enough distance from the ocean, and a freshwater aquifer

Cape Hatteras Lighthouse at its old location

enable the forest to exist. However, it is constantly stressed by wind and salt and doesn't really thrive. Many dead pines are evident on the island. Recent storms have weakened and killed many; insects took advantage and finished off the weakened trees. Although more than half the forest is owned by government entities, the rest is threatened by development.

The easy nature trail takes you through a thick forest of loblolly pine, live oak, dogwood, American hornbeam, yaupon, bayberry, and even the tropical-looking palmetto to the shores of a shallow marsh. Because it is lighter, a lens of fresh water floats on top of deeper salt water, causing shallow groundwater to be fresh. Human use of the water has lowered the level of ponds and marshes in these woods. In addition, the woods were once cut and cleared for lumber, fuel, and pasture. Severe erosion of the loose, sandy soil resulted, causing people to realize the forests' value. In summer, take mosquito repellent and keep an eye open for snakes as you hike the trail.

At the cape, the island and the highway make an abrupt turn southwest. Follow the road through Buxton, which blends in with the next town on the island, Frisco. There is another ocean fishing pier here and a National Park Service campground. Beyond Frisco, the island narrows and the forest becomes scrubby. The road re-enters the national seashore for a short distance, then enters Hatteras, the largest town on the island. This busy place has plenty of lodgings, although they can fill up in summer. Beaches, marinas, and sun draw many thousands of people here every year.

Wind your way through the town to the end of the drive at the Hatteras–Ocracoke ferry, which crosses Hatteras Inlet. A hurricane blasted Hatteras Inlet open, separating Hatteras and Ocracoke Islands. The Confederate army constructed two forts here in 1861 to guard the inlet. When the forts fell soon after, they gave the Union its first victory of the Civil War. Except when storms strike, the inlet is peaceful today. The ferry here began operating in 1953 as a private ferry service. Today the state runs the busy ferry, carrying more than half a million people across Hatteras Inlet every year. In summer, the wait for a ferry can be long. If you have time, consider taking the free, forty-minute ferry ride to Ocracoke Island, which is covered in the next drive.

Blackbeard's Haunt

Ocracoke Island

General description: A paved 14-mile drive across quiet Ocracoke Island, once a hangout of the pirate Blackbeard.

Special attractions: Cape Hatteras National Seashore, Ocracoke Lighthouse, Silver Lake Harbor, Hatteras–Ocracoke ferry, Cedar Island–Ocracoke ferry, Ocracoke-Swan Quarter ferry, Ocracoke ponies, beaches, fishing, swimming, boating, hiking.

Location: Upper North Carolina coast. The drive starts at the Hatteras–Ocracoke ferry terminal on the north end of Ocracoke Island, one of the islands of the Outer Banks.

Drive route number: NC 12.

Travel season: All year. Summer is hot but ideal for beach activities. Spring and fall are less crowded, with cooler temperatures. Winter can be chilly and stormy.

Camping: Cape Hatteras National Seashore manages a public campground a few miles north of the village of Ocracoke.

Services: All services are available in the village of Ocracoke. Lodging can be tight in summer, especially on weekends.

Nearby attractions: Other parts of Cape Hatteras National Seashore, Cape Lookout National Seashore, Portsmouth Island, Fort Raleigh National Historic Site, Elizabethan Gardens, *Elizabeth II,* North Carolina Aquarium, Pea Island National Wildlife Refuge, Cedar Island National Wildlife Refuge, Wright Brothers National Memorial, Bodie Island Lighthouse, Cape Hatteras Lighthouse, Nags Head Woods, Jockey's Ridge State Park.

For more information: Cape Hatteras National Seashore (National Park Service), North Carolina Ferry System, Outer Banks Chamber of Commerce, Outer Banks Visitors Bureau, Ocracoke Civic and Business Association. See Appendix for addresses and phone numbers.

The Drive

This short scenic drive crosses Ocracoke Island of the Outer Banks. Except for the small, quaint village of Ocracoke, almost the entire island is part of Cape Hatteras National Seashore. Industrial tourism hasn't yet arrived at Ocracoke. There are miles of beaches and lots of marshes important to wildlife. The Ocracoke Lighthouse is the oldest operating lighthouse in North Carolina.

Unlike the other Outer Banks islands covered elsewhere in this guide, Ocracoke can be reached only by car ferry. Two long ferries sail here from Swan Quarter and Cedar Island. A shorter, forty-minute ferry connects Hatteras Island with Ocracoke. Any of the ferries makes for a fun trip across the blue waters of Pamlico Sound. The drive starts at the ferry terminal for Hatteras Island at the northeast end of Ocracoke Island, which is the busiest ferry to the island.

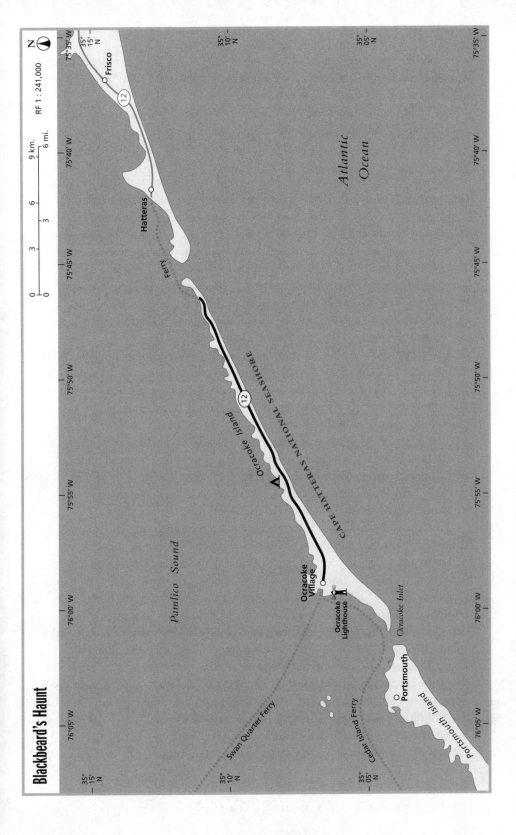

Blackbeard's Haunt

RF 1 : 241,000

From the ferry terminal, head southwest along NC 12 through miles of undeveloped coastline. On the left a dune ridge separates the beach from the highway. Although you won't be able to see the ocean except through occasional storm-created breaks in the dunes, the Atlantic is only a dune-hop away. If you want to go to the beach, wait and park at one of the beach access points. Unless you have four-wheel drive, parking in the soft sand along the road is an invitation to getting stuck.

The dune ridge was created and vegetated in large part by the Civilian Conservation Corps (CCC) in the 1930s to help stabilize the island. Like all barrier islands, Ocracoke was created of sand by wind and waves and is constantly reshaped by storms and currents. Storm waves regularly wash over the dunes onto the road, making NC 12 an expensive route to maintain. Inlets between the Outer Banks islands open and close periodically. Hatteras Inlet, between Hatteras and Ocracoke Islands, was opened by a storm in 1846. Ocracoke Inlet, on the southwest side of Ocracoke Island, has been open since the English first sailed these waters. Because of that, it has been an important navigation route as far back as the first British colony in the New World at Roanoke.

Several possibilities exist for the island's name. *Ocracoke* could be a corruption of the name of a small group of Indians, the Wacocon tribe, who once lived on the mainland across the sound. Another theory says that it's a corruption of an Algonquian word for "fort." One legend says that Blackbeard, impatient to get on with raiding, cursed early in the predawn hours, "Oh cry cock!"

After about 6 miles, you pass the marked Ocracoke pony pasture on the right. A short boardwalk offers views of these horses, which used to run wild on the island. They created both a hazard for themselves and motorists in those days. When the herd was large, it did considerable damage through overgrazing. Today, the National Park Service contains a reduced herd in this large pasture.

How did these small, sturdy horses get to Ocracoke and other Outer Banks islands? Early theories postulated that they were brought by pirates or settlers in the 1700s. A popular local legend says that they are descended from shipwrecked horses that managed to swim ashore. The most likely explanation is that they were brought in 1585 by Sir Richard Grenville during the founding of the Roanoke colony. A narrative from his voyage tells of picking up horses in Haiti and Puerto Rico. Grenville's ship *Tiger* ran aground while trying to get through Ocracoke Inlet and had to be beached for repairs. In such instances, livestock were often pushed overboard to swim ashore. It is likely that some ponies were released on Ocracoke during the repairs and not rounded up afterward. These small horses have all the characteristics of Spanish mustangs, including the proper number of lumbar vertebrae and ribs. This fact lends credence to their early origins.

Beyond the pony pasture, the highway crosses a number of small, marshy channels as it continues down the island. Some woods, filled mostly with pines, start to appear in a little more than 2 miles. On the left is the windy Ocracoke Campground managed by Cape Hatteras National Seashore. Just past it on the right is a parking area for the Hammock Hills Nature Trail. This easy path winds through dunes and pine forest to the marshy shores of Pamlico Sound, then loops back to the start. Interpretive signs along the way tell about various sights.

The highway enters the village of Ocracoke about 3 miles past the nature trail. The quaint little village lies in a wind-gnarled forest of live oaks, pines, and cedars on picture-perfect Silver Lake Harbor. There are no huge waterfront hotels, no fast food places, and no strip malls here. Unlike Outer Banks towns to the north, Ocracoke still looks much like a small fishing village from out of the mists of time. Many of the town's streets are not even paved. Winding avenues lead to old wooden houses, many of them historic. Because of limited parking and narrow streets, walking is probably the best way to see the sights.

The first records showing this settlement date to the early 1700s, when sea pilots stopped here to help with shipping passing through Ocracoke Inlet. Sometime in the early to mid-1700s, a differently located Hatteras Inlet closed, joining Ocracoke Island to Hatteras Island. Until the inlet reopened in 1846, shipping became concentrated in Ocracoke Inlet. During the American Revolution, many of the supplies desperately needed by George Washington's Continental army passed through here.

As shipping declined in the mid-1800s, a few affluent vacationers began to discover the island, seeking to leave the heat and insect-ridden plantations and cities in summer. During the Civil War, the Confederates built a fort on Beacon Island, a tiny plot of land near the inlet. After the forts at Hatteras Inlet fell to Northern troops early in the war, this one was abandoned. Ocracoke remained under Union control for the rest of the long, bloody conflict.

Ocracoke's most famous resident was the notorious pirate Edward Teach, better known as Blackbeard. His fearsome reputation as a successful and brutal pirate spread far and wide. On the west side of town, the shore faces a navigable channel called Teach's Hole. The infamous pirate used this channel as a home harbor while he raided nearby shipping. Blackbeard operated with the unofficial permission of colonial officials in North Carolina, much to coastal residents' chagrin. According to a mix of fact and legend, Blackbeard's demise was brought about by the locals' complaints.

Tired of the reign of terror that Blackbeard brought, locals asked the governor of Virginia for assistance in ending Blackbeard's piracy. In November 1718, the governor ordered two small British warships south to pursue Blackbeard. This small party, commanded by Lieutenant Robert Maynard, arrived at Ocracoke on the night of November 21. The next day, Maynard found Blackbeard's ship, the *Adventure*, moored in Teach's Hole. As Maynard approached the pirate's ship, Blackbeard supposedly greeted him by saying, "Damn you for villains, who are

Silver Lake Harbor, Ocracoke Island

you?" When Maynard raised the flag of the Royal Navy, Blackbeard responded with a broadside from his cannons.

The blast blew one of Maynard's two ships nearly to splinters and killed a number of his sailors. To protect his remaining men from another broadside, he ordered all his crew belowdecks. As Maynard's sloop drifted closer, Blackbeard saw only Maynard and the helmsman. When the ships bumped together, Blackbeard's men tossed homemade grenades onto the deck of Maynard's ship, then rushed aboard after they exploded. Maynard's men boiled up from the cabins below and joined the battle. Guns exploded and sword blades rang together in the melee.

The two leaders pursued each other. Blackbeard's pistol shot missed Maynard, but Maynard's wounded the pirate. Yanking his sword out, Blackbeard clashed with Maynard, seemingly unfazed by his gunshot. Maynard's sword broke under the furious assault, but he was saved when one of his sailors slashed into the pirate's neck with his sword. Undaunted, Blackbeard fought on, the deck becoming slippery with the blood of fallen men. Eventually, the pirates tired, worn down from swinging their heavy cutlasses. The British, with their lightweight rapiers, gained the upper hand. By the time Blackbeard finally fell, he had twenty-three wounds, from gunshots and sword slashes. The rest of the pirates were captured or killed. To prove that he had defeated the notorious pirate, Maynard cut off Blackbeard's head and mounted it on the bowsprit of his ship.

During Blackbeard's exploits along the North Carolina coast, he accumulated a substantial amount of loot. Ever since his death, people have hunted for his treasure, with little luck. Maybe someday a hurricane or storm will rework the North Carolina coast and reveal Blackbeard's lost gold. Remember, treasure hunting is not allowed at the national seashore.

Until the 1930s, the town of Ocracoke remained an extremely remote place to live, little changed in 200 years. The town had no electricity, telephone, regular ferry service, or paved road. When a town native, Stanley Wahab, made his fortune elsewhere, he returned home to bring Ocracoke into the twentieth century. With his support, electric lines were installed here in 1938, followed by an ice plant, movie theater, and other amenities. When Cape Hatteras National Seashore was first proposed, many island residents opposed it. The national seashore eventually covered all of Ocracoke Island except their village. In spite of the national park status, the town was still very remote; the road connecting Hatteras Inlet with the village was not paved until 1957. When state and private entities established regular car ferries, tourism slowly increased. It now is the primary basis of the local economy.

The town's most prominent landmark is the Ocracoke Lighthouse. Although this light tower is considerably shorter and more squat than its more famous neighbor on Cape Hatteras, the 76-foot-tall lighthouse is still impressive as it looms over the village. A light was first built near Ocracoke Inlet in 1803. After it was destroyed by lightning in 1818, the present tower was built. Completed in 1823, it is the oldest operating lighthouse in North Carolina and the second oldest in America. Its interior is closed to visitors, but the site is still worth a visit. A bright white picket fence surrounds the tower and its accompanying keeper's quarters.

Another interesting, but sad, site in Ocracoke is the British Cemetery. In World War II, German U-boats were stationed off North Carolina. During the early months of 1942, before an effective defense could be mounted, these submarines sent many ships to the bottom of the sea. An unpleasant chore for villagers in Ocracoke and other Outer Banks towns was the recovery of bodies washed up by the surf. To help stem the carnage, the British forces sent antisubmarine trawlers to the North Carolina coast. The trawlers helped cut the losses, but one, the HMS *Bedfordshire*, was spotted by a U-boat and torpedoed. The bodies of several British sailors washed ashore and were buried in this small plot in Ocracoke.

Over the years, the cemetery was mostly forgotten, although local residents occasionally trimmed the graves. In the 1970s, the British War Memorial Commission replaced the old headstones with new granite ones. As part of the American

Ocracoke Lighthouse

bicentennial celebration in 1976, the state of North Carolina purchased the small plot and donated it to Great Britain to commemorate that country's assistance in clearing the coast of German submarines. The cemetery is now carefully maintained, and today the buried men rest in a little parcel of Britain.

If time allows, consider making an interesting side trip from Ocracoke to nearby Portsmouth Island. Private ferries based on Ocracoke carry people over to the deserted town of Portsmouth. Like Ocracoke, that town was once a thriving place whose economy was based on Ocracoke Inlet traffic and fishing. Today it is a ghost town with many structures still standing. The National Park Service protects the old village as part of Cape Lookout National Seashore. Inquire at the National Park Service Visitor Center in Ocracoke for information about Portsmouth ferries.

The scenic drive ends at the ferry terminal in town. In summer, the long ferries to Cedar Island and Swan Quarter are very popular. Be sure to book a place on them well ahead of time if you plan to use them to leave Ocracoke.

Beaufort

Cedar Island to Beaufort

General description: A 44-mile paved drive from Cedar Island National Wildlife Refuge, past several picturesque maritime towns and near Cape Lookout National Seashore, to the historic town of Beaufort.

Special attractions: Historic Beaufort, Cedar Island National Wildlife Refuge, North Carolina Maritime Museum, fishing, boating.

Location: Middle North Carolina coast. The drive starts at the ferry terminal of the Cedar Island–Ocracoke Ferry on Cedar Island northeast of Beaufort and Morehead City.

Drive route numbers: NC 12, Old Cedar Island Road, US 70.

Travel season: All year. Summer is hot but ideal for water activities. Spring and fall are less crowded, with cooler temperatures. Winter can be chilly and stormy.

Camping: There are no public campgrounds along the route.

Services: All services are available in Beaufort. Limited lodging is available on Cedar Island and Harkers Island. Food and gas are available in most towns along the route.

Nearby attractions: Cape Lookout National Seashore, Cape Hatteras National Seashore, Portsmouth Island, Cape Hatteras Lighthouse, Ocracoke Island, Fort Macon State Park, North Carolina Aquarium.

For more information: Cape Lookout National Seashore, Cedar Island National Wildlife Refuge, North Carolina Maritime Museum, Fort Macon State Park, Beaufort Historical Association, North Carolina Ferry System, and Carteret County Tourism Development Authority. See Appendix for addresses and phone numbers.

The Drive

This drive is easily done on your way to or from the ferry connecting Cedar Island and Ocracoke on the Outer Banks. It passes through a national wildlife refuge, several interesting old fishing towns, and ends in the historic town of Beaufort. Cape Lookout National Seashore lies just off the route. The drive follows part of an official North Carolina Scenic Byway, the Outer Banks Scenic Byway.

The drive starts at the Cedar Island–Ocracoke ferry terminal on Cedar Island. If you just disembarked from the ferry, start right into the drive. If you haven't been to Ocracoke Island, consider taking the ferry there sometime. Cedar Island is a big island, consisting mostly of undeveloped marsh and forest protected within Cedar Island National Wildlife Refuge. When colonists began to settle here in the late seventeenth century, they were surprised to find white residents. Oddly, these people lived like the local Indians but spoke English. They couldn't read or write and claimed to have always lived on the island. Some of the people had the same

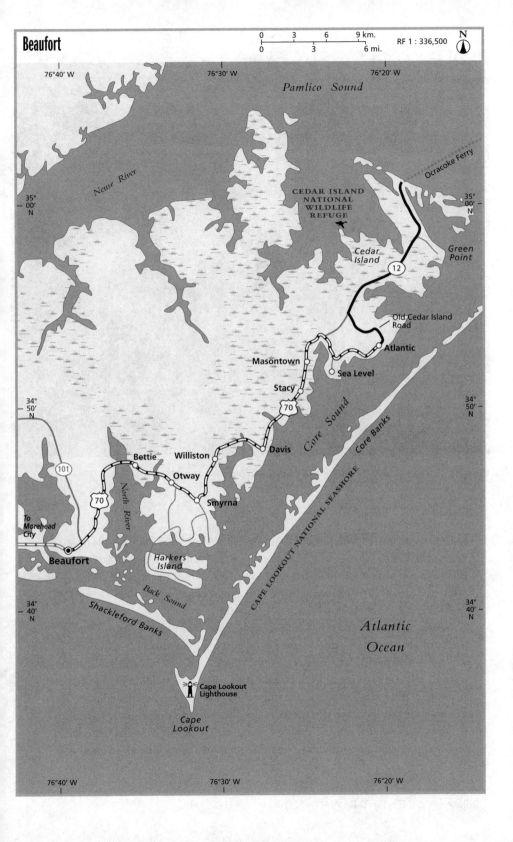

Dunes with sea oats at Core Banks, Cape Lookout National Seashore

last names as the lost colonists of Roanoke Island, and historians have long wondered whether the mysterious residents of Cedar Island were descendants of the Roanoke colonists. Archaeologists have never been able to determine with any certainty the fate of the Roanoke settlers, who disappeared sometime between 1587 and 1590; see Drive #27 for more on the mystery.

After leaving the ferry, NC 12 quickly plunges into pine forest with homes scattered along the way. After about 3.5 miles, Lola Road turns off to the left. It's a short, interesting side trip to Green Point, where the road ends at a boat ramp with a good view of the marshes in the Cedar Island National Wildlife Refuge. Beyond Lola Road, the main highway enters the refuge. Like other coastal wildlife refuges, this one was created largely to protect waterfowl nesting and wintering grounds.

The road soon leaves the wooded island and begins to cross the large marsh separating it from the mainland. Near the other side of this marshy causeway, a bridge arches high over the Thorofare, a channel used by boats to cut through the marsh. The highway then reaches solid land again and more pine forest.

Just after reentering the forest, turn left onto Old Cedar Island Road. This side road makes a scenic loop through the old fishing town of Atlantic. It leads through more of the national wildlife refuge and passes scattered homes. After 3.1 miles, it comes to the edge of Atlantic. Signs at an intersection here direct you to turn right to get to US 70. You will turn here to continue the scenic drive. Before you do so, go straight ahead into town. At another junction, turn left to get good views of Core Sound; turn right to see the back side of Atlantic's harbor. This is a picturesque, working harbor. Fishing and lobster boats fill most of the slips.

Atlantic is one of the largest towns of the area known as Down East Carteret. Although the town wasn't incorporated until early in this century, it was first settled in the mid-1700s. Hunting guide services, tourism, and other forms of employment add to the local economy, but fishing and other forms of seafood production have been a mainstay throughout the town's history. Atlantic has one of the concessions that ferries people over to Portsmouth Island, part of Cape Lookout National Seashore. Private businesses ferry people over from four main locations—Ocracoke Island, Atlantic, Davis, and Harkers Island.

Unlike Cape Hatteras National Seashore, Cape Lookout can be reached only by water. The national seashore at Cape Lookout includes the uninhabited barrier islands of Portsmouth Island, Core Banks, and Shackleford Banks. The National Park Service manages most of it as de facto wilderness. Other than a small patch of maritime forest at the ghost town of Portsmouth and another small tract on Shackleford Banks, there is little at this national seashore but marshes and endless sandy beaches. A few adventurous folks love the isolation and quiet, despite the lack of creature comforts.

If you go over to the island, take everything you need, particularly food, water, sunscreen, insect repellent, extra clothes, and some sort of shade shelter. Crossing the shallow sound is difficult, but years of experience allow the ferry operator at Morris Marina to make the trip safely time after time. All the North Carolina sounds are shallow, but Core Sound is particularly so. Newcomers are sometimes startled to find a fisherman in waders standing in the water far from shore. Morris Marina also manages lodgings in the national seashore, two groups of rustic fishing cabins on North and South Core Banks. There are few other options besides primitive camping.

After you have explored Atlantic, backtrack to the junction marked for US 70 and head southwest. Go left in a mile, following more signs for US 70. In only 0.2 mile go right onto the start of US 70. If you want another view of Atlantic's harbor, go left here. US 70 heads southwest out of Atlantic along the sound. It crosses some marshes and enters the village of Sea Level. Food is available along the highway here. If you have time, take the side road on the left that leads into the heart of the small community on a tiny peninsula.

Drivers now loop back to NC 12 again, the highway that you left some miles earlier. Stay on US 70, which crosses a high bridge over Salters Creek. You will pass through woods and occasional marshes with views of Nelson Bay on the way to the small fishing village of Stacy. After Stacy, the road crosses a long area of marshes, then enters the settlement of Davis. Davis lies on the shores of Core Sound on a small crooked thumb of land that extends outward from Down East Carteret. The town got its name from one of its first settlers, William Davis, who got a land grant from the British Crown in 1763. Until the highway from Beaufort arrived here in the twentieth century, the town was very isolated, accessible only by water.

Davis's isolation led to some real hardships over the course of its history. Little compares to the winter of 1898, however. That year, record cold weather came early and just got colder. Waterfowl, usually hunted in winter to supplement the larder, fled south to warmer climes. Ice choked the sound, preventing fishing boats from leaving the harbor. Passage overland, across miles of frozen marsh and forest wilderness, was impossible. As winter tightened its grip, the sound froze solid and food supplies ran out. Desperate for relief, the villagers gathered for an outdoor prayer meeting led by Uncle Mose Davis, a black leader. He made a short prayer ending with "We've done everything we can for ourselves, and unless you do something to help us, we are all going to starve to death. Amen."

Almost as soon as the villagers raised their bowed heads, they saw a column of smoke rising from Core Banks, the offshore barrier islands. The town residents knew that it was a signal for help, but thought that it would be extremely dangerous to attempt rescue across the frozen sound. Boats could not move through the ice, and people walking on it risked breaking through and dying by drowning or hypothermia. Finally, the group was pushed into action by Uncle Mose. Three stalwart sailors tied lines to their waists, then connected them to a skiff. Slipping and sliding, they managed to drag the boat across 3 long miles from the sound to the island. There they found the seamen of a wrecked ship, the *Pontiac*, huddled on the beach. The villagers took care of the shipwreck survivors and began salvaging the ship. To their amazement, its holds were full of grain and molasses. By risking their lives to save the sailors, they themselves were saved from sure death. This true event is surely a morality tale if there ever was one.

Today Davis is a sleepy village of about 500 people. It still has a busy waterfront, with docks and marinas popular with local fishermen and recreational boaters. There is another Cape Lookout National Seashore concession here, ferrying people over to a fishing camp on Core Banks. From Davis, continue on US 70 through more marsh and woods to the hamlet of Williston. In another 3 miles, the highway enters Smyrna, another small town.

About 1.5 miles past Smyrna is a turnoff on the left for Harkers Island. A few miles of pavement and a bridge lead to the island, the most populous place in Down East Carteret. Harkers Island received a boost in population in 1899 after a major hurricane drove people to the island from several small communities on Core and Shackleford Banks. Unlike the banks across the sound, this island is somewhat protected against Atlantic storms and has developed both its year-round population and its seasonal tourist trade.

Harkers Island is well known for its wooden boat building, but it is perhaps best known as the headquarters of Cape Lookout National Seashore. The National Park Service has a visitor center here, and ferries cross the sound to the seashore preserve. The park's most famous landmark, the Cape Lookout Lighthouse, is best reached from here.

Like Cape Hatteras to the north, Cape Lookout has had more than its fair share of shipwrecks. Early on it earned the name "Horrible Headland" from mariners. To improve safety, Congress authorized a lighthouse at Cape Lookout in 1804, soon after a light was built at Cape Hatteras. As seems to be typical with government projects both then and now, there were long delays in construction, and the tower was not finished until 1812. The lighthouse rose 104 feet above the water, but had a very weak light. A new 156-foot tower with a first-order Fresnel lens built in 1859 greatly improved its usefulness as a navigation aid. Like many lighthouses standing at the start of the Civil War, the Cape Lookout light was damaged by Confederates as they withdrew from the coast. At the time of the construction of the existing lighthouses at Cape Hatteras, Bodie Island, and Currituck Beach, the Cape Lookout Lighthouse was given its distinctive black-and-white diamond paint job.

The lighthouse looms over an excellent natural harbor, the Cape Lookout Bight. This harbor has been used for shelter from the open ocean by everyone from Spanish privateers to the U.S. Navy. Surprisingly, it has never been developed into a commercial port, although plans for such a port have been made over the years.

From the turnoff to Harkers Island, continue the drive along US 70. The highway passes through the small communities of Otway and Bettie. Beyond Bettie, the highway crosses the North River, a large arm of Back Sound. After crossing the river, the road hits a junction with a stoplight. Go left and stay on US 70 here. In about 5 miles you will reach the center of Beaufort. Although Beaufort's modern commercial strip along US 70 is not particularly scenic, it is not representative of the beautiful old parts of town clustered along the waterfront. Turn off the highway and drive down to the harbor. You will want to spend some time here.

North Carolina's third-oldest town, Beaufort was settled in about 1700 and was first known as Fishtown. In 1713, the town was renamed Beaufort for Henry Somerset, the Duke of Beaufort. It was incorporated in 1723. The town's good

Beaufort's harbor

harbor led to its development as a port. The harbor brought prosperity, but it also occasionally brought grief. Pirates and privateers sailed the coastal waters off Beaufort, raiding and looting. In 1747, a Spanish fleet sailed into town, claiming it for Spain. The Spanish sailors pillaged the town before being driven out after several days by an outraged militia of farmers and townspeople.

During the Revolutionary War, the port produced salt and acted as a supply point for George Washington's troops. Residents paid a price for their support of the Revolution after British general Charles Cornwallis was defeated at Yorktown. British navy ships arrived in Beaufort on April 3, 1782, and proceeded to sack the town before being fought off.

Soon after the Civil War began, Beaufort was occupied by Union forces. Because no great battles occurred here, it was little damaged by the experience; many homes and buildings built before the war survive today. Beaufort thrived until the 1960s as a port, fishing, and resort town. Then fishing declined and the town's waterfront area suffered. Though the future looked bleak, residents didn't give up. They restored historic buildings, cleaned up and built a new boardwalk along the waterfront, and promoted tourism. Restaurants facing the harbor opened, and historic homes were converted to bed and breakfast inns. Today the waterfront thrives with gift shops, galleries, and seafood eateries. Sleek motorboats and sailboats moor at the docks here.

Park along Front Street and stroll along the waterfront. Many beautiful, historic homes, some dating well back into the 1700s, line this street along with attractive commercial buildings. To see more old structures, visit the Beaufort Historic Site, one block off Front Street at the corner of Ann and Turner Streets. This historic site includes a small complex of restored buildings; one, the R. Rustell House, dates to about 1732. Of particular note is the thirteen-star American flag housed in the 1796 Carteret County Courthouse.

Many other beautiful homes line nearby streets; the Beaufort Historical Association has registered more than one hundred. Plaques posted in front bear their names and dates of construction. The peaceful Old Burying Ground here has graves dating to the early 1700s. Its ghosts could tell many stories, both happy and sad. People at the Beaufort Historic Site conduct tours of the cemetery, along with guided walks in the historic site.

One modern spot deserves a visit. The North Carolina Maritime Museum on Front Street is a surprisingly large and well-done museum. It would be highly respected in a large city, no less in the small town of Beaufort. It has exhibits on everything from coastal plant and animal life to a giant seashell collection. The story of pirates, fishermen, sailors, and all those who made their living from the sea is told here. Full-size boats, both old and new, are mixed with excellent models. The history of the U.S. Lifesaving Service and coastal lighthouses is chronicled. Excellent coastal art often hangs on the walls of one gallery. Across the street from the museum, on the water, is the Harvey W. Smith Watercraft Center, where you can watch craftspeople restore and build wooden boats.

If the scenic attractions of Beaufort, the end of this drive, haven't worn you out, there is plenty more to see nearby. Highlights include Fort Macon State Park, the North Carolina Aquarium, and the beaches of Bogue Banks.

SUGGESTED READING

Adams, Kevin. *North Carolina Waterfalls: A Hiking and Photography Guide.* Winston-Salem, N.C.: John F. Blair, Publisher, 2005.

Bachman, Karen. *Insiders' Guide to North Carolina's Outer Banks.* Guilford, Conn.: Globe Pequot Press, 2006.

Barefoot, Daniel W. *Touring the Backroads of North Carolina's Lower Coast.* Winston-Salem, N.C.: John F. Blair, Publisher, 1995.

Barefoot, Daniel W. *Touring the Backroads of North Carolina's Upper Coast.* Winston-Salem, N.C.: John F. Blair, Publisher, 1995.

DeLaughter, Jerry, Carson Brewer, and others. *Smokies Road Guide.* Gatlinburg, Tenn.: Great Smoky Mountains Natural History Association, 2005.

Johnson, Randy. *Hiking North Carolina.* Guilford, Conn.: Globe Pequot Press, 2006.

Logue, Victoria, Frank Logue, and Nicole Blouin. *Guide to the Blue Ridge Parkway.* 2nd ed. Birmingham, Ala.: Menasha Ridge Press, 2003.

North Carolina Atlas & Gazetteer. 4th ed. Yarmouth, Maine: DeLorme Mapping, 2000.

Richards, Constance E., and Kenneth L. Richards. *Insiders' Guide to North Carolina's Mountains.* Guilford, Conn.: Globe Pequot Press, 2006.

Sakowski, Carolyn. *Touring the Western North Carolina Backroads.* 2nd ed. Winston-Salem, N.C.: John F. Blair, Publisher, 1995.

Sources of More Information

For more information on lands and events, please contact the following agencies and organizations.

Drive 1

Blowing Rock Chamber of Commerce
P.O. Box 406
Blowing Rock, NC 28605
(800) 295–7851 or (828) 295–7851
www.blowingrock.com

Blue Ridge Parkway
199 Hemphill Knob Road
Asheville, NC 28803
(828) 298–0398
www.nps.gov/blri

Boone Convention and Visitors Bureau
208 Howard Street
Boone, NC 28607-4037
(800) 852–9506 or (828) 262–3516
www.visitboonenc.com

Mount Jefferson State Natural Area
P.O. Box 48
Jefferson, NC 28640
(336) 246–9653

Stone Mountain State Park
3042 Frank Parkway
Roaring Gap, NC 28668
(336) 957–8185
www.ils.unc.edu/parkproject/ncparks
    .html

Drive 2

Asheville Convention and Visitors
    Bureau
P.O. Box 1010
Asheville, NC 28802-1010
(800) 257–1300 or (828) 258–6101
www.exploreasheville.com

Avery/Banner Elk Chamber of
    Commerce
P.O. Box 335
Banner Elk, NC 28604
(828) 898–5605 or (800) 972–2183
www.banner-elk.com

Blowing Rock Chamber of Commerce
P.O. Box 406
Blowing Rock, NC 28605
(800) 295–7851 or (828) 295–7851
www.blowingrock.com

Blue Ridge Parkway
199 Hemphill Knob Road
Asheville, NC 28803
(828) 298–0398
www.nps.gov/blri

Boone Convention and Visitors Bureau
208 Howard Street
Boone, NC 28607-4037
(800) 852–9506 or (828) 262–3516
www.visitboonenc.com

Grandfather Mountain
P.O. Box 129
Linville, NC 28646
(800) 468–7325 or (828) 733–2013
www.grandfather.com

Mitchell County Chamber of
   Commerce
P.O. Box 858
Spruce Pine, NC 28777
(800) 227–3912 or (828) 765–9483
www.mitchell-county.com

Mount Mitchell State Park
2388 State Highway 128
Burnsville, NC 28714
(828) 675–4611
www.ils.unc.edu/parkproject/ncparks
   .html

Pisgah National Forest
Grandfather Ranger District
Route 1, Box 110-A
Nebo, NC 28761
(828) 652–2144
www.cs.unca.edu/nfsnc

Drive 3

Asheville Convention and Visitors
   Bureau
P.O. Box 1010
Asheville, NC 28802-1010
(800) 257–1300 or (828) 258–6101
www.exploreasheville.com

Blue Ridge Parkway
199 Hemphill Knob Road
Asheville, NC 28803
(828) 298–0398
www.nps.gov/blri

Brevard/Transylvania Chamber of
   Commerce
35 West Main Street
Brevard, NC 28712
(800) 648–4523 or (828) 883–3700
www.brevardncchamber.org

Cherokee Visitor Center
P.O. Box 460
Cherokee, NC 28719
(800) 438–1601 or (828) 497–9195
www.cherokee-nc.com

Great Smoky Mountains National Park
107 Park Headquarters Road
Gatlinburg, TN 37738
(252) 436–1200
www.nps.gov/grsm

Maggie Valley Visitors and Convention
   Bureau
P.O. Box 87
Maggie Valley, NC 28751
(828) 926–1686 or (800) 624–4431

Pisgah National Forest
Pisgah Ranger District
1001 Pisgah Highway
Pisgah Forest, NC 28768
(828) 877–3265
www.cs.unca.edu/nfsnc

Drive 4

Blowing Rock Chamber of Commerce
P.O. Box 406
Blowing Rock, NC 28605
(800) 295–7851 or (828) 295–7851
www.blowingrock.com

Blue Ridge Parkway
199 Hemphill Knob Road
Asheville, NC 28803
(828) 298–0398
www.nps.gov/blri

Pisgah National Forest
Grandfather Ranger District
Route 1, Box 110-A
Nebo, NC 28761
(828) 652–2144
www.cs.unca.edu/nfsnc

Drive 5

Avery/Banner Elk Chamber of
    Commerce
P.O. Box 335
Banner Elk, NC 28604
(828) 898–5605 or (800) 972–2183
www.banner-elk.com

Boone Convention and Visitors Bureau
208 Howard Street
Boone, NC 28607-4037
(800) 852–9506 or (828) 262–3516
www.visitboonenc.com

Pisgah National Forest
Grandfather Ranger District
Route 1, Box 110-A
Nebo, NC 28761
(828) 652–2144
www.cs.unca.edu/nfsnc

Drive 6

Avery/Banner Elk Chamber of
    Commerce
P.O. Box 335
Banner Elk, NC 28604
(828) 898–5605 or (800) 972–2183
www.banner-elk.com

Blowing Rock Chamber of Commerce
P.O. Box 406
Blowing Rock, NC 28605
(800) 295–7851 or (828) 295–7851
www.blowingrock.com

Blue Ridge Parkway
199 Hemphill Knob Road
Asheville, NC 28803
(828) 298–0398
www.nps.gov/blri

Boone Convention and Visitors Bureau
208 Howard Street
Boone, NC 28607-4037
(800) 852–9506 or (828) 262–3516
www.visitboonenc.com

Mitchell County Chamber of
    Commerce
P.O. Box 858
Spruce Pine, NC 28777
(800) 227–3912 or (828) 765–9483
www.mitchell-county.com

Pisgah National Forest
Grandfather Ranger District
Route 1, Box 110-A
Nebo, NC 28761
(828) 652–2144
www.cs.unca.edu/nfsnc

Drive 7

Blue Ridge Parkway
199 Hemphill Knob Road
Asheville, NC 28803
(828) 298–0398
www.nps.gov/blri

Mitchell County Chamber of
  Commerce
P.O. Box 858
Spruce Pine, NC 28777
(800) 227–3912 or (828) 765–9483
www.mitchell-county.com

Pisgah National Forest, Appalachian
  Ranger District
Toecane Ranger Station
P.O. Box 128
Burnsville, NC 28714
(828) 682–6146
www.cs.unca.edu/nfsnc

Drive 8

Blue Ridge Parkway
199 Hemphill Knob Road
Asheville, NC 28803
(828) 298–0398
www.nps.gov/blri

Mitchell County Chamber of
  Commerce
P.O. Box 858
Spruce Pine, NC 28777
(800) 227–3912 or (828) 765–9483
www.mitchell-county.com

Pisgah National Forest
Grandfather Ranger District
Route 1, Box 110-A
Nebo, NC 28761
(828) 652–2144
www.cs.unca.edu/nfsnc

Drive 9

Asheville Convention and Visitors
  Bureau
P.O. Box 1010
Asheville, NC 28802-1010
(800) 257–1300 or (828) 258–6101
www.exploreasheville.com

Pisgah National Forest, Appalachian
  Ranger District
French Broad Ranger Station
P.O. Box 128
Hot Springs, NC 28743
(828) 622–3202
www.cs.unca.edu/nfsnc

Drive 10

Brevard/Transylvania Chamber of
  Commerce
35 West Main Street
Brevard, NC 28712
(800) 648–4523 or (828) 883–3700
www.brevardncchamber.org

Pisgah National Forest
Pisgah Ranger District
1001 Pisgah Highway
Pisgah Forest, NC 28768
(828) 877–3265
www.cs.unca.edu/nfsnc

Drive 11

Blue Ridge Parkway
199 Hemphill Knob Road
Asheville, NC 28803
(828) 298–0398
www.nps.gov/blri

Cherokee Visitor Center
P.O. Box 460
Cherokee, NC 28719
(800) 438–1601 or (828) 497–9195
www.cherokee-nc.com

Great Smoky Mountains National Park
107 Park Headquarters Road
Gatlinburg, TN 37738
(252) 436–1200
www.nps.gov/grsm

Maggie Valley Visitors and Convention
    Bureau
P.O. Box 87
Maggie Valley, NC 28751
(828) 926–1686 or (800) 624–4431

Swain County Chamber of Commerce
P.O. Box 509
Bryson City, NC 28713
(800) 867–9246 or (828) 488–3681
www.greatsmokies.com

Drive 12

Cherokee Visitor Center
P.O. Box 460
Cherokee, NC 28719
(800) 438–1601 or (828) 497–9195
www.cherokee-nc.com

Great Smoky Mountains National Park
107 Park Headquarters Road
Gatlinburg, TN 37738
(252) 436–1200
www.nps.gov/grsm

Drive 13

Graham County Travel and Tourism
    Authority
P.O. Box 575
Robbinsville, NC 28771-9442
(828) 479–3790 or (800) 470–3790
www.grahamcountytravel.com

Great Smoky Mountains National Park
107 Park Headquarters Road
Gatlinburg, TN 37738
(252) 436–1200
www.nps.gov/grsm

Nantahala National Forest
Cheoah Ranger District
Route 1, Box 16-A
Robbinsville, NC 28771
(828) 479–6431
www.cs.unca.edu/nfsnc

Drive 14

Graham County Travel and Tourism
    Authority
P.O. Box 575
Robbinsville, NC 28771-9442
(828) 479–3790 or (800) 470–3790
www.grahamcountytravel.com

Nantahala National Forest
Cheoah Ranger District
Route 1, Box 16-A
Robbinsville, NC 28771
(828) 479–6431
www.cs.unca.edu/nfsnc

Nantahala National Forest
Tusquitee Ranger District
123 Woodland Drive
Murphy, NC 28906
(828) 837–5152
www.cs.unca.edu/nfsnc

Drive 15

Franklin Chamber of Commerce
425 Porter Street
Franklin, NC 28734
(866) 372–5546 or (828) 524–3161
www.franklin-chamber.com

Highlands Chamber of Commerce
P.O. Box 62
Highlands, NC 28741
(828) 526–2112
www.highlandschamber.org

Nantahala National Forest
Highlands Ranger District
2010 Flat Mountain Road
Highlands, NC 28741
(828) 526–3765
www.cs.unca.edu/nfsnc

Nantahala National Forest
Wayah Ranger District
90 Sloan Road
Franklin, NC 28734
(828) 524–6441
www.cs.unca.edu.nfsnc

Swain County Chamber of Commerce
P.O. Box 509
Bryson City, NC 28713
(800) 867–9246 or (828) 488–3681
www.greatsmokies.com

Drive 16

Brevard/Transylvania Chamber of
    Commerce
35 West Main Street
Brevard, NC 28712
(800) 648–4523 or (828) 883–3700
www.brevardncchamber.org

Cashiers Chamber of Commerce
P.O. Box 238
Cashiers, NC 28717
(828) 743–5941
www.cashiersnorthcarolina.com

Highlands Chamber of Commerce
P.O. Box 62
Highlands, NC 28741
(828) 526–2112
www.highlandschamber.org

Nantahala National Forest
Highlands Ranger District
2010 Flat Mountain Road
Highlands, NC 28741
(828) 526–3765
www.cs.unca.edu/nfsnc

Drive 17

Crowders Mountain State Park
522 Park Office Lane
Kings Mountain, NC 28086
(704) 853–5375
www.ils.unc.edu/parkproject/ncparks
    .html

Gaston County Travel & Tourism
P.O. Box 2168
Gastonia, NC 28053
(704) 864–2621
www.gastonchamber.org

Kings Mountain National Military
    Park
2625 Park Road
Blacksburg, SC 29702
(864) 936–7921
www.nps.gov/kimo

Kings Mountain State Park
1277 Park Road
Blacksburg, SC 29702
(803) 222–3209
www.southcarolinaparks.com
    /stateparks/parklocator.asp

Drive 18

Hanging Rock State Park
P.O. Box 278
Danbury, NC 27016
(336) 593–8480
www.ils.unc.edu/parkproject/ncparks
    .html

Horne Creek Living Historical Farm
308 Horne Creek Farm Road
Pinnacle, NC 27043
(336) 325–2298
www.ah.dcr.state.nc.us/sections/hs
    /sites.htm

Mount Airy Chamber of Commerce
P.O. Box 913
Mount Airy, NC 27030
(336) 786–6116
www.mtairyncchamber.org

Pilot Mountain State Park
1792 Pilot Knob Park Road
Pinnacle, NC 27043
(336) 325–2355
www.ils.unc.edu/parkproject/ncparks
    .html

Winston-Salem Convention and
    Visitors Bureau
200 Brookstown Avenue
Winston-Salem, NC 27101
(866) 728–4200 or (336) 728–4200
www.wscvb.com

Drive 19

Morrow Mountain State Park
49104 Morrow Mountain Road
Albemarle, NC 28001
(704) 982–4402
www.ils.unc.edu/parkproject/ncparks
    .html

Reed Gold Mine State Historic Site
9621 Reed Mine Road
Midland, NC 28107
(704) 721–4653
www.ah.dcr.state.nc.us/sections/hs
    /sites.htm

Stanly County Chamber of Commerce
116 East North Street
Albemarle, NC 28002
(704) 982–8116
www.stanlychamber.org

Drive 20

Asheboro/Randolph County Chamber
of Commerce
317 East Dixie Drive
Asheboro, NC 27203
(336) 626–2626
www.chamber.asheboro.com

Uwharrie National Forest
789 Highway 24-27 East
Troy, NC 27371
(910) 576–6391
www.cs.unca.edu/nfsnc

Drive 21

Richmond County
Chamber of Commerce
P.O. Box 86
Rockingham, NC 28380
(910) 895–9058
www.richmondcountychamber.com

Stanly County Chamber of Commerce
116 East North Street
Albemarle, NC 28002
(704) 982–8116
www.stanlychamber.org

Town Creek Indian Mound State
Historic Site
509 Town Creek Mound Road
Mount Gilead, NC 27306
(910) 439–6802
www.ah.dcr.state.nc.us/sections/hs
/sites.htm

Drive 22

Bladen Lakes State Forest
4470 NC 242 Highway North
Elizabethtown, NC 28337
(910) 588–4964
www.ils.unc.edu/parkproject/ncparks
.html

Elizabethtown–White Lake Area
Chamber of Commerce
103 East Broad Street
Elizabethtown, NC 28337-9577
(910) 862–4368
www.elizabethtownwhitelake.com

Jones Lake State Park
4117 NC 242 Highway North
Elizabethtown, NC 28337
(910) 588–4550
www.ils.unc.edu/parkproject/ncparks
.html

Drive 23

Bentonville Battlefield
5466 Harper House Road
Four Oaks, NC 27524
(910) 594–0789
www.ah.dcr.state.nc.us/sections/hs
/sites.htm

Cliffs of the Neuse State Park
345-A Park Entrance Road
Seven Springs, NC 28578
(919) 778–6234
www.ils.unc.edu/parkproject/ncparks
.html

Wayne County Chamber of
  Commerce
308 North William Street
Goldsboro, NC 27530
(919) 734–2241
www.waynecountychamber.com

Drive 24

Elizabethtown–White Lake Area
Chamber of Commerce
103 East Broad Street
Elizabethtown, NC 28337-9577
(910) 862–4368
www.elizabethtownwhitelake.com

Green Swamp Preserve
The Nature Conservancy
131 Racine Drive, Suite 101, Box
  Number 5
Wilmington, NC 28403
(910) 395–5000
www.nature.org/wherewework/north
  america/states/northcarolina

Southport–Oak Island Chamber of
  Commerce
4841 Long Beach Road, Southeast
Southport, NC 28461
(800) 457–6964 or (910) 457–6964
www.oak-island.com

Drive 25

Currituck Chamber of Commerce
P.O. Box 1160
Grandy, NC 27939
www.currituckchamber.org

Elizabeth City Chamber of Commerce
P.O. Box 426
Elizabeth City, NC 27907
(252) 335–4365
www.elizabethcitychamber.org

Mackay Island National Wildlife
  Refuge
316 Marsh Causeway
Knotts Island, NC 27950
(252) 429–3100
www.fws.gov/refuges

North Carolina Ferry System
North Carolina Department of
  Transportation
113 Arendell Street
Morehead City, NC 28557
(800) 293–3779
www.ncferry.org

Outer Banks Chamber of Commerce
P.O. Box 1757
Kill Devil Hills, NC 27948
(252) 441–8144
www.outerbankschamber.com

Drive 26

Cape Hatteras National Seashore
1401 National Park Drive
Manteo, NC 27954
(252) 473–2111
www.nps.gov/caha

Currituck Chamber of Commerce
P.O. Box 1160
Grandy, NC 27939
www.currituckchamber.org

Jockey's Ridge State Park
P.O. Box 592
Nags Head, NC 27959
(252) 441–7132
www.ils.unc.edu/parkproject/ncparks
.html

Nags Head Woods Preserve
The Nature Conservancy
701 West Ocean Acres Drive
Kill Devil Hills, NC 27948
(252) 441–2525
www.nature.org/wherewework/north
america/states/northcarolina

Outer Banks Chamber of Commerce
P.O. Box 1757
Kill Devil Hills, NC 27948
(252) 441–8144
www.outerbankschamber.com

Outer Banks Visitors Bureau
One Visitors Center Circle
Manteo, NC 27954
(877) 629–4386
www.outerbanks.org

Wright Brothers National Memorial
1401 National Park Drive
Manteo, NC 27954
(252) 441–7430
www.nps.gov/wrbr

Drive 27

Alligator River National Wildlife
Refuge
708 North Highway 64
Manteo, NC 27954
(252) 473–1131
www.fws.gov/refuges

Elizabethan Gardens
1411 Highway 64
Manteo, NC 27954
(252) 473–3234
www.elizabethangardens.org

Fort Raleigh National Historic Site
1401 National Park Drive
Manteo, NC 27954
(252) 473–5772
www.nps.gov/fora

Historic Bath
P.O. Box 148
Bath, NC 27808
(252) 923–3971
www.ah.dcr.state.nc.us/sections/hs
/sites/htm

Mattamuskeet National Wildlife
Refuge
38 Mattamuskeet Road
Swan Quarter, NC 27885
(252) 926–4201
www.fws.gov/refuges

North Carolina Aquarium–Roanoke
Island
P.O. Box 967
Manteo, NC 27954
(252) 473–3494
www.ncaquariums.com/newsite/ri
/riindex.htm

Outer Banks Chamber of Commerce
P.O. Box 1757
Kill Devil Hills, NC 27948
(252) 441–8144
www.outerbankschamber.com

Outer Banks Visitors Bureau
One Visitors Center Circle
Manteo, NC 27954
(877) 629–4386
www.outerbanks.org

Drive 28

Cape Hatteras National Seashore
1401 National Park Drive
Manteo, NC 27954
(252) 473–2111
www.nps.gov/caha

North Carolina Ferry System
North Carolina Department of
 Transportation
113 Arendell Street
Morehead City, NC 28557
(800) 293–3779
www.ncferry.org

Outer Banks Chamber of Commerce
P.O. Box 1757
Kill Devil Hills, NC 27948
(252) 441–8144
www.outerbankschamber.com

Outer Banks Visitors Bureau
One Visitors Center Circle
Manteo, NC 27954
(877) 629–4386
www.outerbanks.org

Pea Island National Wildlife Refuge
c/o Alligator River National Wildlife
 Refuge
708 North Highway 64
Manteo, NC 27954
(252) 473–1131
www.fws.gov/refuges

Drive 29

Cape Hatteras National Seashore
1401 National Park Drive
Manteo, NC 27954
(252) 473–2111
www.nps.gov/caha
North Carolina Ferry System
North Carolina Department of
 Transportation
113 Arendell Street
Morehead City, NC 28557
(800) 293–3779
www.ncferry.org

Ocracoke Civic and Business
 Association
P.O. Box 456
Ocracoke, NC 27960
(252) 928–6711
www.ocracokevillage.com

Outer Banks Chamber of Commerce
P.O. Box 1757
Kill Devil Hills, NC 27948
(252) 441–8144
www.outerbankschamber.com

Outer Banks Visitors Bureau
One Visitors Center Circle
Manteo, NC 27954
(877) 629–4386
www.outerbanks.org

Drive 30

Beaufort Historical Association
130 Turner Street
Beaufort, NC 28516
(252) 728–5225 or (800) 575–7483
www.beauforthistoricsite.org

Cape Lookout National Seashore
131 Charles Street
Harkers Island, NC 28531
(252) 728–2250
www.nps.gov/calo

Carteret County Tourism
    Development Authority
3409 Arendell Street
Morehead City, NC 28557
(800) 786–6962 or (252) 726–8148
www.crystalcoastnc.org

Cedar Island National Wildlife
    Refuge
c/o Mattamuskeet National Wildlife
    Refuge
38 Mattamuskeet Road
Swan Quarter, NC 27885
(252) 926–4021
www.fws.gov/refuges

Fort Macon State Park
P.O. Box 127
Atlantic Beach, NC 28512
(252) 726–3775
www.ils.unc.edu/parkproject/ncparks
    .html

North Carolina Ferry System
North Carolina Department of
    Transportation
113 Arendell Street
Morehead City, NC 28557
(800) 293–3779
www.ncferry.com

North Carolina Maritime Museum
315 Front Street
Beaufort, NC 28516
(252) 728–7317
www.ah.dcr.state.nc.us/sections
    /maritime

INDEX

ABOUT THE AUTHOR

Laurence Parent was born and raised in New Mexico. After receiving an engineering degree at the University of Texas at Austin, he practiced engineering for six years before becoming a full-time freelance photographer and writer specializing in landscape, travel, and nature subjects. He has visited North Carolina many times. His photos appear in Sierra Club, Audubon, and many other calendars. Article and photo credits include *National Geographic Traveler, Outside, Men's Journal, Backpacker, Newsweek,* and the *New York Times.*

Parent has completed thirty books, including six other guidebooks for Globe Pequot/Falcon Publishing: *Hiking Big Bend National Park, Hiking New Mexico, Hiking Texas, Scenic Driving New Mexico, Scenic Driving Texas,* and *Scenic Driving Wyoming.* One of his latest works is *Texas Coast,* a large format, coffee-table-style photo book produced by University of Texas Press. He makes his home near Austin, Texas, with his wife, Patricia, and two children.